ART, MUSIC & AUDIO-V

5 10

ACPL ITEM
DISCARDED

3 1833 004

P9-EDY-449

DO NOT REMOVE
CARDS FROM POCKET

784.092 C42H   7052735
HARDING, JAMES.
MAURICE CHEVALIER, HIS LIFE,
1888-1972

ALLEN COUNTY PUBLIC LIBRARY

FORT WAYNE, INDIANA 46802

You may return this book to any agency, branch,
or bookmobile of the Allen County Public Library

DEMCO

MAURICE CHEVALIER

By the same author:

Biography
Saint-Saëns and His Circle
Sacha Guitry, The Last Boulevardier
The Duke of Wellington
Massenet
Rossini
The Astonishing Adventure of General Boulanger
The Ox on The Roof
Gounod
Lost Illusions: Paul Léautaud and His World
Erik Satie
Folies de Paris: The Rise and Fall of French Operetta
Offenbach

Anthology
Lord Chesterfield's Letters To His Son

Translation
Francis Poulenc: My Friends and Myself

MAURICE CHEVALIER

His Life
1888–1972

James Harding

*With illustrations from the
collection of André Bernard*

Secker & Warburg
London

Allen County Public Library
Ft. Wayne, Indiana

First published in England 1982 by
Martin Secker & Warburg Limited
54 Poland Street, London W1V 3DF

Copyright © James Harding 1982

British Library Cataloguing in Publication Data
Harding, James, *1929–*
Maurice Chevalier.
1. Chevalier, Maurice
2. Singers — France — Biography
I. Title
784'.092'4   ML420.C47

ISBN 0-436-19107-5

Typeset by Inforum Ltd, Portsmouth

Printed in Great Britain by
Richard Clay (The Chaucer Press) Ltd,
Bungay, Suffolk

7052735

For Gill and Marianne

Contents

List of Illustrations   ix

Acknowledgements   xi

Foreword   xiii

Chapter One   *SLUM CHILD*   1
  i   Old as the Eiffel Tower   1
  ii   Red-nosed Comedian   8
  iii   Working the Cafés-Concerts   16

Chapter Two   *RISING STAR*   24
  i   Mayol and Fragson   24
  ii   Ordeal in Marseilles   28
  iii   A Character by Colette   33

Chapter Three   *INDEPENDENCE*   46
  i   Croix de Guerre   46
  ii   The Golden Age of the
     Casino de Paris   57

Chapter Four   *CRACK-UP*   67
  i   Breakdown   67
  ii   Yvonne . . . and "Valentine"   79

Chapter Five   *HOLLYWOOD*   87
  i   Marriage   87
  ii   Lubitsch and *The Love Parade*   92
  iii   Marlene, Divorce, Exit La Louque   103

Chapter Six   *"MOMO"*   111
  i   *Love Me Tonight*   111
  ii   Mist again – *The Merry Widow*   117
  iii   Stage-fright   127

Chapter Seven   *GREY HAIR*   132
    i   The Most Expensive Artist
        in the World   132
    ii The Cure for Smoking   135
    iii Occupation   141
    iv Silence is Golden   149

Chapter Eight   *DISCOVERIES*   155
    i   Utrillo, Matisse and Colette   155
    ii Patachou, Aznavour and Piaf   160
    iii Momo the Red   167

Chapter Nine   *UNCLE MOMO*   173
    i   Marnes-la-Coquette   173
    ii Thank Heaven for Little Girls   179
    iii Around the World in Eighty Years   191
    iv Easeful Death   197

The Films of Maurice Chevalier   202

Bibliography   212

Index   215

List of Illustrations

Between pp. 46 and 47
At twelve years old
Aged twenty
Wearing the Croix de Guerre
A 1921 poster
La Valse renversante
Mistinguett
On and off stage with Mistinguett
With "La Louque"
The Love Parade
With Douglas Fairbanks and Yvonne Vallée
One Hour With You

Between pp. 78 and 79
With Yvonne Vallée
Love Me Tonight
The Way to Love
Preparing to go on stage
The Merry Widow
At home
With Henri Varna
A typical studio portrait
Le Silence est d'Or
With Nita Raya

Between pp. 110 and 111
At the London Coliseum
With Norma Shearer
With Patachou and Gracie Fields
With Margaret Lockwood
With Patachou

The finale of "Plein Feu"
Meeting the Queen
With Bob Hope
Love in the Afternoon
With Suzy Volterra

Between pp. 166 and 167
With his brother Paul
Showing off his roses
Gigi
Count Your Blessings
Fanny
Can-Can
With Marlene Dietrich and Ingrid Bergman
With Georges Carpentier
With a portrait of "La Louque"
In his sitting-room
Chevalier's last performance
In his eighty-third year

Acknowledgements

I am indebted for much valuable documentation to M. François Vals, who for twenty-two years until Maurice Chevalier's death was his administrator and, with Mme Vals, an intimate of his circle. My good friend André Bernard generously supplied pictures and information from his own vast theatre collection as well as kindly giving me access to the autograph correspondence between Chevalier and Mistinguett. At the ORTF my old friend Maurice Meslier, who remembers broadcasting songs from the Eiffel Tower in the days when it was used as a radio station, took immense trouble to further my researches, as did his colleague M. François Fabre. I am also grateful indeed to M. Hervé le Boterf; Mr Wilfrid Brambell; M. Jacques Cathy, President of the Société Mutualiste des Artistes des Variétés, Fondation Dranem, Maison de Retraite Maurice Chevalier, at Ris-Orangis; Miss Deborah Kerr; M. Henry Lemarchand and Mme Gobert, President and Librarian respectively of the Société des Auteurs, Compositeurs, et Editeurs de Musique; Mrs Mary Relph Powell, the daughter of Little Tich; and Mme François Salabert, Chairman and Managing Director of Editions François Salabert. It is a pleasure to acknowledge the secretarial skills of Miss Winifred Marshall, whose good humour and eagle eye have been undaunted by the most intricate of manuscripts.

Alas, since I began work on this book two people have died whose cordial assistance, both here and elsewhere, I have always prized. One was the composer Georges van Parys, and the other was the film director René Clair.

Foreword

The performer dazzles and is gone. Unlike the artist and the writer, he leaves no solid achievement behind him. We can never experience at first hand the thrill of a Garrick or the shudder of an Irving. Yet we have to accept that dead actors and actresses were great in their time on the evidence of writing by critics like Hazlitt and Agate. When you hear the grainy squawk that emerges from ancient gramophone records made by Sarah Bernhardt, it is hard to credit that her famous "voix d'or" once enraptured audiences. Nor can you glimpse her mastery of the stage in silent films where her gestures appear absurd, even grotesque. If the spell of the long-dead tragedian is almost beyond our grasp, the comedian is still more elusive. Who would imagine, on viewing the scrap of film remaining to us, that Little Tich was the supreme comic of his day and perhaps among the first of all time?

I have, therefore, avoided too much description of Maurice Chevalier on stage. You must take his dominance for granted, as indeed it was by millions of admirers throughout the world. The audience is the performer's raw material, as stone is the sculptor's and paint the artist's, and without an audience his effects evade the attempt of mere words to pin them down. Besides, Chevalier is fresh in the memory and survives in films and on disc – although, technically superior as they are to those of Bernhardt, who can say that a hundred years from now they will not cause astonished disbelief that this was one of the most successful entertainers of the twentieth century?

What I have tried to do is to show how he inherited the technique handed on by music-hall stars of his youth, men like Félix Mayol, Harry Fragson, Max Dearly, and from it evolved his own unique style. He was also a shrewd judge of English music-hall and learned a lot from George Robey and Grossmith. Mistinguett features largely in these pages, not only because, after his mother, she was the most important woman in his life, but also because she taught him much about the craft of the stage. He always welcomed new ideas – in his mid-seventies he was excited by the discovery of *Beyond The Fringe* – and sought novelty to the end. No career that depends on the favour of the public would have lasted for a triumphant sixty-eight years without ceaseless adaptation. Having learned how to master rowdy music-hall audiences, he evolved into a star of operetta. He passed easily from musical comedy to silent cinema, and then into the very different world of the sound film. In middle age he became a character actor. By the end of the nineteen-sixties he had made himself an accomplished television performer. There seemed to be no medium which could resist the tireless patience, hard work and dedication he brought to every challenge that faced him. The jaunty straw-hatted figure who charmed people with that nineteen-twenties hit "Valentine" was to delight their grandchildren with "Thank Heaven For Little Girls" many years later.

His story is worth telling. He himself delighted to tell it, and the passages of direct speech in this book are quoted on the authority of his own autobiographical accounts. Chevalier rose from the vilest slums of Ménilmontant, where he sang in squalid cafés amid pimps and prostitutes, to become the highest-paid entertainer in the world. He began as a twelve-year-old urchin, coarsely made up, red-nosed, singing obscene ditties he was too innocent to understand. He ended as the grand old man of entertainment, ageless, debonair, and universally known by the affectionate nickname of "Momo". When asked the formula of his durable success, he replied simply, "You must love what you are doing." Although he was involved with many women, the public remained his only true love. He lived for an audience to woo, to play on with skill perfected over the years and to draw from it the laughter and applause which were the sweetest sounds on earth. Momo was at his happiest when he set foot on a stage and, as minute succeeded minute, coaxed, wheedled and seduced those who watched and listened out there beyond the footlights. For this privilege he willingly sacrificed everything: love, family, even peace of mind. His doggedness and his strict self-discipline, as harsh as any the austerest monk imposed, earned huge rewards and made him a very rich man indeed. He was noted for his extreme closeness with money. I think, though, he would have been ready to pay large sums for the joy, the fearful exhilaration that possessed him whenever he stood in the wings preparing to make his entrance into a world that meant more to him than anything outside a theatre.

J.H., Bloomsbury, 1982

"My dear Maurice, I want you to know how much your style and your nobility have always impressed me in an age without nobility and without style.

From your old friend in the craft, affectionately,
JEAN COCTEAU"

CHAPTER ONE

Slum Child

"The heart of Paris can never be in the same place for every Parisian. Each one of them has his 'Paris' within Paris. Notice that I deny no one the right to live in Montmartre or Passy, but what do you expect? I don't call that Paris! People claim, I know, that these are districts of Paris, but in reality they're little towns with their own appearance, their own habits, their own customs – and often their own accent. Oh yes. A little boy born in Grenelle hasn't at all the same way of talking as a little boy born in Ménilmontant."

Sacha Guitry

i

Old as the Eiffel Tower

Guy de Maupassant was horrified and left Paris to avoid sullying his view with the ghastly object. Fifty distinguished men, among them the composer Gounod and the writer Alexandre Dumas *fils*, raised a petition in the name of art and civilization to protest against the horrible invention. A retired dragoon captain, equally aghast, declared he would lie on the ground and challenge the workmen's picks with a bosom which even German lances had failed to touch. Bitter passions indeed were roused by the avant-garde monument with which Gustave Eiffel threatened to disfigure Paris.

By 1889, notwithstanding, seven thousand tons of ornamental iron cast a fretted shadow over the Champ-de-Mars. A few months previously the dashing General Boulanger, leader of a noisy populist movement, had exiled himself to England after losing his nerve at the very moment when he could have made himself ruler of France. The Third Republic had also been shaken by the resignation of President Grévy, a corrupt and aged miser who was prised from office after a tenure marked by spectacular financial scandals. His successor, cold of manner but impeccable in morals, was Sadi

1

Carnot. Sadi was a good Republican through and through. Had not his Revolutionary grandfather Lazare voted for the murder of King Louis XVI? Sadi determined to bring back something of the old ideals to a country which had been in danger of forgetting them.

He decreed that a great Universal Exhibition should be held in Paris. Its aim was to stimulate French patriotism and to show the world how rich, how powerful, how enterprising the land of France could be. Although, by a neat historical irony, Sadi Carnot was to meet, at the hands of an Italian anarchist, the same fate his grandfather had proposed for Louis XVI, his presidency helped to restore the confidence of a people humiliated by the defeat of 1870. The Exhibition did much towards this. One problem that caused a deal of thought was to find an appropriate symbol for the event. Among the seven hundred ideas put forward was a "sun tower" a thousand feet high with a giant light-house on top that would illuminate the whole of Paris. Others included a water tower that would sprinkle and refresh the city in times of drought, and an edifice in the shape of a guillotine. Eventually the plan submitted by the engineer Eiffel was accepted. He, like Carnot, was a fervent Republican. His infamous tower – it was bound to fall down within a few years, said critics, and was a mad contraption defying all the laws of gravity – stood precisely three hundred metres high. This, he explained, was because he planned that it should have one thousand, seven hundred and eighty-nine steps to honour the date of the Revolution.

What became known as the Eiffel Tower did not take long to build. Started in 1887, the gaunt framework was already complete in 1888. On the evening of 12 September the electric lights were tested in readiness for the official opening six months later. For the first time the bright silhouette flashed and twinkled through the dusk. Earlier that very day the child destined, at least for foreigners, to symbolize Paris as vividly as the Eiffel Tower, chose by a pleasing coincidence to enter this world.

The scene of Maurice Chevalier's birth was far removed in distance and character from the fashionable neighbourhood of the Eiffel Tower. The rue du Retrait, where he first saw the light of day, was built in 1812 along the line of an ancient vineyard and ran through the old village of Ménilmontant, itself a dependency of Belleville. In 1860 both communities were swallowed up by the devouring monster of Paris. Yet Ménilmontant still preserves something of its original village atmosphere. The houses are built on the highest hills in the capital after Montmartre. At the time of Chevalier's birth the streets were shabby and raucous. Few tourists or visitors came there, and those who did, perhaps on their way to sample the green delights of the Parc des Buttes Chaumont, took care to avoid the dreary rue du Retrait.

The Chevalier family lived at number twenty-nine in a hovel-like apartment. The neighbourhood was rough and populous. The houses in the street sheltered scores of working-class families crammed into tiny rooms between walls that were cracked and glistening with damp. Navvies lived there, and coachmen and labourers and dustmen and all those workers whose existence depended solely on their physical strength. The life they led was vigorous and crude. Perhaps they had heard about and glimpsed the distant illumination of the Eiffel Tower. Perhaps, too, they had for a moment seen in the desperate adventure of General Boulanger a hope of better things to come. It is much more likely that they found in drink what entertainment or political philosophy or culture happened to come their way. However many speeches were made by Sadi Carnot in all his frigid pomposity, however many grand Exhibitions were held to the greater glory of France, the workers in the rue du Retrait were so exhausted by the bare struggle to keep alive that they had little energy to spare for other things, and drink was the supreme consolation. At a time when statistics reported that the average Frenchman drank seven pints of pure alcohol a year, Victor Charles Chevalier, house-painter, domiciled at 29 rue du Retrait, was accustomed in the course of twelve months to swallow much, much more than the official estimate.

When sober he was, employers found, a neat and reliable craftsman. These periods of clarity were, though, not frequent. By his wife Joséphine he had seven children. Only three of them survived, all boys. The eldest son, Charles, was his assistant. Paul had begun to learn the metal engraving trade. Maurice was the youngest and the last of the family. Their mother was Belgian, a small, quiet, gentle woman. She loved Victor Chevalier. As he left for work each morning she would give him a wistful and reluctant goodbye. In the evening, as the time of his return drew nearer, she would hum an excited little tune. Usually he was late. Then the sound of uneven, clattering footsteps was heard, the door lurched open, and he staggered, drunk, into the room. His journey home led him by way of taverns whose invitation he could not resist. After supper he would collapse on his bed in a fuddled stupor. Often Joséphine would sit long into the night while the rest of the family slept, her face covered with silent tears.

During the day there was no time for weeping. She did the housework, mended and washed clothes, ironed them, cleaned the apartment and scrubbed the floors. In her few spare moments she was busy with the lace-making that earned much-needed francs to be thriftily put away against emergencies and out of Victor's reach. She would often have to stitch away throughout the night, moving quietly so as not to disturb anyone's sleep and working by the dim rays of a lamp turned down as low as possible. By morning, the order safely completed in time, her face was pale and her eyes were shadowed with dark rings. She did not complain.

Soon after the birth of Maurice the Chevaliers moved to number fifteen in the rue Julien-Lacroix, another grim narrow street which runs its course between the rue de Ménilmontant and the rue de Belleville. Here they knew the luxury of two small rooms in which to live. Victor continued to drink. His homecomings were occasions of drama and raised voices. In the morning he was repentant, swearing never to touch a drop again. But they all knew that at night he would be back, reeling and cursing with all the familiar violence. Once the child Maurice heard the sound of weeping and saw his mother's face contorted with despair.

"You're crying, Mama," he said in puzzlement.

She smiled uneasily at him and put her finger to her lips. "My eyes are bad because I've been sewing all day in a poor light. It's not good for them," she lied.

There came an evening when Victor erupted more brutally than ever. He shouted and stormed. He covered Joséphine with sneers and abuse. He roared obscenities. She stood through it all and said nothing. Her silence fuelled his anger. As he ranted and swore, her one visible reaction was to stroke her face whence all colour had gone. Her eyes widened with shock and her hand moved in a gesture of infinite suffering. Victor blundered out and slammed the door behind him. She never saw him again.

The room was silent. There were to be no more scenes of drunkenness and uproar followed by moments of pathetic contrition. Joséphine sensed that he had gone for good and no one ever heard her mention his name afterwards. Yet in those few moments of quiet that followed his departure a grimace of inexpressible anguish passed over her features. She forgot all the distress and the hurtful words. She only remembered the man she had once loved.

Charles, the elder son, now became, at the age of twenty, head of the family. He did not remain so for long since he wanted to get married and set up his own home. His mother did not protest and hid her disappointment beneath a sympathetic smile. She was to lose a son and the family to be deprived of a living wage. The only money coming in now consisted of the three francs a day earned by Paul, the apprentice engraver. So she worked harder than ever at her stitching and sewing, slaved as a charwoman and took on every possible task in addition to the labours of running her own home and looking after the two boys who were left. Inevitably she wore herself out. Anaemia set in, blood collected around her eye-lids and she started going blind. Again and again she collapsed and fainted.

The doctor ordered her to hospital. She explained to Paul how he was to manage while she was away. But what about Maurice? The doctor signed a certificate for him to be taken in by the Hospice des Enfants Assistés, a home for children temporarily motherless. Joséphine said goodbye to Maurice and clutched him so hard that she had not the strength to withdraw. She was helped away, and a friendly neighbour took the child to the rue Denfert-Rochereau and the Hospice des Enfants, a place miles away from the slums of Ménilmontant.

There were three other urchins in the waiting-room of the large and mysterious building, and this gave the child a comforting sense of shared experience in the unknown adventures that lay ahead. He was soaped and thoroughly washed. An almoner gave him a medallion with his number on it, and a blue uniform to wear. The girls lived in a building across the way. The boys were huddled together like rabbits, fearful and jumpy, into their own quarters. Some of them had led such awful lives outside that they were overjoyed to find themselves in what was, for them, a paradise, and they trembled at the thought that one day they would have to return to the horrors of their previous existence. Maurice, however, longed for the time of reunion with his family.

The authorities were not unkind, and among the children there grew up a feeling of comradeship. Some weeks later, when they were out in the playground, an orderly told Maurice that his mother had left hospital and was ready to see him at home. The neighbour who brought him there was now waiting in the office to take him back. He sat in the bus with unseeing eyes as the vehicle trundled across Paris on the return journey to Ménilmontant. At number fifteen in the rue Julien-Lacroix he ran up the mouldy, decaying stairs and tumbled breathlessly into the room. Joséphine lay in bed, frail and pallid. She held out her skinny arms. Without a word he rushed over and put his head on her shoulder, nestling down into the hollow where at night he would go to sleep. If they had no money and no future they had, at least, each other.

From the rue Julien-Lacroix Maurice went each day to a charity school in the rue Boyer, a turning off the busy rue de Ménilmontant. Here the priests taught him to read and write. Here, too, he learned more practical lessons. He was a new arrival among the community of small boys and fair game for torment. They gathered round him in the playground. "Grosse tête!" they screeched at him. "Look at him! Big Head!" Others came running up, keen to see the fun and to test out the stranger.

"Is that any of your business, Prune-face?" replied the embattled Maurice. The crowd grew bigger. One boy reached over and grabbed at his hair. Another kicked him with hob-nailed boots. Their prey quivered at the injustice of it all. A wave of anger burned through him. He looked at the ugly, threatening faces that mocked and jeered him, and he bellowed with fury. His sudden roar quelled them for a moment and they stared at him in surprise. Then he lashed out, his legs, arms and fists whirling about in a frenzy. By chance an innocent bystander was caught on the nose. Maurice's head connected with his chin, a flailing boot smashed between his legs and he fell shrieking to the ground. There was a silence and the mob retreated, fearful of the panting, livid child who defied them. The bell rang for classes to start again and they trooped back indoors. It had not, Maurice realized, been courage that won the day but a sense of fear and desperation which galvanized him into action. Yet he had established himself, and the fact that by a cruel chance he had beaten up someone who did not really deserve it simply proved once more the harshness of life.

His education continued. He liked to walk about the crowded pavements of the rue de Ménilmontant and to see the heavy carts rumbling back and forth, the horse-buses clinking their way over the cobblestones and, very occasionally, an elegant carriage bearing people to and from another world of which a slum child could only dream. He stopped to watch a gang of workmen playing cards on an up-turned packing-case and wondered at the money that changed hands, money that to his childish eyes represented wealth untold.

Someone tapped him on the shoulder. He turned and saw a dark-haired man with a hopeful expression. The man handed him a letter and asked him to deliver it to a lady who lived on the sixth floor of an apartment block opposite. With the letter in one hand and a sou in the other, Maurice went on his errand. He found the lady, gave her the message and waited for the answer. She frowned and tore up the letter. He took the pieces back to the man waiting in the street below. The latter's face clouded over and he walked miserably away.

A short while later the man returned. Maurice looked at him anxiously. Did he want his sou back? On the contrary. He produced another letter and another coin.

"What address this time, sir?"

"The same one."

"But the lady was very angry. She'll tear it up again."

"Never mind. Take it up to her," the gentleman insisted.

The messenger shrugged his shoulders and, his new wealth safely in his pocket, gaily bounded up the stairs once more and knocked at the door of the flat. The young woman had been crying and looked at him in a daze. This time she read the letter and her eyes lit up. She blew her nose in her apron and smiled nervously. Rather puzzled by now, Maurice watched her suddenly go out of the room. When she came back she was carrying a flower, a single red rose, no longer very red nor very fresh, but a red rose all the same. She stroked his cheek and asked him to take it down in reply. Maurice pattered down the stairs and handed over the wilting flower. The lover's expression became ecstatic, his gloom transformed into happiness. Pausing only to give Maurice another sou, he rushed off himself into the building. Aloft, on the sixth floor, two lovers made up their quarrel and embraced.

Maurice at last understood. He had sometimes heard his mother speak of such things and now he knew what happened. A lovers' quarrel! The window on the sixth floor held his attention, and for a long time he stood and gazed at it, more fascinated by the little drama than by the workmen's card game. The sadness, the joy, the

swift changes of emotion, the transition from the bitter to the
sweet, all these bewildering feelings told him of an experience more
profound than anything he had known before.

After which he fingered the sous in his pocket and allowed
himself his favourite debauch. His two passions as a boy of eight
were sugared almonds and cigarettes. You could in those days get a
lot of sweets for a sou and two cigarettes for the same amount.
Safely ensconced in the lavatory he puffed madly away at his
cigarettes. An odd sensation of sweating and dizziness overcame
him and he retreated to bed. His eyes felt decidedly peculiar, and he
looked up through a mist to see his mother peering anxiously down
at him. He was, in spite of everything, a child still.

ii

Red-nosed Comedian

Through a window that gave onto the rue Julien-Lacroix he saw
children of his own age twittering along the pavement. The boys
wore black suits and white ties and dazzling white shirts. The girls,
dressed in white too, had new skirts that flounced and rustled as
they ran ahead of the proud mothers and fathers. They were on their
way to the church of Ménilmontant, for it was the day of their First
Communion and the whole neighbourhood came out rejoicing.
For Maurice there were to be no smart suits, no silken armband, no
white shirt. Such things were far beyond the means of the
impoverished Chevalier household. He saw the last of the children
sweep merrily by and tears rose to his eyes. His mother, unable to
find words of comfort, patted his hand in silence.

One harsh winter round about 1896 he played truant from school
and helped the teams of workmen clearing snow in the hilly streets
about Ménilmontant. Wet, cold, tired, he would stumble home
through the slush each night holding a few precious francs in his
hands. As Christmas approached he decided to buy his mother a
present with some of his earnings. He chose the freshest and biggest

loaf of bread he could find, so hot and steaming that it warmed his chapped and frozen hands back into life. He never forgot the sweet aroma of the bread, and all his life he was to remember it as the most delicious he had ever tasted. His mother smiled, kissed him, and then smoothed grease over his raw red hands. After she'd given him a piece of her "Christmas present" he licked the grease with an appreciative tongue. It was a banquet.

Although Madame Chevalier still tortured her eyes long into the night with lace-making and by day went from house to house carrying bucket and mop on cleaning jobs, things began steadily to improve a little. Her son Paul finished his apprenticeship earlier than expected and became a qualified engraver, making seven francs a day – forty-two francs a week – which meant a large boost to the family fortunes. As a sign of their improved circumstances the Chevaliers moved down from the third floor to a slightly better apartment on the first.

At the age of ten and a half, duly furnished with his school-leaving certificate, Maurice too was ready to become a wage-earner. He knew how to read and write, he knew how to do simple arithmetic and how to conjugate most of the irregular verbs. He joined his elder brother Paul as an apprentice engraver. The job lasted only a few weeks. Engraving was not for him, and neither was the electrician's post that followed. Then came a fortnight in a carpenter's shop and a surrealistic episode in an establishment paint-ing toy dolls. The daydreamer inevitably found himself shaping eyes where mouths should have been and noses where by rights Nature had decreed ears to be placed. His longest period of em-ployment was in a nail factory. Little intelligence was required to operate the press that stamped out tin tacks, and the monotonous work could be done with the least thought. Even here things contrived to go wrong. In a moment of abstraction he caught his thumb in the machine. Once again he was given the sack and, as a permanent reminder, an ugly scar on the thumb of his right hand which never vanished.

With a little more money coming in his mother would sometimes take her boys out for an evening's entertainment. They were an affectionate trio, the small, delicately boned "La Louque" as they called her, an affectionate nonsense nickname which had no mean-ing, the skinny gangling Paul, and the plump little Maurice. A

favourite spectacle was one of the circuses which delighted gener-
rations of Parisian children, the Cirque Médrano or the Cirque
d'Hiver. The trapeze performers enchanted Maurice, and he longed
to be an acrobat, one of those heavenly beings in glittering costumes
who defied all logic and gravity with manoeuvres of thrilling grace
high up amid the cross-beams of searchlights. At home he tried out
falls and somersaults. In the streets he performed lively cart-wheels
and bruised himself on the stones. With his playmates he set up
improbable balancing-acts and toppled to the ground with a thud
that knocked all the breath out of his body.

He infected Paul with his raging enthusiasm for the circus. It was
fashionable at that time for music-hall turns to describe themselves
in English as the "Richelieu Brothers", the "Dubarry Brothers"
and so on. The Chevaliers had thought at first that the word
"brothers" was a name. When they realized it meant *frères* in their
own language they were enchanted. Some old posters were
acquired and adapted to bear the legend "Chevalier Brothers". In
the evenings, to the amusement of La Louque, who could see no
harm in the craze provided it did not interfere with the serious job of
earning a living, they practised routines in a nearby gymnasium.

Amid earnest young men who twirled dumb-bells and wrestled
energetically on the sawdust, the "Chevalier Brothers" finished
preparing their act. Paul began with some weight-lifting. He picked
up a dumb-bell and strained to lift it above his head. His bow legs
started to sag, the muscles on his scrawny chest swelled in agony,
and the cords along his neck stood out in protest. He put down the
forty-pound weight and panted with relief. Maurice now scrambled up onto his shoulders and tried a reverse somersault that landed
him sprawling painfully on the ground. The two brothers looked at
each other dolefully. Maurice stared at Paul's white, skinny body,
and a lump rose in his throat. He wondered why his own physique
varied so unstably between bouts of feverish energy and dumb
listlessness, symptoms which, he was later to discover, were caused
by an unsuspected appendix and lung trouble. The "Chevalier
Brothers", he decided ruefully, were just two undernourished slum
children without the strength or the skill ever to appear on a circus
programme. The dream faded.

Yet it did not entirely vanish. If, he reasoned, an acrobat's career
was beyond him, at least he could work for the circus in another job.
He was taken on at the Cirque d'Hiver, which, like the Cirque

Médrano, supplied Paris audiences with a ceaseless flow of clowns, performing animals and high-wire artistes. The engagement was as standby for a trio of acrobats. No salary was paid, and for nothing he happily swept out the cages, sold programmes and refreshments, and helped tidy up after shows. Perhaps one day a member of the trio would be ill – not too ill, he hoped, but unwell enough to be prevented from appearing – and the great moment when Maurice Chevalier took his place would arrive. It did not happen like that. One day, while preparing a routine with them, he fell himself from the tightrope and fractured his pelvis. La Louque, horrified, never allowed him near the Cirque d'Hiver again, and in the long bed-ridden weeks he laid plans to start another career.

For although the circus was denied him, it was probable that he could find an audience at cafés-concerts. In between the boring round of short-lived jobs when he dreamed the days away and the latest songs trotted through his brain to deaden his mind against the tedium, La Louque took him occasionally to the Café des Trois Lions for a Saturday night treat. The Café des Trois Lions was an undistinguished example of the liveliest popular entertainment then favoured by the working classes. Café-concert as an institution already had a long history. As far back as the seventeen-sixties there were cafés on the boulevards where you could take your drink and at the same time watch tumblers, dancers and singers performing. Napoleon, of course, who could keep his hands off nothing, shut them all down when he became Emperor, on the grounds that they were nests of political intrigue. By the time of the Second Empire they were back again and in still greater number. There were scores of them throughout Paris, ranging from the elegant Café de l'Horloge with its flowers and mirrors to the fly-blown Café des Trois Lions in Ménilmontant. Through a haze of tobacco smoke and the fumes of cheap wine blared sentimental waltzes, bawdy refrains and comic songs. The patrons were rough and ready: apprentice lads anxious to impress their girlfriends by shouting down turns they disapproved of; labourers and their wives keen to forget the struggle for life in a blur of harsh liquor and tinkling tunes.

The people who drank at the Café des Trois Lions knew what they wanted. They applauded noisily when they heard patriotic songs calling for the return of Alsace and Lorraine, the lost provinces stolen by the filthy Boche. They swayed in appreciation when Paulette Darty, the queen of the slow waltz, pointed her capacious bosom at them and drifted majestically around to the rhythm of a cheap languorous melody. They loved rudery, and while they cheered songs that were near the knuckle they went mad for the knuckle itself. If, on the other hand, a singer failed to please, a ruthless barrage of pulpy tomatoes and uproarious abuse would drive the unfortunate from the scene. It was very crude and very basic, but somehow an atmosphere of earthy good humour ran through it all. One night, when she had been particularly amused by a comedian, La Louque whispered through the roar, "Look, Maurice dear, that is what you ought to have done rather than trying to be a human fly. You'd have been so much safer!"

Although he could not read music and had no voice to speak of, he instantly agreed with her. He bought the words of songs and studied them closely. La Louque ran up some sort of costume for him, and the Chevalier family arrived at the Café des Trois Lions one Saturday evening in 1900 to request an audition for its youngest son. The manager, who knew them as regulars, agreed to try out the lad.

When Maurice's turn came he walked hesitantly onto the stage. The reek floating up from the audience made him cough. They looked at him curiously, this odd little twelve-year-old in his quaint home-made costume. He began his song in a different key from the one the pianist was using, and after a few lines, as soon as he realized his mistake, he panicked and started to croak away faster and faster. Soon he had left the pianist far behind, and by the time he finished his accompanist was still desperately trying to catch him up. There were boos and mild insults. "Well," said La Louque after he had crept shamefully back to their table, "at least you didn't forget to smile."

For days afterwards he burned from the humiliation of it. The memory of jeering faces haunted him. Neighbours who had been at the Café des Trois Lions that night chuckled when they met him in the street. They might laugh, he thought to himself, but at least they remembered him. His performance, he admitted, had been abominable, yet even so people did not forget it, and that in itself was something. It is significant that not for one moment did he give up his ambition of going on the stage. Somewhere inside that puny frame there must have been a small but resilient strip of steel.

A comic by the name of Boucot, who appeared at the Café des Trois Lions and at other more exalted places, took an interest in the boy. Louis-Jacques Boucot was only four years older than Maurice, though as the son of an all-round comedian he had been in the business almost from birth. When he died in 1949 he had sung and played in all the Paris music-halls, and he wrote songs not only for himself but for many of the leading performers. He felt an immediate sympathy for the awkward beginner and took him on his visits to music publishers, hoping to find songs that might be useful to him. Another singer, Gilbert, heard Maurice at the Elysée-Ménilmontant, a new café-concert that had opened in the boulevard, and persuaded him to take lessons before attempting another public appearance. How could he afford them? La Louque, practical as ever, came to an arrangement with a singing teacher whereby lace was made to order in return for her son's initiation into the mysteries of reading music and reproducing it. After several weeks of practice he was introduced by Gilbert to the manager of the Casino des Tourelles. A public audition impressed enough to ensure "le petit Chevalier" an engagement at twelve francs a week for a fortnight. Up to then he had been grateful to accept a cup of coffee as his only payment.

Once he had absorbed his material and managed to weld voice, music and gesture into a reasonable flow, he was able to concentrate on dominating his audience. This was by far the hardest part of his task. An audience, though spoken of as a whole, is made up of individuals. There are times when it must be wooed and others when it must be conquered by shock. The moods of this many-headed creature change from minute to minute. Sullen and withdrawn at one moment, at the next it can suddenly melt into exuberant laughter. From the nervous tension that builds up between the actor and his audience comes the magic of a successful performance – or the misery of failure. Chevalier was learning how to tame and shape the reaction of the people who gathered each night at the Casino des Tourelles. They challenged him to amuse them. He had to compete with the chink of glasses and the distracting undertone of conversation that buzzed remorselessly. Before he could reach them with his songs he had to catch their attention and hold it. By varying the length of a phrase or emphasizing a certain word he found that he could create an entirely different mood. The timing of a line made all the difference to the reception he got, and on the length of a pause depended the success of an evening. Sometimes he knew the glowing sensation of being at one with his audience. More often he had to fight hard in the grim and ceaseless struggle to make it listen. The duel, though, was worth it if finally he coaxed a laugh from his reluctant hearers. The performer lives by laughter and applause, and there is no happier moment than when he inspires them. Over the next sixty years, even though he eventually brought his technique to a pitch of immaculate smoothness, Chevalier was to realize that each new audience represents a battle to be won. And his relative success as a twelve-year-old comedian was partly due, it must be admitted, to amusement at the spectacle of a child singing adult obscenities.

The engagement at the Casino des Tourelles soon ended and the new programme offered no opportunities for "le petit Chevalier". He frequented the dingy cafés, the back-street music-halls and the theatrical agents where unemployed actors and singers congregated each day with hope eternally renewed. His new status as an "artist" compensated for lack of money. One of the privileges he most enjoyed was being able to stay in bed until a late hour of the morning. The son of a working-class family, he reflected that only soldiers and labourers can fully appreciate the luxury of not having to rise at six on a winter's morning, to shock yourself awake under a cold tap, to swallow a hurried breakfast and to rush off into the unwelcoming dark. The pangs of joy were shot through with guilt as he saw, from under the warm bedclothes, his brother Paul get up uncomplainingly and set off through the sleety dawn for the engravers' workshop. At about eleven the "artist" condescended to get up and drink the café-au-lait which his mother had prepared for him. His new status, he decided, called for grander clothes, and from a ready-made tailor's shop in the rue de Ménilmontant he bought, for a week's salary, a velvet-collared overcoat and a tall stove-pipe hat. The dumpy figure, reminiscent of a gnome in giant's headgear, strode proudly along the street. At his approach conversation died and people giggled. "Here comes His Worship the Mayor!" said a wag. "Good afternoon, Doctor," said another. The insults multiplied and he quickened his pace. Only two hundred yards from home in the rue Julien-Lacroix an urchin jumped out of the shadows and kicked him gleefully. Others materialized from the ambush and surrounded him with boos and blows. The hat was crushed down over his ears, the coat was muddied and energetically ripped. Terrified, blind with tears, he gained at last the sanctuary of number fifteen and told La Louque of the wretched adventure. He had looked such a dandy! He had been so pleased with his smart rig-out! Despite those ruffians, he consoled himself, he remained an "artist", and no one could ever take that away from him.

The glamour survived the company he kept – the third-rate singers, the clumsy acrobats, the unfunny comedians who haunted the bars and cafés of the boulevard de Strasbourg and pestered the owners for the chance of doing a turn. During the day the place was somnolent. At night, when the street lamps were switched on and queer shadows danced along the peeling walls, there was movement and life. Women, alone or in pairs, hovered at intervals, the gaslight throwing into vivid relief their thickly painted faces. They wore feathered hats and shabby furs. The yellow sheen reflected on the brilliantined hair of men who stood not far away and kept a watchful eye on the progress of trade. One of them came up to Maurice.

"Didn't I hear you sing last week in a place round the corner? You were pretty good."

"Thank you, sir," said the flattered child.

"Are you in work, Monsieur Chevalier?"

"I'm waiting for my next engagement due to start in a couple of days," came the reply. He had already learned the euphemisms of the profession.

"Sure you don't need any money?"

The boy shook his head. He recognized the man now as the pimp of a brunette who worked a bar where he had sung recently.

"All right then," said the man, perhaps a little saddened at the reflection of horror that could be seen in the child's eyes and disappointed that his offer of help, genuine enough, should be rejected. Some twenty years later the memory of this curious encounter was to be evoked by a macabre *dénouement*.

Working the Cafés-Concerts

The Villa Japonaise had nothing about it that was Japanese, and neither did it resemble a villa. Its owner, an ancient blonde with dyed hair, looked at the world through faded old eyes that had seen everything. For all her melancholy experience of life, though, she could not help being amused when "le petit Chevalier" strutted in through the door on a day in 1901 and asked to be taken on. She let him make a trial appearance that evening, and the small boy with the big head did so well that she gave him a week's engagement. The audience at the Villa Japonaise was chiefly made up of ageing businessmen with their young mistresses and commercial travellers killing time as they waited for their train from the nearby Gare de l'Est. They were not easy to amuse and they rarely applauded. Chevalier, in his home-made tramp costume, raised a few smiles and worked hard to produce some sort of response by emphasizing the vulgarity of his material. His repertoire included tales of men-about-town who met with grotesque rebuffs in their attempts at seduction, stories of innocent country girls who applied for jobs in brothels, leering anecdotes, and doggerel featuring milk-maids with vast bosoms.

Backstage he was, like the ignorant farm boy in his songs, much disturbed by the charms of pretty chorus girls as they bent closer to the mirror and adjusted their skirts or smoothed out a wrinkled stocking. One afternoon, at the end of his turn, a couple in the audience asked him to join them for a drink. The man was elderly and adoring, the girl young and embarrassingly adored. A few days later she appeared at their table alone. Her friend, she explained, had had to go away on business. Would Maurice have dinner with her? She knew he was not rich, she added in a kindly whisper, and she would ask him to be her guest.

They ate and drank well. As they walked away from the restaurant she held his arm tightly. "You're so sweet," she murmured. "I just have to kiss you."

She pulled him into a dark doorway and kissed him decorously. They emerged and almost immediately went into the next one. This time she clutched him passionately, not at all in the way his mother used to kiss him, which up to then was the only sort of embrace he had known. There were many inviting doorways in that street, and it was some time before they reached the end of it.

The following afternoon her grey-haired lover sat on his own at the Villa Japonaise. He beckoned Chevalier to his table and gave him a strained look. What had happened? he asked, his lips quivering with anguish. Maurice took pity on him. Here was this poor old man in agonies of jealousy. Surely the best thing would be to tell him the truth. He did so, adding, nobly, that of course nothing more would come of it. The man, livid, rose and stalked away in glacial silence.

A day later, still feeling that he had done a noble thing, the innocent child stepped out of the Villa Japonaise after his matinée. A vision of fury awaited him on the pavement. The girl, her face contorted with rage, her voice ugly and strident, moved towards him. "You dirty bastard!" she screeched. "He's thrown me out. Did you know that?" She raised her fist. "You and your filthy lies, I'll kill you for them."

He turned and ran. Passers-by in the street looked round with astonishment. "You filthy pig!" she panted after him, screaming virulence. At last he shook her off. All night her vicious tones rang through his mind and kept him awake. She had been so gentle before, and the old fellow had implored him to tell the truth, had he not?

When next he came out in front of the audience at the Villa Japonaise and sang one of those bawdy songs he did not entirely understand himself, he nearly missed a note at the sight of the man and the girl sitting at their usual table. Their hands were entwined and they kissed each other as affectionately as ever. Fearfully he made his exit near them, and as he did so he heard them whisper together. "Dirty little brat!" they giggled. Another lesson had been learned.

After the Villa Japonaise he played the Casino de Montmartre for three whole weeks. This was a tribute not so much to his artistry as to his stamina, for the audience was notoriously brutal. It largely comprised the pimps of Montmartre, and their game was to reduce each performer to tears. The technique was simple: a sustained barrage of cat-calls, whistles and obscenity normally combined to drown the singer's voice and bring the act to a humiliating conclusion. Perhaps the extreme youth of "le petit Chevalier" spared him the usual rough treatment since he was allowed to perform in an atmosphere of semi-indifference.

He had, by 1902, acquired an agent, who booked him for three successful months at a more sympathetic café-concert in the fashionable avenue de Wagram. The patrons were drawn from among the cooks, butlers and maids who worked in the grand houses nearby. "Le père Hamel", its eccentric owner, would prowl about the orchestra stalls during performances and shout, "Bravo! That's a fine song you've got there!" or else, "I'll have to chuck you out if you go on singing muck like that." But the tone was good-humoured, and at thirty-five francs a week Maurice Chevalier was more than ready to put up with worse.

As the months passed he worked in most of the little café-concerts in Paris. From the boulevard Sébastopol he went out to the suburb of Auteuil. From the rue Montmartre he travelled to the rue Saint-Dominique and came back to the boulevard de Clichy. During a merciless apprenticeship there were few low dives he did not come to know and play in. Life alternated between days of feast and weeks of famine. His brother Paul decided to get married, and Maurice was left alone with La Louque. No offer of work was too humble for him to accept. For three francs and a collection he sang in beer gardens and dreary cafés on the outer boulevards. Never, in all his life, did he know anything more humiliating than the moment at the end of his act when he had to step down among the audience and hold out a saucer for them to throw in their jingling centimes. The shame was almost unbearable. But he thought of La Louque waiting anxiously at home, and he learned to smile as, with death in his soul, he brandished the saucer at reluctant drinkers and their women.

An agent who thought he showed talent booked a small provincial tour for him. At Le Havre he had his first view of the sea, and the Paris urchin gazed in awe at the whirling breakers crashing against the shore. In Tours, city of the ancient and the picturesque, he underwent another initiation. A jovial commercial traveller took him out to lunch with plenty of wine. After coffee they had rum in a *brasserie*, and then more drinks. Maurice had never tasted spirits before, and although the harsh liquor burned his throat he found the warm feeling it created by no means unpleasant. More followed, his companion chuckling to himself at the idea of making the gullible boy drunk. The room began to spin round, strange voices were heard, faces vanished in a blur and reappeared as bizarre shapes.

"Waiter! Two more rums!"

Maurice remembered with horror that he was due to perform soon. He got to his feet and struggled through the mist. In his dressing-room a haggard face stared back at him from the mirror as he began to put on make-up with a shaking hand. It was no good. He collapsed in a pool of vomit and the show went on without him. A kindly girl put him to bed with cold compresses.

"The Chevalier kid's made a good start," people said. "How disgusting for a child of his age!"

Back in Paris in 1902, now that Paul was married, Maurice and La Louque decided to move house. They left behind them the crumbling warren of the rue Julien-Lacroix, its dank stairways and sombre landings, to take an apartment at 15 rue du Faubourg du Temple. It was near the bustling Place de la République and looked out onto a courtyard. The two rooms were quite big enough for the pair of them. At the age of fourteen Maurice was the head of the household and the only support of his mother. He tried out his songs on her, talked about the way his career ought to develop, asked her opinion of what he should do next, and confided everything in her – everything, that is, except his precocious escapades with women, for La Louque was a simple, good-hearted creature, and there are certain things you cannot tell your mother.

After the cheap cafés-concerts which had been his training ground he was lucky enough to be signed on at the Petit Casino in the boulevard Montmartre. In the profession this theatre was looked on as a springboard for young talent, and a discerning audience was quick to recognize promise. He capered on stage and began the coarse patter that had gone so well up to then. No one laughed and no one clapped. His next number, in which he played an errand boy delivering a packet of underwear to a lady, involved his opening the packet and draping himself suggestively with corsets and petticoat. This had always raised a tremendous roar of laughter. At the Petit Casino there was grim silence.

"That's enough!" they clamoured. "Send him back to school. It's shameful. Children shouldn't be allowed to do such vulgar stuff!"

Amid boos and protests he crept from the stage and took refuge in his dressing-room. For an hour he wept bitter tears. How could he face another audience? Why had nobody told him that the sight of a child burbling vulgarities was not, after all, so very amusing? At the evening performance, chastened and trembling, he did a number that would not have offended the most respectable critic. His reception was chill, but this time there were no outraged protests and he managed to complete the rest of his week's engagement without being sent off.

It had been a crushing experience. His confidence was gone and he saw once again the spectre of the tin-tack factory and of all the other places where he had tried in vain to earn a living. Perhaps he was not a real "artist". Perhaps he should never have tried to be anything else but a labourer or a factory-hand who got up at dawn and only returned by late evening, weary from a long day of brutalizing manual tasks. His discouragement increased as the weeks became months and he could find no manager willing to employ him.

An evening in the gallery at the Eldorado revived all his old ambitions. The "Eldo" in the boulevard de Strasbourg occupied the first floor over a tavern, where patrons went down to refresh themselves during the interval. The lower balcony was the preserve of the bourgeois. Immediately above them sat the local shopkeepers and their families. The top gallery, or "gods", was filled with workmen, pimps and prostitutes. Here everyone lolled at ease, the men coatless and in shirtsleeves. The atmosphere was thick with smoke and sweat and gas, for the fumes down below mounted up to gather in a dense cloud at the highest point. In that hot, crowded auditorium condensation gathered on the walls and rivulets of moisture trickled vague patterns across the yellowing plaster. People took swigs from bottles of wine and passed round bits of cold sausage. On the night Maurice went there the star of the show was a young singer called Mistinguett.

As the chorus fell back and made way for the leading performer it seemed to him that a burst of radiance cut through the murk. He glimpsed a vision of whirling chestnut hair and of big, dazzling teeth framed by voluptuous red lips. Mistinguett lobbed friendly insults at the orchestra and then, sitting astride the prompter's box at the middle of the stage, waved her pretty legs back and forth with a shocking but delightful abandon. She was neither tall nor short, her face was not particularly beautiful, yet her personality filled the theatre and her charm lit up the remotest corner of the distant gallery. Charm may perhaps be an odd word to use if one's only acquaintance with this famous artist is limited to ancient gramophone records. One hears a rusty suburban voice pounding out the songs with raw force and a commanding vulgarity, though of charm there is little. But people still exist who can remember her in her prime, and they are emphatic when they declare that her charm was irresistible. She had only to appear on the stage with her mischievous smile and to say a few lines in her gurgling accent for the audience to fall completely under her spell. Those who saw her perform insist that her personality dominated all else and that it was impossible to take your eyes off her.

Quite inappropriately the real name of this impudent child of the Paris streets was Jeanne Bourgeois. Moreover, she had not started life in one of the working-class districts but had been born in the conventional suburb of Enghien-les-Bains, where her Belgian father ran an upholstering shop. She was a tomboy rather than the sedate daughter of a respectable tradesman's family. Whenever she heard music she forgot her deportment lessons and could not help jigging about in an unladylike manner. Hoping to channel her enthusiasm into a more acceptable form her father sent her to Paris for violin lessons. Already her charm had conquered the boys in the neighbourhood, and they would see her off from the railway station, galloping right to the end of the platform and waving their handkerchieves as her train steamed off to the capital. They called her "Miss Helyett", after a fashionable operetta of which the heroine was a young lady whose name had been Gallicized from "Miss Elliott".

"Bon voyage, Miss Helyett! Bon voyage!" they would chant as she appeared at her carriage window and graciously acknowledged their tribute.

In Paris, Mademoiselle Bourgeois often played truant from her violin lessons and hung around the café-concerts and music-halls. She lay in wait at stage doors and enviously regarded the magical beings who came and went there. From earliest childhood she had longed for the theatre as the place which she knew was her true element. She would put on make-up in secret, invent outrageous costumes with the aid of scarves, and act to herself for hours in front of a mirror.

One day in the train to Paris she chatted with her fellow-traveller, a revue-writer called Saint-Marcel. They often talked about the theatre, and Saint-Marcel told her of a new song he'd just written.

As she climbed into the carriage he hummed:

C'est la vertin-quoi? C'est la vertin-qui?

C'est la vertinguette.

"Why, Miss Helyett – hello." He smiled and absent-mindedly continued:

C'est la Tin-tin-guette

C'est la Miss Helyett

C'est la Miss-tin-tin

C'est la Miss Tinguette.

"You know," he said to her, "if you ever go on the stage, you should call yourself Miss Tinguette."

Which is just what she did after running the two words together and dropping the final "e". And it was Saint-Marcel who obtained her first engagement at the Casino de Paris. All her little mates from Enghien-les-Bains were there in the front row to hear her sing "I'm the kid from the Casino". Then she followed the path Chevalier knew so well, from smoky dives to cafés-concerts and eventually big music-halls like the Eldorado. At first audiences were not impressed by her voice, but they enjoyed her sharp mimicry and her zestful impersonations. Her legs, soon to become famous, were at this juncture rather skinny, although even then the once-famous poet Catulle Mendés was able to comment; "If the revue she's appearing in reaches its hundredth performance, it'll be thanks to those legs, those exquisite bare legs. . ." A few years later she was to insure them for half a million francs, a sum which at the time equalled the cost of a mansion in the Champs-Elysées.

Inevitably her name was linked with that of King Edward VII, a monarch who, if all the stories are to be believed, must have enjoyed the favours of several thousand beauties from the aristocracy and the theatre. It is said that after a private dinner "Miss" was discreetly reunited with her royal lover at the home of a woman-friend in a smart quarter of Paris. All went well, according to the anecdote, until the friend's husband chanced to discover the king's top hat on the bedroom floor.

More credible, and more characteristic of "Miss", is the tale of her encounter with King Alphonso XIII of Spain. He invited her to dinner and failed to turn up. A vast bunch of flowers, an apology and a fresh invitation, angrily rejected, were powerless to calm her rage.

"But what will the king say?" asked his worried envoy.

"Exactly what I said when I saw his empty place," roared Miss. "But His Majesty will probably say it in Spanish!"

When Maurice Chevalier first saw her in 1903 from his humble place in the gallery, Mistinguett already had a glamorous name. She embodied, for him, all the grace and humour and courage of Paris. She inspired excitement and fascination. She carried a whole evening's entertainment by the magnetic force of her character alone.

After the show, he contrived an interview with her. He knocked at the door of her dressing-room and heard the warm, throaty voice say, "Come in." She looked at him, her face cleaned of make-up, her eyes still flickering with exhilaration. The compliments he had so carefully prepared flooded out in an awkward torrent of words. She rose and smiled at him.

"How old are you, little Chevalier?"

"I'm fifteen, Madame Mistinguett," he stammered.

"Well, listen to me," she beamed. "You've got a pretty little face. You'll get to the top."

And she went out on the arm of her current lover.

The remark was conventional show-business flattery. The boy did not recognize it as such, and for long afterwards he lived in a trance, in a dream from which he did not truly recover for quite a few years.

CHAPTER TWO

Rising Star

"Quite a lot of folks seem to think a comedian just *happens*.
They have an idea that he grows one night, like a mushroom
– or a toadstool. I know there are folks who think that about
me."

Little Tich

The gusty gaslight shoots a thin
  Sharp finger over cheeks and nose
  Rouged to the colour of the rose.

All wigs and paint, they hurry in:
  Then, bid their radiant moment be
  The footlights' immortality!
Arthur Symons, Behind the Scenes: Empire

i

Mayol and Fragson

Having originated in England, where it absorbed elements of the
circus and the pleasure garden, music-hall travelled abroad and
soon naturalized itself in various countries. By the nineteen-
hundreds it was so firmly established in France that, although it
kept its English name, a Gallic taste for precision had already
classified the various types of performers into neatly defined
categories. The variety bill was made up of *"artistes d'attractions"*.
These were tumblers, acrobats, dancers, gymnasts, conjurers and
the like. Clowns were rigorously subdivided into four types, and
thoughtful provision was made for something called "phenomena"
– ventriloquists, mind-readers, hypnotists, armless wonders and, at
the uttermost reach of fantasy, the *"pétomane"*, whose fundament
was so uniquely shaped that he could play tunes with it.

The singers and top-of-the-bill performers who specialized in
"tours de chant" were also carefully pigeon-holed. Among them were

24

the *diseuses* (of whom Yvette Guilbert was the best-known rep-
resentative), the comic peasants and soldiers, the "swells" and the
"bawlers". One of the most popular *chanteurs de charme* was Félix
Mayol, a plump and elegant man who wore a bunch of lilies of the
valley in his immaculate evening-dress buttonhole. A lovingly
tended quiff of hair always crowned his head, and through his
Cupid's-bow mouth came a strong but oddly fluting voice in which
he sang about maidservants, shopgirls and dressmakers with such
insinuating charm that all the dressmakers, shopgirls and maidservants of France were in love with him.

Mayol claimed to have introduced nearly five hundred new
songs in his time. ("Created" is the modest word he used.) One of
them was "Viens poupoule", an all-pervading hit that even found
its way into Proust's *A la recherche du temps perdu*. He had numerous
imitators all over the country. They copied his dress and manner-
isms to the smallest detail and billed themselves as "The Mayol of
Vaugirard", "The Mayol of Romorantin" and so forth. At the
height of his fame he set up his own music-hall, the Concert Mayol,
which after his death managed to survive as the poor man's Folies
Bergère. It specialized in girls dressed up to the neck in black
evening dresses who, when they turned round, thrilled the audience
with a view of naked rears. After the 1914–18 war Mayol became
very fat and lost his popularity. He made no less than seven
"farewell" tours before retiring to his native Toulon, where he
died, paralysed and poverty-stricken, in 1941. There was only one
mourner at his funeral.

The eloquence and grace of Mayol's gestures were celebrated.
His hands, when he sang "Les mains de femmes", rose and fell and
wavered in delicate arabesques. Maurice Chevalier watched him
often and certainly learned from him. In the mature Chevalier it is
possible to see Mayol's influence on the precise and deftly calculated
use of hands and fingers to underline a meaning or point a phrase.

One evening in 1904, a trifle nervous and perplexed, Maurice
found an invitation from Mayol to dinner. The atmosphere was
jolly, there was good wine to drink, and Mayol talked amusingly
about his songs, his profession, his public. Late in the evening the
other guests unaccountably vanished. A photograph with a flattering dedication changed hands.

"You know," cooed Mayol, "despite my success I'm alone. I
need a friend, a real friend. I'd like us to be more intimate, little

Chevalier, I'd like us to see each other more often. You understand, little Chevalier, don't you?"

Little Chevalier stood up, blushing with confusion. "You're barking up the wrong tree, Monsieur Mayol," he spluttered. He rushed from the room and clattered down the stairs. Mayol subsided into gentle resignation. He had known many such rebuffs and was prepared to wait.*

Another singer whom Maurice admired for his craftsmanship, though he did not have to fear advances from him, was Harry Fragson. Born in Soho, Fragson was classified as a *chanteur à accent*, for he travelled back and forth between Paris and London to sing French songs in the first and English ditties in the second. A number entitled "Les Jaloux" in Paris would become "Canoodling" in London, from which it will be seen that although he sang with an accent Fragson had an idiomatic command of both languages. The name with which he was born, Victor Philippe Pot, was only a little worse than the pseudonym he chose for his début, "Frogson". A colleague pointed out that, most unfortunately, a Paris audience could translate this into "son of a frog", whereupon he prudently changed the first "o" to an "a".

Fragson brought a number of innovations to the music-hall. Dressed in evening clothes he accompanied himself at a grand piano and switched easily from romantic ballads to character songs. He introduced Irving Berlin's "C'est pour vous", better known as "Everybody's doing it", and was an early exponent of the ragtime which suited his light syncopated style. His spies were everywhere on the watch for new hit songs, and the moment something good appeared words and music were hastily noted down and passed on to him, with the result that many a hitherto unknown composer was thrilled to hear the great Fragson singing his work and paying him for it into the bargain. He also wrote his own material, which ranged from the topical "John Bull's Budget" for London consumption to the Edwardian "Oh I say!" and "Ladies Beware!" The rollicking tune he composed for "Hello! Hello! Who's your lady friend?" is probably his most famous inspiration.

Surrounded by a court of admirers who trailed him from music-

---

* The novelist Roger Peyrefitte, who is always ready to claim adherents to the homosexual brotherhood of which he is France's most outspoken advocate, imputes occasional Greek episodes to Chevalier – something which the latter very indignantly denied. Another of Peyrefitte's supposed "discoveries" is a President of the United States.

hall to music-hall, Fragson had only to embark on one of his popular numbers for the whole audience to burst out in chorus. Tall, slim, almost bald except for strands of black hair cunningly held in place thanks to brilliantine, he presided at his piano with humour and dignity. The voice in which he retailed his Anglo-American numbers was clipped and sonorous. At matinées and evening performances he would throw off a dozen songs in a row and leave the audience shouting for more. Off-stage he wore beautifully cut tweed suits and a straw boater, adding a swagger-stick to complete the impression of an Edwardian masher. You would have thought he was charm itself.

Yet there were sombre depths in his character. He was horribly jealous and forced his mistress to telephone him regularly throughout the day so that he could check on her movements during the time they were apart. When his wife Alice Delysia cuckolded him his anguish grew so unbearable that his career almost fell into ruins. His early death resulted from a dispute over a girl with his elderly and eccentric father. Monsieur Pot senior followed his son everywhere and became accustomed to enjoying the favours of the chorus-girls whom Fragson conquered. One of them proved to be not so accommodating as the others, and the old man flew into a rage. Fragson threatened to put him in a home, at which Monsieur Pot drew out a revolver and coolly shot him. Fragson died at the age of forty-four in 1913, and over a hundred thousand people crowded the streets of Paris for his funeral.

Chevalier came to know and appreciate Fragson when they appeared in the same revue at the Parisiana music-hall in 1904. Now replaced by a cinema, the Parisiana had originally been a department store and was so clumsily adapted that stagehands up in the flies had to work lying down. Fragson was a big draw there, and Chevalier viewed him with curiosity and some respect. It was said that he ate cleansing cream with a soup-spoon, and strange rumours circulated about his private life. "I was in a blue funk about him," Chevalier later recalled, "and each time I came across him behind the curtain I shook like a leaf." He need not have worried. Fragson liked to cultivate mysteries, they were good for business, and he did nothing to discourage them. More useful to Chevalier were the lessons he learned each night as, from the wings, he watched Fragson on stage and noted his deceptively simple technique.

The engagement at the Parisiana came after a long summer of unemployment, during which La Louque had had to slave away even more desperately than usual to keep them both in food. It was nothing brilliant, little more, indeed, than crowd-work and parading in the chorus, but it came as a godsend. At rehearsals, in his eagerness to do well, Maurice drew attention to himself with excessive gestures.

"Chevalier!" snapped the producer. "Let me tell you I've never seen anything more awkward than what you look like on a stage. You'd do better to set up as a street-sweeper!"

But they kept him on, and throughout the six months' run he knew the security of a regular wage. When the revue ended he hoped he would be re-engaged for its successor. Unfortunately he had grown so fast that his gawky figure upset the proportions of the chorus line. A registered letter from the management terminated his contract. He was out of work again.

ii

Ordeal in Marseilles

The impression of Harry Fragson remained. The ease and subtlety of his act were examples to be assimilated, and because Fragson also was part of the Anglomania which at the time flourished in the music-hall, Chevalier decided to include in his own act something which he called "The English Jig". He rouged his mouth so that it seemed to stretch to his ears, extended his eyes to the forehead with lampblack, and painted his lashes. At the Eden Concert in suburban Asnières he swayed nimbly as he traced the steps of his new dance, corkscrewing his neck and smartly jolting his hat from one eye to the other. It was all very unlike the sophisticated Fragson, but the audience enjoyed what it took for an exotic piece of Englishry.

The local bookies and shopkeepers who went to the Eden Concert were tickled by his jaunty manner, and their wives became fondly maternal when the boyish figure pranced on stage. His engagement was extended to a week. It turned into a fortnight, then a month, and eventually a whole season. From the start audiences there applauded him and called him back. The songs he sang, borrowed from star turns of the day, he made his own by injecting them with a special flavour of his native Ménilmontant. His style was evolving and gaining a quality individual enough to distinguish him from others. How he blessed Asnières and the confidence it gave him, and the welcoming atmosphere that greeted him as he stepped before the footlights. It helped erase from his memory the anxieties and unease of the Parisiana engagement. He could almost forget the awful moment when, sporting a new suit which he'd thought particularly fashionable, he had been stopped dead by the sound of Harry Fragson's metallic voice. "Is that your grandfather's suit?" Fragson had enquired with glacial English irony. Though he admired Fragson as an artist, Chevalier had never quite forgiven him the sally.

He earned the nickname of "le petit Jésus", "the Holy Child", of Asnières, and was a popular house artist at the Eden Concert. News of his success quickly spread through the little world of café-concert managers and impresarios, and he found himself with a week's date in Brussels that later was extended to a month. Then came two months in Lille at fifteen francs a day. He could hardly believe how easy it all was compared with his earlier years of struggle and humiliation. People liked him, they were ready to clap before he opened his mouth and they were greedy for encores. Back in Paris, to which he returned with two thousand francs in his pocket, the theatrical agents in the boulevard de Strasbourg looked at him with an appraising eye. "Maurice, my boy, they say you wowed 'em in Brussels and Lille. . ."

Better still, the manager of the most famous music-hall outside Paris happened to be in the capital arranging his winter season for 1905 and booked the seventeen-year-old "petit Jésus" for a three-month tour of the South from Marseilles to Algiers. François Esposito, known as Franck, ran the Alcazar in Marseilles and was, though already well established in the profession, only half a dozen years older than Maurice. He had an eye for talent, and one of his protégés in later years was to be the home-grown Fernandel, who, in gratitude, had his own son christened with the name of Franck. Success at the Alcazar would help Maurice to build a reputation in the provinces which should, in turn, help with Paris managers.

Or would it? Music-hall audiences down south were notorious and without pity. Fearful stories were told in Paris about rowdy spectators who exulted in destroying reputations. Once upon a time there was a very distinguished actress who played the rôle of a suffering heroine. She came on stage wearing a night-dress, knelt and said her prayers at the bedside, and then, having outlined the dilemma to which love had brought her, raised her arms heavenward and pathetically declared, "And now, O Lord, what must I do?" A Provençal voice from the gallery advised, "A wee-wee!" But this was mild compared with the experience of a tenor, who suffered from a prolonged bombardment of rotten tomatoes. "They're not being very nice to your husband," said a stagehand to the tenor's wife, who sat knitting tranquilly in the wings. "Oh, this evening's nothing," she said. "Last night in Carcassonne they beat him up."

As he walked from the railway station through streets crowded with a swarthy, gesticulating mob, Chevalier's confidence melted away. The Alcazar was as tough as the old Glasgow Empire on a Saturday night. Except that every night was a Saturday night for the Marseillais audience.

A fearful Maurice began rehearsals in a voice that croaked scratchily throughout the cavernous theatre which yawned before him, dark and menacing. A stagehand paused in surprise while shifting a set. Franck's eyebrows bunched up with a frown. What about trying it in a lower key? suggested the conductor sympathetically. No, said Maurice, he was just tired, that was all. Everything would be fine by evening. Pitying glances followed him as he crept out to his lodgings.

The house was packed that night and the gallery lusted for blood. They talked noisily throughout the opening acts. Then a veteran performer lost his head and, desperate to quell the mounting din, began cart-wheeling. Grimly he whizzed round the stage amid pandemonium and flew off through the wings to crash heavily into a wall beyond. The next turn, a woman singer, was quickly dealt with and sent off in tears. Franck stood by, desolation written over his features.

Chevalier appeared while the audience was still helpless with mirth. The orchestra played his introduction several times over as he waited patiently for the noise to die down. Finally it did. The hysteria cleared, and, wiping away their tears of laughter, the

patrons of the Alcazar looked curiously at the youth in his clown's
outfit and grotesque make-up. They were puzzled by his silence and
let him sing his first song in a menacing hush. There was no
reaction. He tried a monologue and glimpsed Franck in the wings,
his expression as hopeless as ever. A third song evoked a few
solitary giggles. Some hesitant shreds of applause convinced him
that he was winning, and, donning a toy Foreign Legion cap and
blowing into a miniature rifle as if it were a trumpet, he marched
and sang and mimed to increasing but friendly laughter. Each time
he passed the wings and started a new verse Franck would hiss, "It's
all right, you've done it!" He came off to shouts of approval where,
ten minutes earlier, there had only been jeers and mockery.

He was still quivering from the ordeal when Franck burst joy-
fully into his dressing-room. "You've won over Marseilles, do you
realize? They like you, they like you." He did not reply for a
moment, and his trembling hands continued automatically to peel
off the make-up. How narrow, he thought to himself, was the line
between success and failure! Each appearance on stage was a fight in
which he was matched against those vague faces beyond the footlights. The challenge was to conquer them anew, to win them over
by his talent and his craft. Was there, after all, any other way of life
that could give him such thrills and such eventual satisfaction?

Soon the Marseillais had taken him to their hearts. The most
dominant local character, a legendary fishwife of stentorian voice,
more or less adopted him. One evening he appeared in a sketch
playing the part of a small lad being beaten by his parents. The
fishwife rose from her seat and, exuding an aura of bouillabaisse and
red wine that spread throughout the house, bawled, "You dare hit
the kid, you dirty sharks! The first of you to touch him, I'll break his
neck. . . Have you seen what they did to little Maurice?" she
demanded, turning to her neighbours. "You load of filth!" she
hurled at the actors who played Maurice's parents.

After Marseilles the rest of the tour was easy, and he arrived in
Bordeaux to find himself on the same programme as Mayol. The
latter's name dominated the bill, though Chevalier's appeared not
so far down in quite large capitals. Mayol looked at him with a new
respect and took him to lunch at the finest restaurant in the city.
There was no mention of their last encounter. Next day they met
again in the older man's furnished rooms. Although they were

indoors he wore a bowler hat – to keep his wig in place, he explained.

"Listen, Chevalier," Mayol began, "I'm going to make you a final proposal, and if it's not acceptable I promise I'll never mention it again." He smiled, though his eyes had a serious look. "If you like . . . well . . . if you accept, I'll give you a thousand francs."

This was an enormous sum to a child of seventeen. The child shook his head.

"A thousand francs!" Then he gathered himself for the final, dazzling, irresistible offer: "A thousand francs and a bicycle!"

Another shake of the head greeted this tempting proposition. Mayol sighed and talked of other things. Their friendship remained on a professional basis and, unable to give Chevalier anything else, he often passed on good advice. One day, out walking the boulevards, he said, "The opening songs of your act aren't terribly important. People look at you and size you up. 'Well, well, he's got fat! He's well dressed. Isn't his hair grey? Have you seen his bad skin?' It's towards the end of the first third of your act that you have to keep putting on the pressure right up to your climax, and then, quickly, make your exit amid applause . . . if you can!"

As Chevalier's star rose and composers began to write songs for him, Mayol turned wistful. "You sang that new song wonderfully, Maurice," he would say pensively. And, with a philosophical gesture: "You know, five years ago I'm the one they'd have asked to sing it."

Twenty years later they happened to share a sleeping-car on the train to the Riviera. Mayol was now enormously fat, and his young colleague politely ceded the upper bunk to him. In his fluting Toulon accent Mayol remarked, "You know . . . when I see you in such a smart pair of pyjamas I very much want to tell you that . . . I haven't changed my opinion!"

A Character by Colette

As big a star as Mayol in those days was the man who, born Ménard, spelt his name backwards to call himself Dranem. When still an aspiring comedian he had seen, in the window of a second-hand clothes dealer, an outfit consisting of a short-sleeved tail coat, yellow trousers with green stripes and a silly little hat too small for any but the tiniest head. He bought it for six francs on the spot and wore it that evening during his act. It brought the house down and, for the next thirty years or so, was one of the most famous costumes in the French music-hall. Dranem usually sang with his eyes closed, opening them only to simulate a dazed, booby-like terror. Like the English Billy Bennett (invariably credited as "almost a gentle-man"), he gloried in songs of a lunacy which attained heights of inspired surrealism. There was one that celebrated the virtues of green peas. Another, playing with a wealth of botanical terms, explored the vegetable origins of the bowler hat, which in French is a *melon*.

In 1906 this was the man whom Chevalier was suddenly called on to replace in a big new show at the Eldorado. Dranem could fill the place on the strength of his act alone, whereas the Scala across the street had to feature half a dozen big names just to keep up. An important provincial tour summoned him away from the Eldorado. The manager, desperate for a replacement, offered Chevalier a thousand francs a month. It was an incredible piece of luck. Gossip fermented in the agents' offices around the boulevard de Strasbourg. Too much too soon, remarked some. Disaster ahead, predicted others with relish.

Among the latter was a horse-faced comic by the name of Mon-tel. He starred regularly at the Eldorado and did not come far below Dranem on the order of billing. In private life he was, as often happens with comedians, a sullen and violent man. The news that a nineteen-year-old was taking over from Dranem aroused a spiteful anger that was never far from the surface where his colleagues were concerned. On the night of Chevalier's début Montel gained his usual triumph but refused an encore – at which his faithful public clamoured their disappointment and ruined the next act by noisily demanding another song from him. When Chevalier's turn came he was greeted with shouts of "Montel! Montel!" He had been suffering agonies of stage-fright, but a heavy dose of Sauternes gave him courage and he faced the raging audience with a cheerful grin. Deliberately emphasizing the gawkiness of his figure, he ambled round the stage waiting for the din to subside. Anger gave way to curiosity, and in the silence that followed he sketched a few eccentric dance steps. The audience laughed in sympathy, forgot about Montel and warmly acclaimed the new discovery.

"Mister Chevalier," snarled Montel, acrid with jealousy when he saw his trick had failed, "you're just a great big flop! You've no talent at all! All you can do is waggle your ass about. Make the most of it while you can – it won't last."

A few nights afterwards members of the cast peeped excitedly through the curtain to spot a visiting celebrity out front. This was P.L. Flers, tall, lean, monocled, a donnish-looking author who was director of revues at the Folies Bergère. Everyone that evening played at the top of their powers and with many a sidelong glance at the impassive face in the stalls. Twenty-four hours later an envelope from the Folies Bergère arrived for Maurice. He looked around the "green room". There was silence. No one else had heard. Montel said nothing and his features tautened.

Chevalier could not resist a desire for revenge. With the cruelty of youth he went over to Montel and exulted, "We agree, don't we, Monsieur Montel, I'm the worst performer in the café-concert, and among all the artists whom you excel by far, it's me, the flop, who's chosen to play in the next big Folies Bergère revue. And at a salary of eighteen hundred francs a month rising to two thousand five hundred, at my age. Three times what you're earning with your great talent after years of café-concert!"

The shot went home. For a moment Chevalier thought Montel was going to hit him. A sudden regret for his malice invaded him and he almost felt like embracing his victim as he saw an expression of unspeakable sadness flit across the other's face. Then Montel became himself again. "You won't stay there three months, Mister Chevalier," he groaned. "They'll chuck you out after the first season because . . . you're just a great big flop!"

Others were as jealous as Montel. In a café much frequented by music-hall people an ageing, embittered comedian stopped by Maurice's table and jeered, "Well, star of the century, it's very gracious of you to mix with unworthy folk like us!" He was drunk and his mocking approach turned to fury when Maurice did not rise to the bait. "Star, my foot!" went on his tormentor. "Come outside and settle this. I'll put an end to your bragging."

The crowded café looked on with gleeful interest. Maurice, plain scared, muttered that he did not fight in streets and the comedian slouched off. The watchers giggled and were rebuked by Madame Félicie, the proprietress. "That's right, Maurice," she said with a maternal beam, "if you fight him you'll have to take all the others on. They're jealous, that's all." But he went away hot with shame at his cowardice.

The English style of boxing was just then very popular and, still blushing at the memory of the poor figure he had cut, Maurice took lessons for a month. Though bruised and not a little battered, he learned from the expert that his speed and attack were well above average. He also acquired an interest in the sport that was to last all his life.

With a plan clear in his mind – hold off with the left, go into the attack, make for the nose and then lead with a one-two to the jaw – he revisited the café and found his old antagonist playing cards. Quiet descended.

"You said some very insulting things to me a month ago," he began. "I don't see how an oaf like you can do much harm," he went on, after taking another deep breath. "Let's go outside and settle it."

"Bravo, Maurice!" chuckled Madame Félicie.

The man spluttered excuses. The drink had made him touchy, he had nothing against him, he had meant no harm. The hush was broken as the other patrons, their hope of drama unfulfilled, returned to their drinks and conversation.

"Why not have a drink and forget the whole thing?" mumbled the comedian.

"I don't drink with little girls," said Maurice loftily.

At the Folies Bergère there was little of the jealousy that festered among the third-rate. Famous ever since the eighteen-eighties, the theatre soon acquired a prestige that was to last. Here Charlie Chaplin, still an obscure mime, had played in the early nineteen hundreds, a lowly member of Fred Karno's troupe. As early as 1894 the Folies Bergère had introduced a daring attraction which, many years later, was to come back across the Atlantic under the name of "strip-tease".

The theatre was built on the model of the Alhambra in London and could accommodate two thousand spectators drinking and smoking as the show proceeded. It employed nearly four hundred stagehands, dressers, musicians, chorus-girls, electricians, painters, upholsterers and front-of-house people. Along the notorious *prom-enoir* there circulated a few hundred ladies of inviting mien. They paid the management a small fee of twenty francs each and were strictly forbidden to re-sell the chocolates and flowers presented to them by admirers. The Folies Bergère being a respectable insti-tution, it was a house rule that they should always be decorously clad in feathered hat and gloves and that the same dress should not be worn too often. If a girl could not afford new robes the benevolent management would lend her the required sum.

The theatre already had an international reputation. Its chorus-girls, costumes and settings were more spectacular and more lux-urious than those at any other French music-hall. Its audience was unique too. The women, dressed in fashionable gowns and daz-zling with jewellery, sipped champagne. Their men wore evening dress and smoked dynamite-stick Havanas. Chevalier bounced cockily into the spotlight and launched into his first number. The stalls turned a frozen face towards him, bored and disapproving. He started another song, equally robust and suggestive. With growing horror he realized that he had misjudged his public as he had at the Petit Casino. He could not wait to finish his act and vanish into the friendly darkness of the wings. "Where," wrote the critic of *Figaro*, "can they have found this clumsy oaf and let him loose in our leading music-hall? His act is vulgar beyond belief."

Flers was known to be particularly sensitive to criticism and had once fought a duel with a journalist responsible for a bad review of one of his shows. Chevalier went to see him, shaken, distressed, expecting the sack. But Flers proved indulgent. "You haven't found your own style, my boy," he said. "It's early yet. Just listen carefully to what I say and you'll be the star of the winter show by the time of the dress rehearsal. Tone things down a bit. Don't make such an effort. Cut down on the business. And when it comes to the revue, do as I tell you."

As Flers had promised, the winter revue went better. Chevalier danced and sang the lyrics Flers wrote for him with a lightness of touch he could never have brought to the crude material he had been using up to then. Contact with the other leading names at the Folies taught him the virtues of polish and understatement. Since he could now look forward to more seasons there, he and La Louque moved into a new flat at 18 passage de l'Industrie which, though still in the same area of the boulevard de Strasbourg, offered modest luxury compared with their earlier homes. Moreover, the Ambassadeurs and the Alcazar d'Été, which were open-air cafés-concerts in the Champs-Elysées, engaged him for summer seasons to alternate with his winter appearances at the Folies Bergère.

With a sudden pang of excitement he learned that Mistinguett had been signed up for the next Folies revue. Since their meeting several years ago at the Eldorado he had not been able to get her out of his mind. Admiration mingled with affection, and affection turned into an emotion not far short of longing.

"Do you know Mademoiselle Mistinguett?" asked Flers at the rehearsal Chevalier had been waiting for so impatiently. Did he know Mistinguett! He thought she was the most ravishing woman in the whole of Paris.

Flers and his team of writers and directors took their places on the wooden platform covering the empty orchestra pit. Chevalier and Mistinguett were to perform a comic number called "La Valse Renversante". They were, Flers explained, lovers who quarrelled. After some amusing dialogue, of which Mistinguett as the star had the most to deliver, she was to slap her partner's face. Then they fell into each other's arms and began to dance frenetically around the stage. They sent chairs and tables flying in their increasingly dizzy waltz. Eventually they tumbled over a sofa and fell onto a rug in which they rolled themselves up. After which the rug unrolled and, still clutching each other tightly, they waltzed out through the window.

It was not very subtle but it made excellent theatre. Maurice knew why they had chosen him for the number. He was young, agile and with a good constitution toughened by boxing. He did not care. What really mattered was that each morning he was to dance with the woman whose strange and unsettling enchantment fascinated him utterly.

Their rehearsals were moments of delight. She was exuberant yet tender, full of high spirits yet oddly sensitive. "Madame Mistinguett" became "Mist", and "Monsieur Chevalier" became

"Maurice". The hours between rehearsals seemed empty and dull for him. He looked forward passionately to the time when he would have her to himself, whirling around in their crazy waltz and pressed closely against him within the friendly rug.

Their number by now was as smoothly co-ordinated as they could make it. The dialogue crackled, the slaps in the face were perfectly timed, the waltz flowed with tireless brio. They rolled up inside the rug, she tightly compressed in his arms. He kissed her and she responded. As the rug fell away they went on embracing.

Rehearsals continued that day until close on midnight. He took her from the theatre to a cab that waited outside, the driver perched aloft, a muffled silhouette, and the horse a patient shadow in the murky street. They climbed in together and soon became oblivious to the clatter of hoofs on cobblestones.

The following day he came from the wings to greet her on stage. "Je t'aime, Mist," he said. She did not speak, but her big eyes gave him the answer he sought. There were to be clandestine meetings, brief encounters in little restaurants, for Mist's evenings were devoted to another man with whom she appeared in those fashionable places where a star of her magnitude was expected to be seen and admired.

At the opening night of the *Grande Revue d'hiver* the "Valse Renversante" was the hit of the evening, and this despite an accident which upset their split-second timing. In the confusion that inevitably accompanied a *première* a stagehand altered slightly the position of the scenery. A projecting ledge bumped unexpectedly against Maurice's head and drove his forehead into Mist's face. Her chin and her throat ran with blood. Off-stage a doctor hastily dressed the wound and assured her that all was well.

"It was all my fault, Mist," said her inconsolable partner. "What awful luck they chose me to dance with you."

"Don't ever say that again," she said sharply. "The day they picked on you was the luckiest day of my life."

Flers appeared at the door. "It's a smash hit, Maurice," he enthused. "A terrific success."

Chevalier registered the words but barely paid attention. As he left the dressing-room his thoughts revolved around Mistinguett and her wide-open eyes, her supple body vibrant with magnetism. Despite the professional triumph they had enjoyed his mind brimmed over with melancholy. He was in love, truly in love, for the first time, and he could not forget the man who continued to share Mist's life with her. At their secret meetings, stubborn and perplexed, he urged her to drop him. She explained that she still had affection for his rival and that she could not end the relationship so brutally. He did not understand. Jealousy made him bitter, and his anguish deepened.

In this dejected mood he almost welcomed the cancellation of his summer contract in 1908 at the Alcazar. Although it meant touring the provinces again he looked forward to release from Paris where his affair with Mist coloured every minute that passed. Once more he knew the tedium of long journeys on slow trains, of waiting for connections at dreary junctions, and of dawn arrivals, crumpled and sleepy, in silent unwelcoming towns. The people never changed. The musical director was usually a failed composer, a middle-aged man of lightning talent and versatile brilliance who looked back nostalgically to his youthful dreams of writing great symphonies and operas. There was the young dancer, her face caked with dead-white powder, her eyelids thick with mascara, who, despite the offers of jewellery and motor cars from admirers, stuck coldly to her theatrical ambitions. Perhaps she could see herself, twenty years later, as the ageing actress only too grateful for duenna parts and swearing always that this was her last tour, though she knew that she would go on wandering the provinces until she dropped. At the other end of the scale was the child prodigy, the permanent eleven-year-old cursing whenever she found she had grown a little and reproaching her mother for not having given birth to a dwarf.

At the Casino de Lyons Chevalier's name appeared next to that of Colette Willy. Under the tutelage of her much older husband, the notorious critic and man-about-town known as Willy, she was the author of sensuous novels. She had broken free of his tyrannical régime and taken to the stage in a dramatization of her book *Claudine à Paris*. Accompanied by a Sapphic friend to provide consolation at off-stage moments, she displayed her talent for dance and mime in a number entitled "Flesh". It was very scandalous. At one point her male partner ripped her costume to reveal her naked breast, a spectacle to which provincial theatregoers at that time were not wholly accustomed.

"Flesh" was played each evening before Chevalier's turn came to go on. He watched it spellbound. Colette was a fine example of a nineteen-hundreds beauty, well-fleshed as the criterion of the day required – rather thick-set and plump but by no means fat. She had wide shoulders and, he decided, the most appetizing bosom in the world. Every night in Lyons he waited eagerly for the exciting moment. He was never disappointed. Full, round, firm, the tempting sight always evoked a fresh and pleasurable shock of voluptuousness.

Far from Paris and Mistinguett, he thought he might well fall in love with Colette. She rather frightened him though, and in her presence he felt a daunting sense of mystery. As he stood, alone and a shade depressed, awaiting the cue for his entry on stage, she came up to him.

"Why do you always look so sad?" she whispered. Taken aback, he muttered that he did not have much to be happy about. She laughed, and told him that he was only a child with the whole of life ahead of him, that things were better than they seemed.

What he did not know was that her quick eye, which took in everything as material for her writing, had seen him as a character in one of her novels. Some time later, when he read *La Vagabonde*, he was startled to recognize in the man she baptized Cavaillon a portrait of Maurice Chevalier. Cavaillon, she wrote, was young still but already a famous name in the music-hall, a big earner and the envied rival of Dranem. The lanky singer moved as if he had no bones, like a snake, and though his hands were large they swung from thin wrists. The face was almost pretty but his restless eye betrayed acute, maniacal anxiety. The young recluse did not drink or enjoy himself on nights out. Instead he carefully put his earnings away and passed the hours in solitary boredom. Gloom and silence enveloped him off-stage. She saw him through the doorway of his dressing-room, head in hands before his make-up mirror. The vision made her shiver, and she tried to suppress the memory of that lost, wretched man hiding his face in solitude.

Colette intrigued him. She was so tempting, so strange, and yet he could not bring himself to make the first advance. Desire flowered and was stifled. She became another might-have-been. And although she was later a famous author, for him the glory of her shapely bosom was always to outshine by far her reputation as a leading novelist.

*   *   *

From Lyons and the tantalizing image of Colette he moved on in 1909 to other towns and other theatres. The heat of the South melted cold cream and reduced make-up to the state of rancid butter. Of Nice and Carcassonne and Toulouse he knew only the road that led from railway-station to music-hall. While he rehearsed at morning sessions to the strident tinkling of an old piano on a bare, echoing stage, cleaners moved in a haze of dust round the auditorium collecting cigarette-ends, toffee-papers and all the sad rubbish left by the previous night's house.

After the last performance he would saunter home through the warm night, deliberately slowing his pace so that the time he had to spend alone in a bare, impersonal hotel room would be that much less. Half-way through the tour on one such evening he walked along the corridor and found his room lit up and the door open. He stepped inside and saw Mist coiled up in a chair.

"Aren't you even going to say hello?" she chirped at the astonished figure that stood over her.

She knew he had been unhappy, she explained, and she had taken the train on an impulse. She had understood! Now she could spend the rest of the tour with him, and the bleak memory of the past few weeks would be forgotten!

But no. There was the other man. Yes, she loved Maurice, but she had loved his rival too, once, and she did not want the final parting to occur in an ugly atmosphere. He accepted, with baffled reluctance, this odd feminine reasoning.

Soon after the tour was over and he returned to Paris he had a note from the actor who had been Mist's lover. They met, and Maurice recognized the elegant character he had seen hovering in her dressing-room nearly ten years ago when, a mere boy, he had stammered his first words of admiration.

He had had an anonymous letter, said the other, which revealed that Chevalier and Mist were lovers. His eyes blazed and his features hardened. Chevalier looked at him curiously and felt, despite himself, a lurking sympathy for a man suffering the tortures of a jealousy he knew only too well. Out of misplaced kindness he lied that there was nothing between him and Mist. His rival's face cleared. They shook hands.

Near the end of the current Folies Bergère season they had another meeting, stormy this time and full of threatening words, for the truth had come out. There were angry charges of cowardice and deceit. They agreed to meet by the stage-door at midnight to settle the matter.

The news spread quickly through the theatre. "Are you really going to fight in the street?" asked the young Yvonne Printemps. "How exciting it'll be!" At one minute to twelve, by the spluttering yellow gas-jet outside the stage-door, a dimly perceptible crowd of vague figures gathered round – singers, dancers, chorus-girls, musicians – all agog to see what happened.

The chimes pealed and the two contestants met. Chevalier's opponent was heavier and bigger, though he lacked speed and the ability to manoeuvre quickly. Within minutes he ran into a hard right and an implacable left. Very soon he had had enough and was helped away by a friend. Chevalier walked off and glanced up at a window. There was Mist, anxious and alert.

A few days later she invited him for the first time to her legendary apartment high up over the Boulevard des Capucines. By an historical irony which she may not have appreciated, this grand thoroughfare owed its name to a Capuchin monastery whose boundary it followed. The monks and nuns who once perambulated there were succeeded by raffish journalists and men of fashion attracted to the famous Café Napolitain at Number One. It was entirely suitable that Offenbach, leader of the Second Empire's frenzied revels, should have died at Number Eight. The link with show-business continued at Number Fourteen, where the first public film show was given in 1895. Mistinguett lived at Number Twenty-four.

On entering you were liable to bump into the wax effigy of a Negro boy sitting astride a tabouret. Nearby stood a red model of a temple where Chinese gods slumbered in shiny gilt. On the wall hung a picture of Mist in revue costume amid an avalanche of white feathers and beads. The drawing-room contained a violet sofa and a Venetian mirror. The gleam of a rococo chandelier illuminated a vast full-length portrait of the thirty-eight-year-old Mist when young – a comic little urchin wearing clumsy hobnail boots, ragged clothes and an absurd hat. She carried a cheap brolly and looked the embodiment of sauciness. The grown-up Mist received her callers while reposing on a panther-skin rug beneath a flowering tree. Around the room were cages full of singing birds. Dolls, cushions and photographs lay about everywhere. A marmoset played in a corner with a chattering monkey. A brace of lap-dogs, their hair elegantly curled, their necks decorated with ribbon, frisked and barked. An ice-bucket containing Mumm champagne, the hostess' favourite drink, was ready at hand. Through an open door you could glimpse a magnificent bed. After Mist's death in 1956, when she had lived in the flat for over half a century, that bed was destined to become the most celebrated feature of a left-bank hotel.

This baroque shrine to the queen of the Paris night was Maurice's introduction to the extravagant life led by his mistress now that he had become her acknowledged lover. Her day began at eleven in the morning when she emerged from her gymnastic exercises. While she ate a quick lunch her secretary went through the morning's post. Would she give a newspaper interview? No. Would she like to dine with the Countess of X? "No," said Mist, sipping her Mumm. She answered No more often than Yes to the requests that flowed in by the hundred.

Then she would go off to afternoon rehearsals, where she swept on stage and passed a critical eye over everything to do with the production. The set would not do, the costumes were ugly, the lighting was poor, the black-out came too soon. In her wake she left a trail of crestfallen designers and mutinous producers. Rather like Napoleon reviewing his troops, she went on to inspect the chorus. Now and again she would stop in front of a girl.

"Look, darling, if you hold yourself like that you'll soon be sweeping the floor with your tits. Stand up straight! And show your teeth. All performers who get through to the audience show their teeth. That's my secret!"

Throughout rehearsal she dominated the scene: hectoring, commanding, revising. Her authority was absolute and producers rarely dared contradict her, for they knew that she was, more often than not, right. Having stiffened up the sinews of all involved, from leading players to the humblest member of the chorus, she abruptly turned her back and, escorted by a faithful cortège, ordered a taxi en route for her dressmaker.

There she charged through the salon and parked herself in a gilt chair.

"Send me Janine!'

An apprehensive model appeared accompanied by women bearing pieces of material.

"What I want, my dears, is a dress in pink georgette. Where's the georgette? Don't wait about – jump to it!"

It was brought by a girl who, in her haste, slipped and slid on the polished floor.

"Forgive me for making you wait, Janine. I'll send you a couple of tickets for the Casino. Now, are we ready?"

Mist rolled up the sleeves of her dress, called for pins and began to drape the cloth over Janine, now quite trembling with fear. "Pass me a belt. All you have to do is sew it up. I'll come back tomorrow and try it on at four o'clock."

It was the same at her shoemaker's and her perfumer's. No one refused her anything, even when the only form of payment they received was, to everyone's astonishment, an unblushing announcement on stage, in the middle of her current revue, that she bought her shoes from X and her scent from Y.

She made-up for her evening performance in a dressing-room half-filled by a massive suit of Samurai armour and lit with a Japanese lantern. At last she emerged with her dazzling smile, her bright eyes, her gigantic waving plume of feathers, and swooped on stage. After the show there might be a rehearsal that continued until two in the morning. With a sigh of relief the cast heard her say, "That's all for today! Goodnight, children!"

Half an hour later, in evening dress, she was at her favourite night-club. "I'm starving hungry!" she declared. She engulfed a massive dinner and, still fresh and energetic, danced tangos until breakfast time.

Mist loved glitter and luxury and champagne. Her new lover, awkward in the dinner jacket she insisted on his wearing, went with her to the smart restaurants and modish clubs where she delighted to exhibit herself and her man. Chevalier felt ill at ease there. His life and background so far had not prepared him for these surroundings. The café-society of which Mist was so shining an ornament made him uncomfortable and gave him a complex. She thought it feeble of him and tried to bustle him out of it.

There could, of course, be no question of marriage, and neither of them considered it for a moment. A star must be single to preserve his or her glamour, for domesticity would spoil the mysterious aura that attracted the public. Audiences liked to think that the men and women whom they adulated were theirs and theirs alone.

Despite a liaison that might well have shocked her conventional ideas, La Louque took to the woman with whom her son had fallen in love. Sympathy quickly grew between them, not least because they shared Belgian ancestry. More to the point, Mistinguett had been denied a close relationship with her own mother, a woman who became increasingly odd with age and of whom she saw little, and in La Louque she found a warm maternal affection she had not known until then.

So the days and the nights passed in a happiness unflawed. On the professional side things were not so idyllic. Mistinguett was what is technically known as a *meneuse de revue*, that is to say the pivot around which the show was built and revolved. However talented her male partners, it was in the order of things that they should be eclipsed by her overpowering brilliance. Chevalier began to feel it was time he moved on. His Folies Bergère engagement had been fairly rewarding, though in the last weeks he found himself cast in the shade not only by Mist by also by a new American comic called W.C. Fields. People were losing interest in him, he thought, and there was little future at a theatre where he tended to be submerged in cohorts of beautiful girls and scenery. He had the luck to be taken on for a new revue at the Théâtre de la Cigale, where a famous dancer from the Opéra-Comique, Régina Badet, planned to make her début in music-hall. Once the contract was signed he rushed to tell Mist the news.

"This dancer Régina Badet is a charmer," he enthused.

"And young?" enquired Mist in a rather odd tone.

"Probably, why?"

"Oh, nothing, nothing at all," she said, turning away.

"Yes, there must be some reason," he blundered on. "Why do you ask?"

"It was just an ordinary question, nothing more," she replied sharply. "Let's not think about it."

Only afterwards did he recall that Mist was fifteen years older than himself.

CHAPTER THREE

Independence

Mistinguett (making her entrance at the Casino de Paris):
"Bonjour, Paris!"
Audience (in unison): "Bonjour, Mist!"

i

Croix de Guerre

Régina Badet proved as charming as he had described her, though
Mist need not have worried about a possible rival. The show at the
Cigale was a hit, not least thanks to an inspired parody of the quartet
from Verdi's *Rigoletto* sung by Maurice and a young comedian from
Toulon. The latter had been christened Jules Auguste César
Muraire, a string of imperial cognomens which his father inflicted
on him perhaps out of revenge for the baptismal names of Mucius
Scaevola with which, in turn, his own parents had burdened their
child. Young Jules had ambitions to be a singer like Mayol. Shy,
taciturn, rather big for his age, he failed to please and was consigned
to the lowly job of prompter – until one evening, when the leading
player fell ill, he stepped in at ten minutes' notice and, following the
best theatrical models, gained ovation after ovation.

He went on to play in tenth-rate revues and, if engagements were
scarce, worked as a croupier in the casino at Nice, where his
delivery of the traditional "Faites vos jeux!" was enhanced by a rich
and resonant voice. His fellow Southerner Mayol launched him in
Paris at a salary of twenty francs a month. Jules Auguste César
Muraire by then had decided to call himself Raimu. In search of
better pay he abandoned the Concert Mayol and signed up at the
Théâtre de la Cigale. That was the year of the sensational theft of
"La Gioconda" from the Louvre, and at the Cigale audiences were
amused to witness the celebrated portrait brought to life again by

46

As an "innocent" twelve-year-old entertainer

In stage costume, aged twenty

Wearing the Croix de Guerre,
awarded him in 1917

A 1921 poster

With Mistinguett in the film *La Valse renversante* (1914)

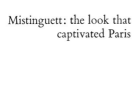

Mistinguett: the look that
captivated Paris

Off and on stage with Mistinguett

With "La Louque" in the late 1920s

The Love Parade (1929)

On the eve of his Hollywood career in 1928, with Douglas Fairbanks and Yvonne Vallée (Madame Cheva

With Jeanette MacDonald in *One Hour With You* (1932)

the lugubrious features of Raimu.

Chevalier partnered him in the finale, which included the Verdi number, and thought him an amiable companion, though their relationship was apt to vary. Sometimes they were the closest of friends. At others a trifling detail, a word out of place, could unleash a storm and Raimu's colossal bad temper would explode in all its fearsome magnificence. For although that great actor specialized in comedy, off-stage he was liable to be full of dangerous moods, ultra-sensitive and prone to sudden bursts of majestic anger. Chevalier acquired the prudent habit of leaving him the last word. Since, in the course of their respective careers, they were not thrown together a great deal, occasions for disagreement rarely materialized, and they continued to regard each other with a cautious admiration.

The leader of the Cigale revue was an actor whom Maurice venerated. Max Dearly had become famous through performing with Mistinguett a number entitled "La Valse chaloupée" in which, to Offenbach's music, he danced as an apache from Montmartre. In his youth he had toured England with a circus troupe and, perhaps as a result of this, like Harry Fragson he sang in an English accent. He dressed with Anglo-Saxon elegance and had three overwhelming passions: the theatre, horses and women. His face looked as if a flat-iron had been passed over it, and his voice, still to be heard in films made before his death in 1942, had an unforgettable huskiness which recalled the scrunch of a rake on gravel.

To be playing opposite Max Dearly, whom Maurice had long admired and from whom he learned much about the art of timing and gesture, was an honour indeed. From the music-hall Max graduated to operetta and straight plays where, acting with the most famous names of the day, he more than held his own by a technique that was wholly original. Women everywhere adored him. He made them laugh and gave them the feeling that, for the moment at least, they were the only people in the world who mattered. Max was reputed to have made conquests throughout the whole of Paris. There was a legend that told of him sitting in a box at an important first night with a friend who pointed out to him all the beautiful women in the fashionable audience.

"How many, Max, out of that lot?"

Max, adopting a thoughtful air, let his glance rove round the stalls, the boxes, the balcony and the gallery. He sat back in his chair and, as if already thinking of other things, murmured, "All except for two."

The triumph of the Cigale revue brought Chevalier back to prominence after several years of relative obscurity at the Folies Bergère. Towards the end of 1911 he was "re-discovered" and, securely in favour again with the public, invited to star in the next production. On that occasion he rehearsed a new number in which he and his partner dressed all in white. After an initial tremor of surprise the audience applauded this unexpected touch of refinement. He decided to leave behind him, for ever, the red-nosed clown costume.

Outside the stage door he had to make his way through an enthusiastic crowd. He heard a timid voice mutter, "Bonjour, Maurice."

Politely he acknowledged the gesture. A vague, half-forgotten memory rose to the surface. He looked more closely at the man who had spoken. Although seventeen years had passed since last they saw each other, he recognized his father. The elderly man was small and thick-set. He eyed Maurice with a look of infinite sadness. A distant remembrance came to the son of a family picnic, of his father buying him a red kite, of walking in a park beside a river.

"Let's go down here," said Maurice, leading him into the now deserted boulevard de Clichy. They stopped beneath the wavering light of a street lamp. The face which had been so contorted when Victor Chevalier walked out on the family now looked softer and benevolent.

"I saw in the paper that you had to do your military service," Victor said, uneasily, "and I wanted to see you before you went, to talk to you a bit."

He continued, with an embarrassed smile, "I've often seen you and heard you from up there in the gallery. It's funny, you know. While you make other people laugh, you make *me* cry."

"Do you need money?"

"No, thank you," came the proud reply, "I can manage. I only came because I wanted to see you. I'd just like to think you had no hard feelings after what I did."

Maurice thought of all La Louque had had to endure because of this man who stood in front of him: the poverty, the wretchedness, the desertion by the husband she so dearly loved. Had Victor appeared only because his son was famous and making money?

"Listen, father," he replied harshly. "I don't want to see you again. We never talk about you at home. It's too late. We've forgotten you. If you need anything, write to me at the theatre, but don't come back again. It'll be better like that. Goodbye."

Victor did not seem to understand. Then he nodded several times and said, "Yes . . . yes." A tear stood in his eye. He held out his hand, and for what seemed an age they looked at each other. Victor turned and Maurice watched him stumping off on his bandy legs into the night.

He never saw him again. Victor neither wrote nor called nor asked for money. Maurice told no one of the meeting. Afterwards he often thought of him, with a growing pity rather than bitterness, and he remembered a certain air of nobility in the old man's humble attitude. Later he tried to find him and talk with him more intimately. No trace of him was left throughout the whole of Paris. Had he changed his name or gone to live elsewhere? A curious regret began to influence the son's memory, and the wish grew to have done something to provide for his old age. As the years passed, regret turned into a feeling of genuine remorse.

The military service Chevalier's father spoke of had been put off several times until, in August 1913, the call-up papers were finally delivered and the chore could be postponed no longer. Mist became tearful and urged Maurice to seek yet another deferment. He shook his head – what was the use? She broke away from his arms.

"You're going out of my life and it doesn't mean anything to you?"

She was appalled at the thought of living without him.

"Look, it's only military service, it's not war. I shall get leave and spend it all with you." He had never seen her so upset before, and he tried to distract her from her misery.

"Listen, I've a week before the first night of the next revue. What would you say to a trip to London?"

"Will it be fun?" she asked hesitantly.

"Of course it will, since we'll be together."

"We don't know a word of English."

"We'll speak sign language."

Her smile came back and the tears vanished as he showed how to mime an order for tea and buns. She laughed, and the cloud of his departure was for the moment forgotten.

Their week in London turned out to be a joyous adventure. Everything delighted the wondering tourists – the trim hop-fields of Kent as the train sped up from Dover, the crowded thoroughfares they saw from the window of their taxi on the way from Victoria Station to the Savoy, and, in particular, the music-halls they glimpsed with a thrill of curious anticipation.

Once their bags were unpacked they started on an arduous programme of theatre visits. This would begin with a two o'clock matinée at the Coliseum followed by the first evening performance at the Holborn Empire. Two hours later they were at the Palace for the current bill, and the time from midnight until far into the morning was spent at a night-club, still watching and evaluating the turns that came before them. English music-hall was a revelation for Maurice. Now at last he realized where Max Dearly found his inspiration. Dearly had taken from the English a solid basis of Anglo-Saxon humour and built upon it an airy structure of Parisian wit. The styles of George Robey, of Grossmith and Wilkie Bard revealed the element of novelty which Max had skilfully blended with his own type of mime and French sparkle. Maurice began to see the possibility of an international music-hall which, though he did not know it then, was to become reality with the arrival of the sound film.

At the Hippodrome he sat enthralled with *Hello Ragtime!* and its American star Ethel Levey. Tall, angular, not very beautiful, she lacked Parisian charm but dominated the audience with her relentless energy and superb dancing. His inability to understand what the comedians were saying made their polished technique all the more impressive.

Each morning, while Mist slept on, he set off alone to explore the streets of London. The history and the atmosphere of the place enchanted him. He loved to walk through Bond Street and St James's, revelling in the window displays of luxurious leather travelling cases, glossy hats and hand-made boots and shoes. He savoured it all and strolled at a deliberately measured rate to take in the sights properly. If sometimes he was in danger of losing his way he could always rely on the dome of St Paul's as a landmark to guide him to the Savoy.

On the journey back to Paris, Mist was taciturn and distant. She clung to him pathetically. "There's so little time left to us, Cio," she murmured, using the affectionate diminutive she often called him by. "It goes so quickly."

It was not long before the time came at the beginning of December 1913 for Maurice to join the army. The eve of his departure fell on a cold, chilly night. As he was about to leave her flat Mist cleared a patch on the foggy window to peer out over the Boulevard des Capucines.

"What time does your train leave tomorrow, Cio?"

"At seven."

She turned and seized his hands. "I know influential people," she cried, "people high up in the army. Why do they have to send you so far away? I can pull strings for you." She buried herself in his arms and wept.

The frigid December morning saw him on a train to an infantry regiment barracks in the unglamorous town of Belfort. Life there, warned an adjutant who had seen him on the stage in Paris, was hard and disciplined. His hair was cut short and he bundled himself into a graceless uniform. The adjutant watched him wrestle clumsily with a rifle.

"They tell me you were a success in Paris, Chevalier," he began. "How much did you earn in that business?"

"Four thousand francs a month," Maurice replied innocently.

The adjutant, who earned a tenth of that sum, frowned ominously. "You like to sing, Chevalier. Very well, you can sing at your leisure . . . while you clean out the latrines."

Belfort was, as the adjutant had told him, a dour and inscrutable town. But he made a good friend there, a conscript like himself called Maurice Yvain, who was destined to play quite a large rôle in his career. Yvain was an excellent pianist who had just graduated brilliantly from the Paris Conservatoire. They spent their free evenings together in a café where Chevalier sang to his friend's accompaniment. Their reputation spread and they began to appear at charity concerts and in the private homes of industrialists who lived nearby, Yvain discoursing Liszt and Chopin, his companion singing the latest songs from Paris. Maurice thought back to what he had seen in London and took a decision to remould his act

entirely. At the café one night he stepped up to the piano wearing
full evening dress and top hat. He had turned himself into something which, in France at that time, was rare indeed: a comic *jeune
premier*. This unorthodox approach did not displease the audience
and gave, in fact, an air of novelty to his songs. It dawned on him
that he had taken another step forward – and what made it all the
more agreeable was that he had done so while in the uncongenial
surroundings of the army.

Yet at the same time he was obsessed with thoughts of Mistinguett in faraway Paris and of the admirers who crowded round her.
Jealousy made him wretched, and he waited impatiently for his first
leave to be granted. It came, after an age of longing, and once more
he was in Paris with Mist to find that nothing had changed, that she
adored him as much as she ever had, that he could not, no, he really
could not, live without her.

In the spring of 1914 he was posted to Melun, a livelier place than
the gloomy town of Belfort. Mist rented a villa close at hand where
La Louque came to join her, and nearly every day he was able to see
˙the two women who counted for most in his life. In June they read
in a newspaper about the assassination of Archduke Franz Fer-
dinand. Where, they asked themselves idly, was this place called
Sarajevo? A few weeks later the army mobilized for war and
Chevalier's regiment was ordered to the front.

Mist reproached him anxiously. "I knew this would happen! I
wanted to prevent it but I didn't dare. Why can't you just stay in
Melun? Or even in Paris?"

"When all the regiment is leaving? What do you mean?"

"I've got friends, Cio. You didn't want me to talk to them about
you . . . and now it's too late. . ."

He interrupted her. "Remember, every day when I shave I have
to look at myself in the mirror."

They parted in silence. At Melun railway station the regiment
entrained and he saw from the distance, amid a heaving surging
mass of khaki green, the tense, unsmiling faces of Mist and La
Louque.

In the autumn of 1914, after weeks of feint and manoeuvre,
contact was at last made with the German army. Behind the wall of
a village church, Infantryman Chevalier and a comrade loaded and
fired, loaded and fired again at the advancing enemy. Maurice

turned to see the man beside him stagger back, a small red hole in his forehead gushing blood down his face. Suddenly there was a thunderous explosion and Maurice crumpled to the ground with an agonizing pain in his back.

He was aware of being carried on a stretcher and of quick hands extracting the shrapnel and dressing his wound. He fell into the deepest, most exquisite sleep he had ever known and drowsed for days. When he awoke he saw all around him a crowd of German officers brandishing guns. They took him prisoner and sent him with others in a cattle-truck to Alten-Grabow, a vast camp near Berlin. Once he got on his feet again he trained as a male nurse. It was, he found, a job at which he proved rather good, especially with syphilitic patients who blessed him for the deft and gentle technique he evolved of giving them injections without pain.

And Mist? Her image, for the moment, was almost blotted out by the misery of imprisonment. On his free afternoons he learned English. Some vague idea lay at the back of his mind that it might come in useful one day, and that at least he would be able to understand what he heard on future visits to London music-halls. His teacher was a Sergeant Ronald Kennedy, to whom he gave eager and industrious attention. There were books to read and, at weekends, camp concerts to arrange. A wave of typhoid hit the camp, and he sat at the bedside of dying men to comfort them with an optimism which, as an experienced actor, he knew how to make tender and believable.

In autumn 1916 the Red Cross organized a prisoner-of-war exchange and he heard that he was among those to go home. He was still incredulous as the train steamed into Paris beneath the smoky roof of the terminus. A military band drowned the hiss of the engine and a pompous captain made a speech of welcome. Mist was there, laughing and weeping at the same time, and as they embraced the curious crowd recognized her and gathered around them. She spoke quickly and nervously. For some strange reason her vivacity annoyed him and he felt uneasy. She had not changed. Her talk was of what had happened in Paris during the war and of how he would have to get to know the city all over again. The voice rattled on with the familiar guttural warmth and her eyes flashed the allure which he remembered from earlier days.

Why, he asked himself, did he feel that they were almost

strangers? Perhaps the two years in Alten-Grabow, cut off from new ideas and outside stimuli, had thrown him too much on his own resources and left him exhausted. Was that the reason for his sense of listlessness beside Mist's overpowering energy?

They reached the door of his flat. La Louque awaited them and he clasped her frail body to his. She made a typical motherly remark: "How thin you've got, Maurice! You need to eat." He laughed for the first time that morning.

Early in 1917, billed as a returned prisoner wounded on active service, he made an appearance at the Casino de Montparnasse, where at other times he had done well. There was a moving welcome for him and the audience prepared to enjoy itself. Somehow, though, his jokes did not get across. His songs brought only tepid acknowledgement. A barrier cut him off from the people of Montparnasse with whom he had once been so close. He could not make contact and he left the stage in a sweat of despair.

His appetite fell away. On stage, during a brief and unsuccessful tour that followed, he had bouts of dizziness. A feeling of exhaustion dogged him all the time and he began to dread the confrontation with an audience. The money he put by before the war had kept La Louque up to now and had been enough to repay what Mist had lent him, but the moment had come when he must start earning again at the only trade he knew – and it seemed that he just did not have the will or the energy. Even the award of the Croix de Guerre for his "valorous conduct" while under fire three years earlier brought little consolation.

Then suddenly, while he was picking his way through a meal, his appetite came back. He ate with relish a piece of Camembert cheese, ripe and savoury, and from that moment on was able to enjoy food again. The army invalided him out and in March 1917 he started to work on new projects with Mistinguett. Among them was an operetta, in which he intended to display for the first time his gifts as a light comedian. The big scene placed hero and heroine on a sofa watched over by a china dog with spotlights behind its eyes. Chevalier was to kiss his partner, who, seemingly embarrassed by the dog's stare, then squirted a soda syphon over the intrusive beast. At that point Chevalier had to murmur "I love you" and, operating a hidden switch on the sofa, black out the stage.

At first the action built up nicely. Then Maurice felt for the switch only to realize that it was not there. He fumbled, in rising panic, and discovered with horror that he was sitting right on top of it. The audience watched him deliver a passionate speech while anxious wriggles seemed to indicate that he was scratching his bottom. They began to chuckle. Amusement turned to open laughter, and for some time after the stage at last went black riotous giggles could be heard.

In his dressing-room afterwards Maurice burst into helpless tears. Mist shrugged her shoulders.

"You're too sensitive," she said. "It's not the end of the world, Cio."

"It is, for me."

"You're behaving like a child."

"Really?"

"Just because people laughed at you. So what?"

"What would you say if people laughed at the great Mistinguett?"

Instantly he regretted the jeer which, in spite of himself, crystallized an emotion that for quite a time had been simmering within him. He was tired of her caprice and her demanding temperament. The youth who once had willingly accepted her imperious ways had grown up. The war, his shrapnel wound, his captivity, had changed him. He was no longer ready to submit without argument to her domineering moods. Though he still loved her, though he continued to admire her as the most talented of all music-hall stars, in heart and mind he was her equal and meant to be treated as such.

Early in 1919 a chance offer of a hundred pounds a week opposite Elsie Janis at the Palace Theatre in London gave him the opportunity to escape from an atmosphere that had become more and more trying. For a week he did not talk to Mist and spent gloomy evenings at home with La Louque. They made it up, of course, and hostility melted away in a reunion that seemed to strengthen their love. But the first hairline crack had appeared in their relationship, and henceforward there would always be a weak point ready to yield at the slightest extra tension.

The news of his London engagement quickly spread through the theatre. Rumours were heard – and their origin was easily to be traced – that without Mistinguett he would never have got where he was in the profession and that she had taught him all he knew. Their farewells were cold.

"Well, you've asked for it," she snapped.

Alone at Victoria Station he felt a shiver of doubt. Once again he saw the lights of Piccadilly Circus and the Savoy Hotel where they had spent a crowded and happy week those few years ago. He was tempted to drop the idea but for Elsie Janis, who, generous and open-hearted, rehearsed him for hours alone. When he spoke English on the stage of the Palace his intonation set up quaint echoes through the empty spaces of the huge auditorium. He emphasized the wrong parts of a sentence and his words came out in a jumble of wild incoherence. Cosy lessons with Sergeant Kennedy in Alten-Grabow had not taught him to project his English in a way to be understood by a gallery of Cockneys.

Patient, sympathetic, Elsie Janis took him through the script and helped him learn it by heart. She showed him every step of every dance and taught him the exact intonation of each word. He realized, when the moment came to walk out in front of an English audience, that there was simply no chance of improvization and that he must do everything as he had been told, babbling in a foreign tongue to people who had never heard of him before and who were unlikely to do so again. And he thought, wryly, that, just as at home, he was once more at the mercy of a woman.

With disaster in his heart he sang "On the level you're a little devil", a new song by the young Cole Porter, and tap-danced his exit. In the sketches he had to play with Elsie Janis his worried mind kept thinking ahead to the next cue and the words and accents he had to produce. A boxing turn came next, and this, being chiefly in mime, went a little better. He thought of Mist's remark – "You've asked for it!" – and when it was all over he went up to Sir Alfred Butt, the manager of the Palace. Ignoring the polite congratulations of those around him Maurice asked to be released from his three-month contract. The steely-eyed Sir Alfred pointed out that a contract was a contract and that as he had signed for three months he would work for three months.

"But they liked you, Maurice," the faithful Elsie put in. "Anyway, the Monday matinée is the coldest house of the week. Tonight will be terrific."

It may not have been terrific, but it was a little warmer, and the improvement continued while the run lasted. As Sir Alfred owned the Mogador in Paris as well, he engaged Maurice to appear there afterwards for another three months. The experiment had worked. Mist became docile and, in secret, marvelled at her lover's command of English. His success made her thoughtful.

ii

The Golden Age of the Casino de Paris

Paris wanted to forget the horror and anxiety of war. In the heady days that followed 1918 the capital was avid for new sensations and glamour. The golden age of revue had dawned and impresarios vied with each other to create the most luxurious and spectacular entertainment Europe could offer. The formula was simple. You took the best *meneuse de revue* you could find and surrounded her with an army of beautiful girls, acrobats, comedians and specialities, the whole being set in a kaleidoscope of lavish costumes and beautiful stage pictures.

No turn lasted long enough to bore. A revue was a cocktail in which the sweet and the sour, the strong and the frothy, were mixed and blended in cunning proportions. Before the audience had time to stop laughing at a comedian the stage blacked out and lit up a few seconds later to reveal Pompeii engulfed in a torrent of red-hot ashes, or a triumphant Napoleon on the march to conquer the world. No sooner had the spectators feasted their eyes on such marvels – which were likely to range from Balinese temples to Turkish harems, from Cossack festivals to waltzes in old Vienna – than they were plunged abruptly into semi-obscurity as a male dancer with heavily oiled muscles gyrated in a blue spotlight and pretended to whip a cringing female. There was no place for satire in a revue. Everything was organized to appeal to the broadest range of audience. For the men there were regiments of girls rushing naked from the wings or floating down from the ceiling in golden cages, and for the women there were handsome young lads who displayed their physique in what passed for artistic attitudes. The illusion of beauty, excitement and richness was all. Electricians devised lighting schemes of inordinate virtuosity. Dressmakers explored the outer limit of fantasy with robes of an elaborateness rarely known before or since. Fortunes were spent on tinsel, gold leaf and brocade.

Of all *meneuses de revue* Mistinguett was the most forceful. In later years her only rival was Joséphine Baker, the dark beauty from Missouri whose charms were as exotic as Mist's were eminently Parisian. Mist's presence in a revue was enough to ensure its success. She was an expert in the art of presenting herself to the best advantage. Every scene, every sketch that preceded her first appearance contained a reference to her and skilfully built up expectation. She never made her entry until about half-past nine in the evening. At the given moment a spotlight centred on a vast staircase descending from a vertiginous height way up at the back of the stage. On the top stood Mist. In a blaze of light and colour, sparkling with jewellery and feathers, a spangled train floating out behind her, she began to walk down to an accompaniment of frenzied trumpets. Simply to put one foot in front of another on this monstrous contraption demanded perfect judgement and balance, while at the same time wearing a head-dress as big as a grand piano and a costume that billowed and wreathed in filmy clouds all around. On the highest of high heels she had to negotiate steps which were a foot deep and only a few inches wide. A slight inclination to the left meant disaster. A moment's hesitation would bring the danger of a humiliating fall. There was no question of looking down, for all the time she had to stare out at the audience with her famous smile. At last she reached the final step and, amid total silence, walked onwards to the front of the stage. She stood there, beaming her toothy grin at an adoring audience, and before she had said a word or sung a note she knew that she could do exactly what she liked with them.

Few of her male partners in revue could avoid being submerged by the flamboyance of her personality. Chevalier was one of that small number, and in the *Grande Revue des Folies Bergère* he managed to keep his individuality despite her overpowering presence. She was impossible as usual. The Franco-Russian designer Erté produced a typically extravagant costume for her – a sunburst helmet of pearls and blue and green aigrettes with a collar of ermine tails and a velvet cloak, gold-lined, its tassels of gold and silver. Enormous plumes and yard upon yard of rich material went into it. Mist was delighted and asked Erté to design more things for her. He asked her about terms. "What terms?" said she. "I never pay for anything." He replied that though he willingly helped performers down on their luck, he did not do the same for those who could afford to pay. His impertinence was never forgiven.

It had become a tradition that revues should have titles which in some way or another incorporated the magic name of Paris. If, by a macabre chance, *Boum!* was to be the name of a production in which Mist and Chevalier appeared while bombs were still falling on the capital, others included *Paris qui chante, Paris qui danse, Paris qui jazze, Paris en l'air* and even *Para-kiri*. The Chevalier-Mistinguett partnership was now the biggest draw in the French music-hall, and their love affair added spice to a topic which daily nourished the gossip columns in all the newspapers. Soon after the war the couple left the Folies Bergère and launched a series of revues at the Casino de Paris, then the fief of Léon Volterra. He was a dominant impresario between the two wars who not only made his theatre a high temple of revue but also was to achieve distinction as the owner of a racing stable among the finest in Europe.

He had started his business career as a penniless ten-year-old on the streets of Paris. His earliest venture was to collect discarded newspapers which he found in litter bins and, shouting the most dramatic news his fertile brain could imagine, sell them to the crowds. By the time his customers realized they had bought a second-hand copy of yesterday's paper he had disappeared round the next corner. Another trick of his was to frequent Les Halles in the early hours of the morning when the market gardeners were delivering consignments of flowers. He would pick up the roses, carnations and violets that fell on the pavement. "Clear off, kid!" shouted the wholesaler. "They're for my Mummy, sir," quavered the pathetic little fellow. Annoyance gave way to tenderness, and he was allowed to gather the flowers amid sympathetic smiles. He made them into little bunches and would go off to the fair. On the roundabouts he would spot a young lady enjoying a ride while her sweetheart stood below and watched her affectionately. Young Léon sprang up beside her on the quivering platform. "From the gentleman over there," he said, proffering the flowers. "Thanks, dearie," said the delighted girl, plunging her nose into the faded blossoms. Léon jumped down and went over to her young man. "The lady over there bought a bunch of flowers, sir." The startled sweetheart paid up and Léon vanished into the crowd before anyone could ask questions.

He hung about the entrance to the Théâtre de la Cigale, fascinated by the gleaming Panhards that drove up and the pretty women in evening clothes who stepped out of them. Once a car door opened suddenly and he automatically put up his hand to protect himself. A richly dressed man got out and, seeing the extended palm, slipped a coin into it. Léon gazed at him in stupefaction.

"Isn't it enough?" asked the man, surprised. "Don't tell me this is the first time you've opened a door!"

Léon shook his head, perhaps annoyed with himself for not having thought of such an easy way to make money.

The man turned out to be the owner of the Cigale and he offered Léon a job as page-boy there. In his red uniform and with a pill-box hat on his fair hair, the child found it a more remunerative and dignified way of earning than his last venture – which had been to buy up a useless stock of right-hand shoes and sell them as pairs, being careful to let customers try on only one shoe. He had not been long in his new job before he was outlining to his employer, with much eloquence, a scheme for vending programmes during the interval.

"You're joking. Everyone's already got a programme by then."

"Ah, but I shall also offer them trial bottles of scent which I can get as free samples from the manufacturers. The gentlemen will want to please the ladies with them . . ."

He was right – they did, and another of his enterprises flourished. When a new dance-hall was opened in Paris he asked the owner for its programme concession. But, objected the latter in astonishment, there was no need for such a thing at a dance-hall. Never mind, replied Léon, he would finance the printing by the sale of advertisement space and throw in the names of the orchestra. He went ahead, and at the end of the season, by dint of selling nothing but advertisements to tango fanatics, he had made five or six thousand francs, the basis of his fortune.

The proprietor of the dance-hall was a man called Jacques-Charles who, like Volterra, became a celebrated name in the world of French music-hall. He developed a talent both as writer and producer, and during a triumphant career, which included ownership of some of the biggest music-halls in Paris, he created over a hundred revues in his native country as well as in London, New York, Rome and Buenos Aires. Jacques-Charles and Volterra were made for each other. Their partnership bloomed in the fierce jungle of theatre management, where native wit and animal vitality brought them huge rewards. By 1917 Volterra was a millionaire. At that precise moment he risked everything he had by purchasing, with Jacques-Charles, the lease of the Casino de Paris. Even more daringly, he mortgaged a vast sum by engaging the famous Gaby Deslys for his first production. He and his partner met her to sign the contract. When the time came for Volterra to add his own name he looked around him in embarrassment. The others waited expectantly. Léon then explained his hesitation. He could neither read nor could he write.

By the time of the dress rehearsal he had not a penny left in the bank. A chorus-girl sat weeping in one of the stalls. She had just received a telegram with news of her husband's death at the front. "Dear me," said Volterra, "you're going to need money." And he gave her a hundred-franc note. It was the last he possessed.

On the morning after the first night he knew his hair-raising bet had succeeded. The Casino de Paris now rivalled the Folies Bergère, and in its early days provided a lustrous ambiance for the talents of Chevalier and Mistinguett. Maurice remained a close friend of Volterra for many years. "It's extraordinary," he said, "how much work this apparently indolent man can get through in a day. Unable to read or write, he carries the details of every business deal in his fantastic memory. He's a very sympathetic type and engages artists like a bookmaker accepting bets on a café table. He keeps his word once he's given it, but he knows a thousand ways of getting round people. . ."

Between 1918 and 1923 Mistinguett was the *meneuse de revue* of no less than eight shows at the Casino. She had made her début there in 1895, though now she had difficulty in recognizing the place which Volterra had transformed with a capacious auditorium and a stage of immense proportions. Her ornate dressing-room was a mass of feathers and flowers and mirrors. In one of her revues she wore on her head a waving tower of paradise plumes worth a hundred and twenty thousand francs, and two dressers were needed to hold up the jewel-encrusted paniers of her costume as she got ready to make her entrance. There was one finale in which dozens of girls flashily dressed as wrens, sparrows, eagles, chaffinches and even an ostrich or two gambolled madly with Venetian nudes and Spanish dancers in enormous hats. She queened it over "fashion" parades symbolizing the variations of the barometer – dry, wet, snow, storm, cloud, changeable, and running through all the grades right up to tropical, which last was a perfect excuse for exotic undress. Homage was paid to opera by the Muse of Song who rose naked from an enchanted piano, and the dance was immortalized by dozens of couples whisking around in measures that ranged from the waltz of Napoleon's era to the shimmy of the nineteen-twenties. In all this glorious flood of *kitsch* it was Mist who set the pace and drove everyone else to exhaustion with her endless animation.

She had still not forgiven Chevalier for his London escapade and the independence he had shown. For her, Elsie Janis was that "chilly-looking blonde", and she felt lancinating pains of jealousy when he came back from London with two trunks full of suits from Savile Row. Yet look at what she had done for the ungrateful youth! Volterra was only offering him a hundred francs a day for his engagement at the Casino. It was she, Mist, who had persuaded the mean impresario to add another hundred by deducting them from her salary without Maurice knowing.

In the summer of 1919 she went on holiday with him to a villa on the Normandy coast. They were accompanied by Chevalier's army comrade, Maurice Yvain, the musician who, by then, had realized that his gift for popular songs could be more fruitful than his talent for writing symphonies. Also in the party were Jacques-Charles and Albert Willemetz, who planned a working holiday to prepare the numbers for Mist's next show. Willemetz, a lawyer by training and a former private secretary to Clemenceau, had long since devoted himself to the stage. He was, like Jacques-Charles, a consummate man of the theatre and a prolific writer, who in his time threw off a hundred and fifty revues and over a hundred operettas.

The English Channel, in that abnormally hot summer weather, began to resemble the Mediterranean, and perhaps for that reason inspiration was lethargic. While Maurice and Mist played out the drama of their dying love affair, the composer and his two writers huddled grimly together in a room dim with the fumes of cigarette smoke. They worked all night, filling ash-trays with mounds of stubs and emptying interminable cups of coffee. One bright day, while doodling at the piano, Yvain found a quick fox-trot emerging under his fingers.

"Play that again," ordered Jacques-Charles, suddenly attentive.

Willemetz wrote some words to the tune.

"They're stupid," ruled Jacques-Charles. Everyone agreed.

Next day they still had not found the verses for this striking melody. Willemetz, who as usual was writing half a dozen things at the same time, remembered the title of a play he was currently adapting – *Mon Homme*, "My Man."

"This is it!" he exclaimed. He and Jacques-Charles spent another feverish night writing, crossing out, rewriting and starting again.

At twelve o'clock the following day Mist and Chevalier returned from the beach.

"Listen to this!" said Willemetz jubilantly.

"I don't like it," said Mist.

Twenty-four hours later Yvain suddenly found himself playing the tune at a much slower rhythm.

"You've got it!"

Willemetz turned to Mist. "What do you think now?"

Mist grimaced. "Oh, hmm. . . ."

"If you don't take it," put in Chevalier, "I'll keep it for myself."

"Listen to him!" bellowed Mist on the defensive. "He wants to pinch all my successes. It's *mine!*"

Such was the birth of "Mon Homme". It was her most famous number of all, this sombre plaint about the agony of love set to a melody that strides forward in a heavy and remorseless rhythm. "My man" is not handsome, he is not rich, he is not even much to look at. He knocks her about and he takes money from her. But she has got him under her skin, she is mad for him, she will do anything he wants. He only has to call and she will run to him like a dog. It is the worst possible hell that can be imagined, yet it is the true face of love:

> Mais c'est connaître l'amour
> Sous son vrai jour . . .

The revue that had cost such agonizing hours on the sunny coast of Normandy brought fresh renown to Volterra's empire in the winter of 1919. The show was costumed by the famous couturier Paul Poiret, a designer who scorned imitation materials and insisted on real silk, real velvet, real brocade, for his evocation of the

Arabian nights. Mist appeared as a street-singer, as a bird-woman and as a passionate courtesan. The greatest sensation of the evening, though, was when, clad in a simple black dress, she stunned the audience with her powerful, dragging accents as she hammered out the insistent metres of "Mon Homme".

Yet despite full houses each night, despite the delirious applause that greeted sensational tableaux like "The Gates of New York" or "The Opium Den", a vision of sinister blues and greens and yellows, Volterra fretted uneasily about his two leading players. From behind the closed doors of dressing-rooms came the babble of angry voices and noisy quarrels. Suppose, he thought fearfully to himself, Chevalier and Mistinguett separated at this very moment just when he had one of his most successful and expensive productions under way? He remembered the wages he had to pay his cast of four hundred and the massive costume bills that remained to be settled, and he groaned.

Even before the curtain rose on the first night there had been arguments over billing. Maurice demanded bigger lettering for his name, and Mist, with a thin smile, told him he was making a fuss about nothing.

"Why?" he demanded. "I'm not asking for the same size of type as you have. It can't do you any harm."

"People will think I'm slipping."

He began to understand. "It's the contrast you want, isn't it? If the others are reduced in size you're sure of being the dominant one!"

Next day Volterra, anxious to keep the peace, granted his wish.

They all knew that this was only a truce. Not without misgiving Volterra allotted Chevalier a ten-minute number on his own. Since he feared this might slow down the pace he had cautiously timed it for the beginning of the second half when people were still returning to their seats. If, he reasoned, the experiment did not work, he could drop it. Maurice accepted, confident of his power to hold a large audience over a period of time on the strength of his unaided skill. In the event he won encore after encore.

"That was a highlight of the evening, Maurice," declared Volterra happily. "Give people something new, something original, and they'll always go overboard for it. Isn't that true, Mist?" he enquired turning to the other star of the show.

"Always," said she, walking briskly away.

Maurice only had one number in which he appeared with her. In the others she was partnered by Earl Leslie, the young American dancer. If, with mingled feelings, Maurice had become her open rival, he had also shown the self-confidence to break out on his own.

Alone in the corridor back-stage he savoured his enjoyment.

"Monsieur Chevalier?" said a timid voice at his side. He turned and saw a chorus-girl whose dark-haired attractiveness he had noticed before.

"You were magnificent this evening," she went on.

And so, he thought, was she, for "Simone" had an effect upon him as troubling as only Mist had been able to exercise until now.

Later on he joined Mist for a celebration party.

"I've brought along my other friend, Cio. You don't mind, do you?" she said, indicating Earl Leslie, who now basked in her radiant smile. Maurice looked at him benevolently and realized that he did not feel at all jealous. In future, when Mist embarked on one of the night-club rounds she delighted to make, he was quite content for Earl Leslie to be her solitary squire.

In public, though, the two darlings of the music-hall continued to act the comedy of their love affair. They were still seen and admired on the boulevards and in restaurants. For the journalists who arrived to interview them they were able to sustain, with the practice of years, a convincing and touching representation of two lovely people who adored each other. Of all the performances for which they were responsible this was, perhaps, the most adroit and the most skilfully managed.

Behind the scenes – and the theatrical metaphor is apt – the involvement with Simone became profound. She could not, by the very nature of things, rival Mistinguett in those areas of Chevalier's life which for ever remained the property of the older woman. He had, after all, grown up under Mist's jealous eye and learned so much from her about life and about his profession. What Simone gave him was uncomplicated and direct. Her sensuality fed a liaison based on violent physical attraction. She asked only for love, and although with Mist there had been shades of emotion and delicate variations of feeling, with Simone there was animality and little else.

One evening Maurice was out front and heard Mist sing "Mon Homme". With fire and bitterness she hymned the ravages love caused and the hurt of an unforgiving passion that chained her without hope to the man who possessed her body and her soul. Although he had heard her perform the number many times before, he suddenly realized that the man in the song was himself, that he in truth was "her" man. "Mon Homme", he reflected, was a dirge for their dead love.

Mist once wrote: "Chevalier lives the way he dances. He doesn't dance, he hops. His presence never brought me very much. Maybe it was my fault that he left me? . . . I didn't lift a finger. I'm incapable of throwing anyone out, even a servant. If he left, he left. If he chose to come back, well and good. I was unhappy, but that was my affair." This was some thirty years later, yet she could not resist adding: "And our story is perhaps not over yet . . . I have only to pick up the telephone and I think I know what would happen." Or did she? The feelings of resentment and affection, of anger and love, did not cease to torment her until death came as a release from them, thirty years later, in 1956.

CHAPTER FOUR

Crack-up

"MADNESS.   [from mad]. Distraction; loss of understanding; perturbation of the faculties."
Samuel Johnson, A Dictionary
of the English Language, 1755.

i

Breakdown

As soon as the current revue ended Mist left the Casino de Paris for
other theatres where the billing and the glory would be hers alone.
Her protégé stayed on and added to his reputation as the star of three
consecutive productions. His fortunes prospered, and so did those
of Léon Volterra. The impresario usually spent sixteen hours a day
in his office and only left it to indulge his new passion for racing. He
happened to pass near an enclosure at Auteuil and overheard someone shout, "Ten thousand I'm bid!" A reflex action inspired him to
cry out automatically, "Eleven thousand!" before going on his
way. An attendant rushed up. "Sir! Sir! Where shall we deliver it?"
"Deliver what?" "The horse you've just bought, sir."

This absent-minded purchase, acquired almost by chance on that
afternoon at Auteuil, laid the foundation of Volterra's success on
the turf. Some years later he bought a hundred or so horses from the
Rothschild stables and then a famous stud which had gone bankrupt. The latter included a stallion called Admiral Drake which
sired Phil Drake, a horse that won the Derby in 1955 for Madame
Volterra. From the very start Volterra enjoyed the fabulous luck he
had known in the theatre. His Auteuil purchase was entered under
the name of Roi Belge for the Grand Prix steeplechase at Brussels. It
won easily. The news came through just as the evening performance at the Casino de Paris was under way. Everyone in the cast

had bet on Volterra's mount. The chorus abruptly halted in mid-step and the curtain fell. An excited compère explained what had happened. The revue gathered speed and rattled on to a climax of multi-coloured parachutes raining down from the roof on to the stalls below.

Roi Belge had won, as the idiom goes, *dans un fauteuil*, or "at a canter". *Dans un fauteuil*, Volterra decided, would be the title of his next revue with Chevalier. It celebrated not only his début as a race-horse owner but also an important innovation by his star. For the first time Maurice performed his act in a dinner-jacket. He had some difficulty, though, in deciding the type of hat to wear with it. In London, at a shop By Appointment to King George V, he had tried on a topper. But no, it would not do for the Paris stage. A felt black hat? Too sombre. Then he had an inspiration: the white straw boater that holidaymakers wore on the Seine in Impressionist paintings and that Parisians still sported on outings in the Bois de Boulogne. It would go well and serve to light up his face.

On a May evening in 1921 the Casino orchestra burst into a wild fortissimo and the curtain edged slowly upwards. A girl came forward wearing a royal blue dress and a gold spangled tiara whence there sprouted huge ostrich plumes.

"Maurrrrrrice . . . Chevalier!" she announced, overcome by the shout of welcome that rose from the audience. On came the hero of the evening, his boater tipped rakishly forward over gleaming black hair. The ovation was renewed at the end of his act. He had found his trademark and from then on the straw hat was to be an emblem with which he was for ever associated.

The Chevalier name had also established itself as an excellent box-office draw and was, as people in the business would say today, highly bankable. For this reason he was approached by the authors of a new musical comedy planned to follow up their hit *Phi-Phi*, which had won great popularity during its very long run. The authors were Albert Willemetz, whom we know already, and Henri Christiné, who wrote the music. Christiné was a Swiss-born schoolmaster who had already composed the famous "Viens Poupoule" for Mayol. In the raffish world of the theatre, so different from the prim confines of his native Switzerland, he found, to the sorrow of his wife, many chances of dalliance. She, on the rebound, fell in love with Harry Fragson, though the triangle, or rather the square, was broken when Fragson met his death at the hands of his father. Christiné left her for a twenty-year-old chorus-girl and she committed suicide. Years later Henri went stone-deaf and died of chagrin when, by an ironic pattern of events, his chorus-girl, still much younger than he was, in turn deserted him.

But in the nineteen-twenties Christiné was a light-hearted musician who composed scores of melodies that effervesced with joy and optimism. *Dédé*, supplied by Willemetz with his usual brand of catchy verse and neat rhymes, was full of tunes that quickly became as popular as those in the legendary *Phi-Phi*. The style of the new musical comedy echoed the post-war atmosphere of *je m'en fichisme*, a characteristic nonchalance born of the deliberate resolve to enjoy oneself and to ignore anything that got in the way of pleasure.

The offer of the leading part in *Dédé* was a challenge to Maurice. Instead of applying his artistry within the compass of brief sketches and songs, he had to use a quite different technique that would enable him to sustain the character he played throughout a whole evening of dialogue. He would need to keep the audience's interest with long speeches and to react as well as act.

The plot of *Dédé*, light as air and twice as insubstantial, concerned a rich tycoon who, infatuated with a sales girl in a shoe shop, buys up the place so that he can continue his secret assignations with her. There was, of course, a troop of beautiful saleswomen to curvette back and forth, and the shop was of a splendour to rival the palatial establishment of Paul Poiret himself. This was well in the tradition of Offenbach, who, at the Bouffes-Parisiens where *Dédé* started life, had made that theatre a byword for lavish production values.

At the first night of *Dédé* in November 1921, Maurice thought how quiet was life back-stage when compared with the atmosphere of a music-hall première. There were no chorus-girls noisily clattering up and down the iron stairway. No stage-hands shouted wearily to each other as they manoeuvred complicated scenery into position for the hundredth time, and no crowds of extras filled the corridors with their chatter as they hurried to change costumes and freshen their make-up. Although a last-minute conference of authors and producer had decreed a cut of no less than a third in the script, the theatre remained calm and free of panic.

The cue Maurice had been waiting for arrived. He walked on feeling a strange lack of excitement. A few hand-claps of polite

curiosity greeted his entrance. After the initial exchanges of
dialogue he began to sense that the piece was catching fire. Speeches
that in rehearsal he had not expected to raise so much as a smile were
received with uproarious laughter. His first song, "Dans la vie faut
pas s'en faire", a carefree piece of advice that nothing in life is worth
worrying about, was an instant success, and as he went into the
dance that followed it he could not help wondering at how easy it
had all been. The three acts of *Dédé* continued amid scenes of rising
enthusiasm with encore after encore for each song. It proved to be
the biggest success in Paris and for two years played steadily to full
houses.

Everywhere that season people were humming "Dans la vie faut
pas s'en faire". Its jaunty tune was heard in the street, in cafés-
concerts, in music-halls, at tango-teas, in dance-halls and at night-
clubs. All the critics agreed that *Dédé* was the hit of the year – and
even more so its young leading man, a revelation, they said, who
could act, sing and dance with superlative professionalism. His
humour, his verve, the impish grace of his movements were irresistible. A musician might say that his voice was little to speak of and
that his vocal range was sadly limited, but audiences were so
fascinated by his variety of expression and the playful tang of his
Ménilmontant accent that they would not have agreed. Girls
dreamed of him as the ideal seducer. Women cherished in their
hearts a secret image of him that sustained them through a boring
marriage. None was proof against his impudent smile and his
inviting eyes.

Whereas in the music-hall everything depended on a rapid, quick-
fire attack that aimed at speedy conquest of the audience, in the
theatre it was necessary to spread out one's effects, to build them up
in carefully graded phases over an extended period of time. At first
too impetuous in his anxiety to woo the spectators, Chevalier
quickly learned how to pace himself. He had discovered yet another
talent. The manager of the Bouffes-Parisiens acknowledged this in
the most practical way. The morning after *Dédé* opened he called on
Maurice and cancelled the contract which guaranteed him six
hundred francs a night. In its place he gave him a new one offering a
thousand a night for the first year of the run and five hundred on top
of that for the second.

"We'll probably run for ages," he said, "and you're the one

people come to see. Other managements will be after you next season with big offers and I'm just getting in first. I want you to have your proper share too, and with a fair deal you'll probably be happy. And that's good for your work and it'll make you a bigger draw than ever. See what I mean?"

A startled Chevalier saw only too well. In later years, he was to learn, managers did not often act like this.

His dressing-room each night after the show became a port of call for the famous. Those who six months earlier would not have deigned to look his way now came and knocked hopefully at his door. Mistinguett was an early visitor. "I'm so happy about it for your sake, Cio," she cooed. "What a long way you've come since the time we were rolled up in the carpet, eh?" The tone of nostalgia awoke little reaction in him. He no longer needed her approval or her support. For the sake of old times, though, he went out to dinner with her and let himself be seen in her company from time to time.

Other callers back-stage included Douglas Fairbanks and his wife Mary Pickford. The American actor's films *The Mark of Zorro* and *The Three Musketeers* were just then enthralling Paris with their dash and vitality. Born Julius Ulman, a name he prudently changed early on, Fairbanks was playboy and magnate, athlete and swash-buckler, a nimble and mercurial being who duelled against villains of the screen with the same deadly assurance he exhibited in closing business deals. His bronzed features shone with enjoyment and a hearty relish for existence. In life as in his films, he created around him a feeling of movement and exhilaration.

"You must come to New York and play *Dédé* in English," Fairbanks enthused. "It would be a sensation."

Chevalier demurred. Though flattered, he recalled with a qualm his early experience of the Anglo-Saxon stage in London. Fair-banks' confidence and Mary Pickford's smile, which had captivated millions, failed to make him change his mind.

A little later the celebrated couple tried again, this time through C.B. Dillingham. The latter was at the peak of a career which, a few short years later, faded into death and bankruptcy. He was a man of restless initiative, part-founder of the celebrated Globe Theatre and the first manager to build a moving electric sign on Broadway. Sometimes he would have half a dozen plays running at the same time, and his quick eye for novelty led him to introduce Shaw,

Lonsdale and Anna Pavlova on the New York stage before he went into eclipse. Dillingham materialized in Chevalier's dressing-room at the Bouffes-Parisiens with a tempting contract: fifteen hundred dollars a week plus a percentage that might well double that figure. Who could refuse? As soon as *Dédé* finished its run the Frenchman would come to New York. Convinced that they had a potential hit, Dillingham and Fairbanks were happy to wait.

Now that he had made his decision about America, Maurice was keen to see the country. Why not spend his holidays there? Incautiously, he spoke of his plan to Mist. "I'd like to come with you!" she announced to his consternation. What was more, she would bring Earl Leslie with her, for he was a New Yorker and could show them around the place of his birth. Maurice bit his lip regretfully. The damage was done, and the strange trio set off on the crossing in the summer of 1922.

Luckily they reached New York before the tensions they strove to suppress had exploded. The skyscrapers of Manhattan and the myriad glints of sunshine striking on windows high up over the city dispelled the unease of the journey. Mist proposed a tour of the night-clubs. Maurice made his own Declaration of Independence and insisted that he had come to America to see the music-halls, the singers and the dancers. So while Mist and Earl Leslie, her partner and now her lover, went off on their own explorations, Maurice followed the path he had chosen for himself.

It led him to Harlem and a Negro revue that electrified him with a new sense of rhythm, a new vibrancy. Among the dancers he noted a girl of outlandish beauty who pulled grotesque faces that dissolved instantly into expressions of ravishing softness, her lithe body meanwhile bouncing to the music in frenzied contortions. Her name, he saw in the programme, was Joséphine Baker. This foretaste of the whirlwind soon to hit Paris astonished him. She and her troupe did their breathtaking routines at three times the speed of French music-hall artists. Here was a challenge that had to be met and equalled.

Next morning his impresario Dillingham put him in touch with a modern-dance teacher. Originally he had planned simply to modify his style for America. Now, however, he found himself, under the American influence, changing it for Europe. For three weeks he worked hard absorbing novel techniques and rehearsing steps of intricate difficulty. During that time, he felt, he had learned more than he would have in three years of France.

It was time to go back. He lazed away the final afternoon on the hot sand of Atlantic City with Dillingham, Mist and Leslie. The air was warm, a gentle breeze ruffled the ocean, and he basked in the contentment of all this fabulous country had revealed to him.

Dillingham had lost none of his enthusiasm. "*Dédé* will be a success," he crowed, "it's something quite new for us. And who knows? Perhaps we'll take it on tour after New York. America will go mad about it, don't you think?" he went on, turning to Mist.

"Yes, yes," she replied, closing her eyes.

"The problem is how much longer Maurice will have to go on playing it in Paris. Another season or more? What do you think?"

"Why ask *me*," huffed Mist. "You've got the star beside you. Ask *him*!" She got up and stalked away leaving Dillingham speechless.

In Paris the long, long run of *Dédé* continued. So did the affair with Simone. She was young, she loved night life and champagne. Together, after the evening performance, they would go out to drink and dance late into the morning. At the same time Chevalier was making a film out at the Vincennes studios, which meant an early rise in addition to three hours of *Dédé* at night and six hours on matinée days. Sudden bouts of ill-temper started to punctuate his life. A badly sewn button threw him into a tantrum and he cursed his dresser. When he apologized she said gently, "Never mind, Monsieur Maurice. We all have our nerves."

La Louque brought him his ritual breakfast in bed and worried about his restless manner. He tried to keep up appearances with airy chat, but his hand trembled as he put the coffee cup back on its saucer and the china rattled.

"You're ill, Maurice!"

"Ill? What on earth put that idea into your head? Of course I'm not ill!"

On one of the rare evenings when he was not going out with Simone, a journalist friend came to see him in his dressing-room. The journalist had to cover the execution of a criminal who, by chance, was called Dédé. It would be an interesting experience, would it not, to come with him? They sat in a café near the place of execution drinking the hours away until dawn. In the cold, bleary light the stark outline of the guillotine loomed through the morning mist. A crowd of some fifty people gathered, mostly officials, policemen and journalists. The executioner tested his machine. The blade fell smoothly, efficiently.

Maurice looked at the men standing beside him. One of them glanced impatiently at his watch. An icy sweat of terror rolled down his back. He heard the rattle of horses' hooves on the cobblestones and the clash of iron-rimmed wheels as a closed wagon arrived. A priest got out, followed by a man whose arms were tied behind his back.

The man lifted his head and walked calmly onward. With a start of horror Maurice recognized him. In a flash his mind went back over the years to see himself as a poor boy in the boulevard de Strasbourg where a kindly pimp came up to him. "Didn't I hear you sing last week in a place round the corner? You were pretty good," the pimp had said. "Are you in work, Monsieur Chevalier? . . . Sure you don't need any money. . .?"

This Dédé, so unlike the *frivol* whom Maurice played on stage, had killed a mate in a squalid brawl. And now the man who, in a sudden impulse of generosity, had offered to help the child Maurice all those years ago, was meeting death with a courage he had probably never shown in life.

Each time Maurice closed his eyes and tried to sleep he saw again Dédé's face in the harsh morning light, the walk to the scaffold and the glitter of the falling blade. The images pursued him through the day and haunted him all night. To dispel the sombre visions that gathered round him he thought he would give a lunch party. His guests were people like Raimu and Max Dearly, and the atmosphere crackled with good humour and vivacity. The food was so good, the wine so cheering, that the party went on late into the afternoon and did not end until six o'clock that evening. Alone once again Maurice looked into a mirror. His face had turned very red and he was staggering a little. He decided he had drunk too much and went to bed for a few hours' rest.

At eight o'clock the maid woke him up in time for the evening performance. His head was spinning. When he tried to walk he could not feel the ground under his feet. It took an enormous effort just to put his make-up on, and he sat staring blankly at the pot of cream in his hand. The voices of his fellow-actors came to him as from a distance and muffled in cotton wool. A doctor arrived a few moments before curtain-up and told him that an excess of rich food and alcohol was the cause of the symptoms. He left a powder to be taken in water and reassured his stupefied patient that all would be well.

Yes, all would be well, Maurice whispered to himself hopefully as he made his first entrance to welcoming cheers and laughter. The face of his partner on stage went in and out of focus, the lips moved and only a tendril of sound came out of them. Maurice uttered his first line of dialogue and prepared for his next cue. It came, but then he suddenly switched to lines he had to say in the third act. He could move, he could walk, but his brain seemed permanently frozen. The other people in the cast did what they could to cover up, hissing cues at him under their breath and trying to distract attention from his fumbling gestures. For the rest of the evening he was tortured by the fear of not remembering his lines. His fist clenched so tight that the nail bedded deeply into his palm, and he fought on through a mist of despair. He spent the intervals shivering with anxiety while the other actors crowded round him trying to help. The curtain fell at last after the third act and ended an eternity of suffering.

He went to Simone's flat and collapsed on a sofa. He heard a piercing noise and realized that she was laughing. She chatted gaily and thought it rather fun that he should have been so drunk as to mix up his speeches. How she would have chuckled if she had been in the audience!

Word by word he went over his lines and the verses of his songs in an attempt to prove that his memory was unaffected. He did not see how he could survive as an actor. A strange voice ranted and declaimed, and he suddenly awoke to the fact that the voice was his own. He raised his head and saw Simone standing at the end of the room.

"Tell me, *chéri*," she said gravely, "do you think that perhaps you're going mad?"

It was the sort of remark that only a noodle like her could have made at such a point. For weeks the nightmare thought obsessed him. At night he dreamed of his wartime experiences and saw himself left for dead on the battlefield as his comrades marched away ignoring his shouts. He awoke drenched with sweat, exhausted, surrounded by sinister shadows that clustered about his room.

Specialists in nervous maladies were consulted. They put him on a diet and told him to give up smoking and drinking. A series of

gland injections was tried, and then massage and then electrical
treatment. None of these made any difference, and his tortured
nerves created yet more terrifying hallucinations. He wondered if
there was something in his heredity that would explain it all. From
La Louque he had inherited stability and a sense of the practical.
With those, perhaps, mingled the heritage of his alcoholic father, a
tendency to swing between moods of black depression and phases
of shrill exuberance. There were also the experiences of a hard
childhood which had influenced his character without giving him
the one quality he needed so badly: confidence.

At every performance he knew afresh the awful terror of forgetting his lines. There was nothing for it but to employ a prompter
who would watch over him at all moments should his mind wan-
der. He broke off his affair with Simone. Against his will he denied
himself the ardours of her passion because he knew that in his
present state they would end by shattering what little composure
remained in him. The notion of going to America was renounced
and he bought himself out of his contract with Dillingham.

Dédé ended its run and he learned, with no enthusiasm at all, that to
fill up the last three months of the season the management planned
to launch a new production in March 1923. Rehearsals began
immediately for *Là-Haut* ("Up There"), a comedy with music by
Maurice Yvain, Chevalier's one-time army comrade. Yvain had
quickly made a name for himself in the French theatre since the days
of his infantry service at Belfort. "Mon Homme", which we have
seen him writing for Mistinguett, was only one of his many successes. These included *Ta Bouche*, a full-length musical comedy which
domesticated American jazz and became for a moment the rage of
Paris. He showed genius for writing music cleverly adapted to the
small orchestras which a post-war economy demanded. The score
of *Là-Haut* was one of his best and brightest, ingeniously put
together and written with rather more imagination than was usual
in popular music at the time. The plot concerned a newly married
young husband who dreams that he dies and goes to heaven,
whence he descends to see what his widow has been up to since his
departure. One of the scenes occurred in Paradise and gave
Chevalier the opportunity to sing a number that stopped the show
at each performance: "Le premier, le seul, le vrai Paradis, c'est
Paris!" This primping fox-trot, which celebrated Paris as a heaven

on earth, was a modern version of the genial legend which Offenbach had first carolled in *La Vie Parisienne*.

Là-Haut contained a part which was second only in importance to
Chevalier's. It was for the "Guardian Angel", and the producer
congratulated himself on obtaining Dranem for the rôle. Dranem
had reached the sunset of his career and was touchingly grateful for
this chance to experiment in a new field, since up to then he had
worked almost exclusively in the music-hall. Chevalier, too, was
pleased to welcome Dranem for old times' sake as a performer
whom he had always admired. Dranem showed great humility,
often asking his younger colleague for advice and consulting him
on problems that came up in rehearsal. Soon after the opening
night, however, it became clear that Dranem, with a lifetime of
stagecraft behind him, had adapted so well to the genre that the rôle
of the Guardian Angel threatened to overshadow everyone else.
The sly old veteran, in fact, was up-staging Maurice and creaming
off the applause. In his present state, and even no doubt had he been
in perfect health, this was something Maurice could not bear, and he
resigned from the show in a fit of temper. Dranem did not for long
enjoy his victory. He and his wife Fifi were very friendly with
Yvain, so friendly indeed that Fifi became the composer's mistress
and left her husband. It was a terrible, brutal shock for the unsus-
pecting Dranem, although he may well have rued the loss of his pal
Yvain more than he did that of his wandering Fifi.

The reviews of *Là-Haut* commented that Chevalier seemed to be
taking more trouble than usual but to no better purpose. Critics had
sensed the effort it cost him to give even an average performance.
Paralysed by the fear of drying up, he was subject to an added
peril: that of dizziness which made it hard for him sometimes to
keep upright. Dranem's triumph gave him a further reason for
withdrawing, and he left the Bouffes-Parisiens with relief.

His problem was still not solved. The doctors found that he
had chronic appendicitis and recommended an operation in the
hope that it might put a stop to the cause of the mysterious illness.
Two days after the appendix had been removed in 1924, he knew he
was no further along the road, for the dizziness and the melancholia
persisted. Then he struck on a solution which had the merit of
neatness and simplicity: he would kill himself. The event called for
meticulous organization. There was La Louque to be provided for
and a will to be drawn up. He would need her out of the way and

would suggest that in summer, Paris being too hot and uncomfortable, she should move to the country for a while. After some argument she agreed and left him the freedom he needed to complete his plans. With prudence, with hypocrisy, he carried on a semblance of ordinary routine while arranging the details of his project. All that remained now was to choose the date of his suicide.

One factor alone hindered his scheme, and that was his friendship with a girl who played a small part in *Là-Haut*. She was called Yvonne Vallée, had come to Paris from her native Bordeaux and begun her modest career in the long-running *Phi-Phi*. He noticed her each evening as she sat patiently in the wings knitting a jumper and awaiting the cue for her entrance. They regularly passed the time of day to each other and he noticed, automatically, the charm of her smile and the deep brown of her eyes. There was, too, a serenity about her that promised comfort and assurance. He asked her out to lunch. Her knitting needles paused for a moment, and she said, without raising her eyes, "Yes, that would be nice."

When they met for lunch at Saint-Cloud he already regretted his invitation. They sat at a small table by a window overlooking the park. It was, he said to himself, foolish to think that this young and inexperienced girl could ever understand his predicament. She told him how she came to Paris and took dancing lessons, returning after every session, duly chaperoned, to her sister with whom she lodged. Among the few men she knew in the capital was an artist called Pablo Picasso, who used to wait at the door for one of his girlfriends. After singing and dancing in the chorus of *Phi-Phi* she had joined the cast of *Là-Haut*.

He listened to her simple story and relaxed. His earlier unfavourable impression dissolved and was replaced by a feeling of companionship.

Chevalier and Yvonne Vallée the day after their divorce in 1933

Love Me Tonight (1932), with Jeanette MacDonald

On the set of *The Way to Love* (1933) with the director, Norman Taurog

Preparing to go on stage

With Jeanette MacDonald in *The Merry Widow* (1934)

At home, surrounded by some of his trophies

At rehearsal with Henri Varna, impresario of the Casino de Paris, in 1938

A typical studio portrait—the trademark known to millions

With René Clair and François Perier on the set of *Le Silence est d'Or* (1947)

At the Club des Champs-Elysées with Nita Raya in 1948

Yvonne . . . and "Valentine"

After the Saint-Cloud lunch they met regularly. She asked no questions and, when his turbulent chatter died away, respected his moody silence as quite natural. He went, reluctantly, to see yet another doctor, who spoke at length of nervous exhaustion. While the learned talk about obsessions and tensions flowed on he broke down into tears. His doctor told him that he needed rest under the guidance of a nerve specialist in the country. He must go as soon as possible. La Louque was too old and frail to accompany him, so he should ask Yvonne for her help.

Of course she agreed and persuaded La Louque that all would be well. Her calm and her gentleness won over the old lady and dispelled her fears. She set off with Maurice on the six-hour journey which she would have to retrace that same day so as to be back in time for the evening performance of *Là-Haut*.

"Are you hungry?" she said at one point. "Would you like to stop for lunch?"

"I wouldn't be able to eat anything," he mumbled ungraciously.

"Then it's not worth stopping. I'm not hungry either," she replied, tender and unruffled as she was to remain throughout the whole period of his illness.

Like a man preparing for his own funeral he took up quarters in the old country house, not at all like a clinic, where he was to follow the treatment prescribed by his advisers. It was at Saujon, the little resort in the Charente Maritime where invalids for years have been soothed by the gentle climate and restful atmosphere. His consultant was the psychiatrist Robert Dubois, son of the man who founded the establishment.

Twice a week Chevalier had a meeting with this patient, elderly man, who listened tranquilly as he poured out his breathless talk. Dubois recommended sleep, walks, conversation. The countryside, he remarked, was very pretty and there were many agreeable views to be enjoyed on one's rambles.

"I want you to sleep as much as possible," he went on. "And if you can't sleep, then rest."

After a month of these anodyne counsels Maurice gave up hope.

One rainy afternoon in the summer of 1924 he could not resist entering a gunsmith's shop he passed on one of his boring walks. There he bought a gun and some bullets. That night, sitting on the bed in his room, he loaded the weapon and stuck the barrel into his mouth. His finger slipped on the trigger and he willed himself to press it. But he could not. He tried a second time. Again his finger refused. He threw the gun away and collapsed into an armchair.

Yvonne called one day unexpectedly and raised his spirits. Summer gave way to autumn and the leaves yellowed and fell to the ground, where they crackled underfoot. He went on with the monotonous round: walks, rest, conversation . . . and conversation, rest, walks. "This routine can cure you, even though you don't like it much," said Dr Dubois.

Some weeks later he told Maurice of an entertainment being got up in the village hall. "It won't be a very select audience," he added, "but I want you to come and sing for us."

"Sing?" replied his astonished patient. "How can you ask me to do such a thing? You know I can't rely on my memory any more and I'm totally incapable of acting. It's absolutely impossible!"

"That's no longer true, Maurice. You *can* sing and you must. I'm not asking you – I'm ordering you."

For a week he rehearsed his songs, stumbling over the words and suddenly drying up. He was to do two numbers with Yvonne, for he needed her at his side and, without her, felt unable even to make his entrance. She coached him with patience, with love, with encouragement. On the evening of the show he walked nervously up and down. One of the nursing staff brought him a letter from Paris. He opened it and saw that it contained a press cutting. Why, wrote the author of the article, had Maurice Chevalier stayed away from Paris this winter? The reason was that the famous star had worn himself out with drinks, drugs and women. He was now nothing more than a ruin bereft of memory and reason. Friends who came to see him in the asylum were wasting their time because he could no longer recognize them. He was finished.

The shock of the press article and the effort of preparing his act made him shiver uncontrollably. He longed to vanish into the night. But the little amateur band had already struck up the opening bars of his number.

"Je t'aime," whispered Yvonne as he faced the audience. He sought in his memory for the first line of the song. It came, and so did the second and the third and the fourth until he got to the end of it. His routines with Yvonne were just as agonizing, yet he managed to get through them.

"Congratulations, Maurice," said Dr Dubois afterwards.

"For what?" he muttered bitterly. "For having got the words out of my mouth?"

"You've proved your memory is good now. That's a big step towards the complete cure. And I didn't hear any booing."

Next day he felt remorse for his irritation. A subsequent engagement was fixed for Melun, the scene of his military career a few years back, and in a shabby, moth-eaten cinema he repeated the programme with Yvonne. The same anguish gnawed at him, the same horrid fear gripped him, but he completed the performance without breaking down. His old patron Franck, owner of the Alcazar in Marseilles, asked him to appear there.

"Remember, Maurice, the last time you played the Alcazar it led to success in Paris. Why shouldn't it be the same this time?"

The long and wearing journey to Marseilles was followed by appearances which exacted a terrible effort. Each night he had to force himself to approach the footlights, and when it was all over he dreaded the next confrontation. After Marseilles came the supreme trial of Paris. On 29 February 1925 the Empire music-hall was packed to the ceiling with an audience that came to watch him as they would a bull-fight or some contest in which a gladiator was fighting for his life. Malice hung heavy in the air, and knowing smiles betrayed an eagerness to see this once popular figure humiliated.

"Five minutes to go, Monsieur Chevalier!"

The sweat beaded his thick make-up and ran in pearls down his cheek. He looked at Yvonne, prettier than ever in the first of the dresses she was to wear for their three numbers together, and he prayed silently, "May she be spared for once the sorrow of a disappointment!"

Half-way through the first verse of the song he could hear his voice, which was never very powerful, resounding throughout the auditorium and penetrating to the very back of the gallery. The acoustics of the newly built Empire were superb, but so was his performance. Confidence flowed back in a rush and he swaggered across the stage with all his former buoyance. Storms of applause erupted and thundered, silencing with their enthusiasm the doubters in the audience. Encore followed encore while people shouted to each other, "For a man on his last legs he's certainly done wonderfully tonight!" The miracle had happened and he had never felt better in his life.

During the four weeks of his season at the Empire he smashed all box-office records. Another contract speedily followed at the Casino de Paris, where Volterra engaged him as leading star for three years in succession. The ghost of failure was banished and ecstatic, unbelievable triumph had taken its place.

His relationship with Yvonne grew closer. She shared in every aspect of his life, both public and private, and although there were moments when he thought with nostalgia of his earlier independence, his gratitude for her loyalty overrode all other emotions. With Mistinguett he had known exhilaration, and with Simone the raw pleasure of sensuality. With Yvonne he experienced a tranquil contentment.

They set up home together at Vaucresson, that agreeable and leafy neighbourhood on the wooded slopes outside Paris. Their house, as neat and trim as its surroundings, he baptized "Quand on est deux" (Just the two of us), after one of his songs. The idyll was perfect. Most nights they would drive home to Vaucresson immediately the curtain had rung down at the Casino. They spent little time in Paris and would hasten away from it as quickly as possible to be alone together.

"What does it feel like, Maurice, to be a star who succeeds in everything?" Léon Volterra asked him with a smile.

To Maurice it seemed extraordinary, rather like a fairy-tale which happened to be incredible but true. He was earning ten thousand francs a night. Whatever he did, wherever he appeared, he met with adoring crowds. It is true that he had little competition from other men in the French music-hall of the time, and the younger ones in any case were imitating him and aping his routines with flattering zeal. Yet he still could not explain the dominance he enjoyed nor the immense popularity which aureoled his name. The reason was most likely to be found in a combination of circumstance, hard work, and the charm of a personality which caught the imagination of the public at just the right moment.

His appearance at the Empire had coincided with the inauguration of the new theatre itself. Before an audience of three thousand he led a revue which also starred forty horses caracoling in manoeuvres of finicky precision across a stage a hundred feet wide. Other attractions on the programme included Little Tich, who was ever a favourite in Paris, and not only because he had taught himself to speak fluent French. Jack Hylton and his orchestra provided music, and there were songs from the volcanic Sophie Tucker. If the troupe of "Musical Elephants" on the bill performed wonders, they were closely rivalled by the mermaids and learned seals which came after them.

In the following year of 1925 Maurice introduced at the Casino de Paris the song with which he was to be identified for ever. Albert Willemetz and Henri Christiné had written for him, with "Valentine", something that could not be bettered as the model of a popular song. You always remember your first mistress, says the opening verse, and in this case her name was Valentine. His straw hat perched at the back of his head, the bow tie pertly knotted, Maurice detailed the charms of Valentine: her twinkling feet, her neat little bosoms *"que je tâtais à tâtons"*, and the dimpled chin. She was not very intelligent and she tended to be rather bossy . . . but what does that matter when you are eighteen and madly in love?

With a rueful grin he went on to tell how yesterday in the boulevard he came across a fat woman with big feet and the waist of a hippopotamus. She threw her arms around him saying, "Hello, my pet!" Startled, he asked, "Excuse me, but who are you?" "It's *me*, Valentine!" Faced with her double chin and her triple bosom he could only wonder at the change in her since their youthful love affair. Yet just think, in those days she had had such twinkling feet, such *tout petits tétons que je tâtais à tâtons*. . .

Christiné's tune, lively but garnished here and there with mild dissonances to point up the light cynical tone, is a perfect match for the words. The dapper rhymes and scampering metres tell a tale that everyone knows, but re-present it with a freshness and a boulevardier humour that make it unforgettable.* Maurice was to sing it thousands of times in his career. Sometimes he would leave out the second of the three verses, as on the gramophone record he made in 1928, an omission which tightened up the song and increased its impact. His singing of "Valentine" shows the adroit-

---

* The English version, by an author called, strangely enough, Eric Valentine, is completely different and maunders on with lines like: "To my queen I'll strum the mandoline . . . Where skies are always blue, with you it's paradise for two", etc.

ness with which he had perfected his technique. The voice was thin and needed careful husbanding over notes that went above middle C, but he had made it a supple instrument for the expression of all the qualities the words implied. The opening verse was taken straightforwardly and with no attempt to embroider. Having prepared his listeners for what was coming, he could afford, in the last stanza, to vary the rhythms and speak the lines almost conversationally. After which, as Mayol had always advised him, he abruptly increased his speed and hit the climax almost before the audience realized.

In Paris he had already made a point of singing a few songs in English for the benefit of the Anglo-Saxon tourists who continued to swell music-hall audiences. To his gratification not only they but also his French admirers approved. It was a logical step for him to appear in London again, this time at the invitation of the American producer Lew Leslie, who planned a sequel to his popular Negro revue called *Black Birds*. The new production, inevitably christened *White Birds*, was launched with a barrage of American-style advance publicity, something then very novel, and worked up interest to a hysterical pitch. Maurice began to have qualms. He remembered that on his last visit to London he had been under the wing of Elsie Janis. On this occasion he played the leading rôle and could expect competition from the best native performers. Neither was he very confident of his English. He was not Harry Fragson, and if Parisians were impressed by his singing in the language he doubted whether Londoners would properly understand his attempts to wrestle with the cursed "th" sound and all the subtle intonations that made Shakespeare's tongue so difficult. Still, Lew Leslie had agreed to pay him five hundred pounds a week, and so he crossed the Channel with Yvonne – but in a cloud of apprehension.

As the train drew into Victoria Station a band of well-drilled chorus-girls rushed forward to welcome him. Reporters and photographers milled around, and the man of the moment was caught up in a riotous happening of a sort quite foreign to him. No one remembered his earlier début in *Hello America*, for which he was thankful, and few of the reporters could spell his name correctly, at which he was not so pleased. Then he posed for photographs with Leslie Henson and George Robey, photographs which publicists captioned as the three "greatest comedians in the world".

Afterwards he protested to Lew Leslie. "What if we don't live up to all this hullabaloo? The public will murder us." Lew smiled an enigmatic smile. He knew what he was doing.

He did not really. From the wings Maurice and Yvonne could hear the ugly murmur of a restive house. They managed to calm the spectators with their "Cuddle up" song and an eccentric dance number, but the second half of the evening collapsed in disorder. Maurice, on his own, sang "Valentine", and then repeated it in various amusingly different ways: aristocratic, plebian, mincing. patriotic. He made his exit as speedily as possible. The high hopes raised by Lew's barnstorming tactics were disappointed. Whistles and jeers interrupted the music, and people threw things on the stage. When the curtain fell the stalls were practically empty and only the gallery remained in force to bellow its outrage.

"It'll all be forgotten tomorrow, *chéri*," Yvonne consoled him. "The critics will be favourable to us, I'm sure, and then we can start thinking about next year."

Her forecast was right, and although the reviews were pitiless about *White Birds* they had good things to say of the French visitors. He embraced her, thankful yet again for her unfailing tenderness, her understanding, her support.

Back in France, while on a tour of the South, they passed through La Bocca, a little place overlooking Cannes, which ravished them with its eternally blue sky and its grandiose prospect of the Mediterranean. Though he knew it was an occupational hazard of theatre people to build houses at an absurdly inconvenient distance from their place of work, Maurice could not resist the temptation. The air was so pure, the sparkle of the water so inviting, that in 1925 he bought a small farmhouse and some land up in the hills. The farmhouse expanded into a villa, which cost half a million francs alone. Then he added many more acres to his holding and planted flowers all over them. He called his new property "La Louque", and escorted his mother from their Paris flat to install her, proudly, in the home which he had named after her.

He knew that his venture cost him a great deal more money than he should have spent. Whereas he ought to have been satisfied with the little doll's house at Vaucresson and its few square yards of lawn, its nearness to Paris and the theatres where he spent his working life, he had chosen to set up on the Riviera, hundreds of miles from the capital, a home which defied all common sense and practicality. He said to himself that he would pass whole months there in summer, forgetting that that time of year was usually spent on provincial tours. Other engagements even further afield were to come his way over the next few years, but meanwhile he luxuriated heedlessly in the pleasure of La Bocca and "La Louque". He sat on the terrace and stared out over the bay flecked with the white sails of boats that looked, in Valéry's phrase, like doves on a quiet roof. While Yvonne sunbathed he listened to new records sent from Paris, and when he wound up the gramophone the steel of the handle was unbearably hot. They swam, they played tennis, they lounged beneath a vast garden umbrella. And all the time the sun flooded the bright white walls of his dream home amid the thousands of vivid blooms that made your eyes quite ache with their brilliance.

Had a photographer taken a picture at that very moment of the host and hostess of "La Louque", the result would have been peculiarly redolent of the nineteen-twenties. For he, in his white sporting cap, snowy ducks and "co-respondent" shoes, and she, in her belted one-piece swimming costume, together symbolized the spirit of the age. Young ladies no longer hid their delicate complexions under parasols but faced the sun openly and aspired to a bronze tan. It was the era of Bugattis and Hispano-Suizas, those chunky motor cars heavy with chromium that swished along the high road in a proud flurry of dust and petrol fumes. The *Train Bleu* carried Parisians in luxury to the South, and was itself destined for immortality in one of Diaghilev's ballets. André Citroën, the adventurer from Warsaw, decked the Eiffel Tower with his name in letters forty yards high and illuminated them by night to advertise his automobile empire. Fashionable women deserted Paul Poiret, master of the voluminous robe, and wore the skimpy creations of Coco Chanel. She persuaded them to cut their hair short and to wear imitation jewellery. Her jackets were comfortable, her trousers very practical, and the new freedom of the nineteen-twenties inspired clothes which, as Poiret lamented, made women resemble "underfed little telegraph boys". Mistinguett and Yvonne Vallée were not alone in their passion for the georgette and shantung which, at Coco's urging, now superseded the thick velvets and natural silk Poiret loved. The old grandeur of pre-war days had vanished and was replaced by the tinselled thrill of night-clubs, the blare of jazz bands, and a rage for the crude but vigorous steps of the Charleston.

CHAPTER FIVE

Hollywood

"I won't hear a word against Hollywood. Hollywood
means to me cash, courage, and climate."
Mrs Patrick Campbell

i

Marriage

La Bocca shimmered in the heat haze. A telephone rang within the
cool depths of the house. Maurice walked along the gravelled path
between beds of roses and violets and entered the hall. He passed the
large oil painting of La Louque that dominated the wall, and the
pictures and ornaments and furniture he had bought with his carefully hoarded francs, and he liked what he saw. His caller was a local
tradesman.

"Was that the call you were expecting?" asked Yvonne when he
rejoined her.

"Yes."

"Won't you tell me who it was? Were you speaking to a
woman?"

"Why should it have been a woman?"

"If it wasn't, why refuse to tell me who rang you?"

He was annoyed by her strange tone. "I didn't refuse, but I do
now!"

They quickly made up the stupid tiff, but the memory lingered.
Odd little remarks and peculiar turns of phrase began to ruffle the
harmony between them. Most times Yvonne was the loving,
thoughtful companion. At others she turned into an adversary. He
puzzled over the matter for weeks. A friend enlightened him.

"What's probably upsetting her is being in love with a man who
never talks of marriage."

Yvonne, he realized, was not a Mistinguett, a volatile creature whom it would have been impossible to bind with marriage. She was quite different, a girl who expected him to recognize formally her total attachment to him.

More surprises awaited him. When he proposed to her she was hesitant. Instead of a gentle "yes", she replied that she wanted to continue appearing on stage with him rather than withdraw into domesticity.

"The part I'm asking you to accept, *chérie*," he said, "includes a much better contract. It's a booking for life!"

This was the first time he had proposed to anyone, and her reaction left him crestfallen.

Eventually, one spring morning, she agreed, and they were married in the little town-hall of Vaucresson with a church ceremony afterwards. La Louque was there, a tiny figure beside her son in the front pew, her eyes shining with happiness. "She's a wonderful girl," she said to Maurice. One of the most successful numbers he and Yvonne had included in their act together was one modelled on the American vaudeville routine of "Mr Gallagher and Mr Shean". At last, in the words they had so often sung, they could tell the gossips of Paris for whom their affair had been a long-running topic of speculation:

Et c'est vrai, M'sieu Chevalier?
Absolument, Mam'selle Vallée!

Within a short time Yvonne was pregnant. Her mood changed from one of querulous uncertainty to one of contentment. The disquieting undercurrents that occasionally troubled their relationship seemed to have faded. On the evening of 21 May 1927, he came home from the theatre and found Yvonne haggard in bed. It was nothing, she insisted, just a passing phase of weariness, there was no need to call a doctor. Next morning she felt worse and had to be rushed off to a clinic in Paris. There were complications, he was told, and she needed to be kept under observation.

In the waiting-room the surgeon came up to him.

"I've had her prepared for the operation, Maurice. I must act immediately."

"An operation? But what about the baby?"

"I'm very sorry, Maurice, but it's no longer a matter of saving the baby. I'm operating to save Yvonne."

A few hours later he was at her bedside watching her sleep, her pale face expressionless on the pillow. He moved nearer, and as he did so her eyes opened and tears ran down her cheeks. His comforting words had no effect.

"It's no use trying to hide anything from me," she said. "I overheard the nurses talking . . . and I know everything."

"Believe me, Yvonne," he insisted, "everything will work out." He suddenly realized that these were the very words she herself had used to him at the darkest moment of his nervous breakdown.

If the baby had lived it might have given their marriage a firmer base. As it was, their life together resumed once again the familiar pattern of tension and quarrel. He sought relief from the strained atmosphere at home by working harder than ever on a new revue at the Casino de Paris, which opened early in 1928.

As he sat in front of his mirror taking off the last traces of make-up, a pageboy announced that a Mr Irving Thalberg of Metro Goldwyn Mayer was in the corridor with his wife. They wanted to see him – and the lady, added the messenger, was very beautiful. With a sigh Maurice agreed to let them in. He was tired, he had a headache after a difficult evening's performance, and he did not feel like exchanging small-talk with fans.

The wife, Maurice thought, was certainly very attractive. Norma Shearer, an actress of modest ability and chiselled features which provoked an unfriendly critic to speak of her "face unclouded by thought", had worked hard for success. In this she was guided by her husband, then one of the most powerful men in Hollywood. Thalberg himself had iron reserves of strength within a frail and often sickly person. At the age of twenty-four he battled with and defeated the flamboyant Erich von Stroheim, whose extravagance threatened to bankrupt the company's fortunes. While Louis B. Mayer directed the commercial and administrative side of the business with Napoleonic flair, Thalberg was left to concentrate on artistic matters. His personality was such that the impression he made on Scott Fitzgerald, that sad whisky-sodden genius, inspired the hero of the novel *The Last Tycoon* – a romanticized portrait which owes more to the force of Thalberg's haunting character than to any great artistic talent on his part.

"Your English is very good, Monsieur Chevalier," Norma Shearer brightly observed.

Maurice beamed at the conventional compliment and made polite conversation.

"Which is very important now that films talk," said her dark, intense husband. "If you agree to make a test and it's satisfactory, I'm ready to offer you a contract for Hollywood."

The star of the Casino de Paris looked at the small, thin man who stood before him, a fellow no more than twenty-eight years old, and decided that he was much too young to be of any importance.

"I'm sorry, Mr Thalberg, but there's no question of my making a test. People sign me up or not, as the case may be. I'm past the stage of auditions."

Thalberg's sombre eyes betrayed no emotion. He expressed courteous regret and departed with the beautiful Shearer. A moment later Maurice's secretary came in, aghast. Did Maurice know that he had snubbed the king of the American film industry? The Thalbergs were recalled in a welter of apologies and a test was made the following day. The verdict declared Maurice to be photogenic. At which point no one could agree on contractual terms and the reel of film was put away in a drawer.

Less than a fortnight afterwards it was taken out again. To Maurice's dressing-room came Jesse Lasky, another magnate from Hollywood. He had been a cornettist, a sideshow barker and a panhandler in the Yukon gold rush before going into vaudeville and rising to the top of Paramount Pictures. His sister married Sam Goldfish, later Goldwyn, and for years the two brothers-in-law struggled viciously against each other in monumental board-room warfare and corporation battles. Lasky was not so much a film producer as an expert fixer, a virtuoso of Wall Street and a master hand at arranging complex financial deals, which he balanced and shaded with the delicacy of a mosaicist.

When Lasky proposed a screen test, Maurice, who this time had learned his lesson, brought out the one he did for Thalberg. Within the hour Lasky gave him a six-week contract. The salary was enormous and promised further rises. Delighted by such quick and practical methods, the new Paramount recruit sped home to Vaucresson.

"Are you taking me with you, Maurice?" enquired Yvonne after studying the contract in silence.

"Of course. Travelling expenses for two are included in the agreement."

At last she smiled, but his euphoria had vanished.

He was no stranger to the camera. In France he had already made a dozen silent films, the earliest dating as far back as 1908 when he appeared as an extra and was grateful for the handful of francs he earned. There followed three one-reelers with Max Linder, for a time one of the most popular French comedians, who brought to slapstick routines an elegance and even a certain well-bred melancholy which can still move and entertain sixty years later. In common with Charlie Chaplin and others, Maurice picked up useful ideas from Linder's timing and smooth comedy. During the war he made two films with Mistinguett, one of their celebrated "Valse renversante" number and another, shot in the surroundings of the Folies Bergère, for which he was paid a thousand francs.

By the nineteen-twenties he was making full-length films for Henri Diamant-Berger, a producer who may, or may not, go down in history as the sponsor of René Clair's first venture, *Paris qui dort*. This was shot between the months of June and September 1923, on days when Diamant-Berger was able to provide the money. Lack of finance did not prevent that buoyant entrepreneur from launching a total of seven films in which Maurice played a part. The casts were not undistinguished and included Marguerite Moreno, then a beautiful member of the Comédie-Française and years away from the Gothic ruin she was later to become; Albert Préjean, the former stunt-man who was already building a career that flowered in Clair's *Sous les toits de Paris* and prospered right up to the nineteen-fifties; and Pauline Carton, a witty and intelligent character actress who for the rest of her life was condemned to play eccentric housemaids and dotty cooks. Two of the films Maurice appeared in for Diamant-Berger had ideas good enough to be taken up later by the American pioneer Hal Roach. He adapted one of them for Charley Chase. The other was fashioned into a vehicle for Laurel and Hardy.

As soon as he heard that Lasky had signed Maurice for Paramount, Diamant-Berger nobly released his star in the spring of 1928 from the long-term contract he had with him. He did not wish to prevent his gaining international fame and earning much, much more money than he would have from small-scale French productions. Maurice himself thought little of his early movies. "Those films were nothing," he once remarked. "I was a straight man for Max Linder or just a partner for Mist . . . If you put all my scenes together from those silent films I doubt you'd have more than thirty or thirty-five minutes of film." Up to then he had little regard for the cinema. Jesse Lasky changed all that.

Lubitsch and The Love Parade

The sound film was in its heroic age. A mammoth industry had grown up over the past twenty years at a speed which amazed everyone except the rough, gruff buccaneers who powered it. Splendid old monsters like Sam Goldwyn, Louis B. Mayer and Adolphe Zukor founded, merged, split up and took over companies in transactions of Byzantine intricacy. Boardroom colleagues turned overnight into scheming foes. The man who had been your friend on Monday was your dedicated enemy by Tuesday. The stakes were too high for good behaviour.

Louis B. Mayer had started as a scrap-metal dealer and Sam Goldwyn as a glove-merchant. Their prosperity was based on one enchantingly simple fact. As a scrap-dealer or a glove-merchant you sold your product and then had to find more stock. With the cinema, they were quick to discover, you took your customer's money, showed them your film, and kept both cash and picture. You could go on exhibiting the film over and over again and collecting the money without ever having to let go of your original product.

As men of the people themselves they knew what the public wanted. They made mistakes, expensive ones, but on the whole they were so successful that Mayer was for long the highest paid executive in the USA. Yet despite the gigantic scale of their operations they were, at heart, no different in their instincts from Mr Vincent Crummles, Dickens' travelling showman. For Mr Crummles the whole of life was a theatre and everything that happened in it an excuse for showmanship. Even his horse was a member of the company. Declared Mr Crummles, "Many and many is the circuit this pony has gone. He is quite one of us. His mother was on the stage. . . She ate apple-pie at a circus for upwards of fourteen years, fired pistols, and went to bed in a nightcap; and, in short, took the low comedy entirely. His father was a dancer."

The Hollywood tycoons would have loved a horse that fired pistols. Their background of fairs and circuses taught them that people adored the freakish, the odd, the sensational. Romance and escapism were essential, too, and these were supplied with a generous hand. Hollywood dealt in dreams. So did Mr Crummles and old-time music-hall managers like Volterra. The only difference between them and Hollywood lay in the vast technical and financial resources the latter enjoyed.

This was the bizarre world Maurice prepared to enter. On 28 June 1928, he embarked with Yvonne to cross the Atlantic on the maiden voyage of the French liner *Île de France*. Paramount had booked them into a first-class cabin full of giant bouquets and greetings telegrams. In his fashionable plus-fours Maurice stood on deck for the photographers with Yvonne in a sleek fur coat and Chanel toque. The studio's publicity man arranged for them to dine that night at the Captain's table. "Relax and be sophisticated," he advised Maurice with a cheery smile. The slum boy from Ménil-montant wrinkled his brow. He was forty years old but he realized that life still had many surprises in store for him.

The last night of the crossing brought a friendly telegram from Douglas Fairbanks, which he read and re-read in the attempt to stifle those all too familiar sensations of disquiet that nagged him at each new step he took in his career. Journalists and photographers mobbed him on arrival in New York. "Give us a big smile, Maurice!. . . Wave your hat in the air!. . . Where's Mrs Chevalier?" The publicity man stood watchfully at his side.

After New York and a dazzling round of parties and receptions, a train journey lasting nearly a week delivered them over to the Californian sunshine. The locomotive rumbled into the station while a band thundered out the ear-splitting din of the *Marseillaise*. He felt like a hero passing under the Arc de Triomphe. And the memory of *White Birds* and its ill-starred ballyhoo returned to unsettle him.

Yet another grand dinner was arranged in his honour. Douglas Fairbanks, Charlie Chaplin and Gary Cooper came along to encourage him. The newspaper magnate Citizen Kane, alias William Randolph Hearst, was there too, and he gave a speech about his recent travels in Europe. He had not liked what he saw in France, nor did he approve of the French. In calm, even tones he spoke of his distaste for that country and its people, and as a good American he deplored their graceless manners. The diners roared with laughter at his sallies and Maurice wriggled uncomfortably, for he was supposed to follow this speech with his act. When his turn came he decided to introduce his songs in English before singing them in

French. The notion was successful, his accent and manner intrigued the audience, and what might have been a diplomatic incident turned into an agreeable occasion.

"They all like you, Maurice. You're going to be a big hit in America," said the jovial Adolph Zukor, clapping him on the back.

The Hungarian Zukor, by trade a fur salesman, ran the Paramount film studios in an uneasy partnership with Lasky, whom he usually succeeded in out-manoeuvring. Although in 1912 he had broken new ground by helping to set up and distribute a remarkable film in which Sarah Bernhardt played Queen Elizabeth – it lasted an hour, an unusually long time in those days – he was not really interested in the nature of his product. He employed other men to look after what went into the tins of film and concentrated on the battle for power and money. Paramount had a reputation as the stylish home of people like Cecil B. De Mille, John Barrymore, Gloria Swanson and the Marx Brothers, and had also cast its net over the foreigners Marlene Dietrich, Ernst Lubitsch and Josef von Sternberg. Zukor went steadily on, avoiding whenever possible the need to set foot in a projection-room or cinema, and, having resolutely placed his trust in nothing and nobody, was in the end to die a happy man at the age of a hundred and three.

Since the change-over to sound was not yet complete, the studios were fully occupied during the day in shooting silent films which had been on the stocks before the new technique evolved. Maurice's production would therefore have to be filmed at night. It was not, strictly speaking, his first American film. While in New York he had spent three days on a little travelogue, *Bonjour New York!*, which the thrifty Paramount company intended for French-speaking countries. A tour of Wall Street, the Bowery, Fifth Avenue and Greenwich Village was linked to a commentary in which the Parisian joked with smiling brio. Now, however, he had to face the real thing.

A ritual tour of the studios brought him face to face with Clara Bow, the embodiment of contemporary sex-appeal which was then known as "It". Her red hair and black eyes, enough to damn a bishop, troubled him exquisitely. He had always admired her on the screen, and the view in real life of her too, too solid flesh proved even more electrifying. The "It" girl took him back to the days before he had known Yvonne and the nights of his carefree bachelordom. But he was married, he reminded himself, and Miss Bow received from him nothing more than the tribute of gallantry.

In a dressing-room he met Emil Jannings, another alien whose acting in classic German films had led him to Hollywood and *The Way of All Flesh*, though his finest achievement came later with *The Blue Angel*, that characteristically Teutonic analysis of human degradation, a field where Jannings excelled. With much gesticulation and a thrilling guttural accent, he advised Maurice, "Act as if there weren't any screen. Don't bother about wrinkles or double chin. Never think of your profile or anything else. Be sincere. The talking film has greater need of character than of male or female beauty without substance." It was not, perhaps, the best of advice, for Jannings' skirmishes with his Paramount employers were Homeric.

Dinner with Charlie Chaplin left Maurice goggling in embarrassed silence. The presence of this legend was overpowering. Though only the same age as Chevalier, he had bushy hair that was already white. He spoke gravely of politics and international relations. His wide-ranging soliloquies hid the alarm of a man worried by the challenge of the sound film and still undecided on how to meet it, and his well-informed talk about world affairs avoided reference to a private life that was tragic and disordered. Often Maurice saw him afterwards at parties. "Hello, Charlie," "Hello, Maurice," they would greet each other with the smiling, empty formality of Hollywood convention.

Far less intimidating was Adolphe Menjou. A dignified ladykiller in dozens of long-forgotten films, he was, despite his name and Latin looks, a thoroughgoing son of Pennsylvania. From *The Amazons* of 1917 to *Pollyanna* in 1960 he acted with an easy grace that was the despair of his fellow-players. Paramount had given the small-town Menjou international fame. Would it, Maurice thought, do the same for him?

For a while Maurice and Yvonne stayed at the Beverly Wilshire Hotel and then settled for good in a rented bungalow. From there he travelled to the studio in the inevitable Ford car, passing through and wondering at the exotic setting of Beverly Hills and its flamboyant pseudo-Spanish architecture. Professionalism is always admired in Hollywood, and he was to show it in full measure. Having taught himself as a young music-hall performer how to work on a big scale with ample gestures and broad grimaces in order to reach the distant galleries of large theatres, he now had to reverse the technique and un-learn much of what he knew. His experience of silent films was not very helpful either, for the same over-theatrical style had been required to convey meaning in the absence of dialogue.

He soon realized that the cinema, both visually and audibly, magnified to an alarming extent. A raised eyebrow, a tremor of the lip, were all that was needed to express what, in silent films, would have demanded frantic mime. Instead of pitching his voice to reach the ears of people sitting hundreds of feet away from him, he learned to talk as if in a conversation, natural and intimate, with his partners. Yet although his audience now consisted of little more than a handful of cynical technicians, and although he no longer had to fight for a hearing and impose himself on unwilling listeners, the challenge to his craftsmanship was, if anything, greater. Without the stimulus of live spectators he had to generate his own excitement and impress men and women who would not be seeing his performance for many months yet. But at least at this stage he pleased his employers. Ever ready to accept guidance in the novel and rather terrifying medium, he was punctual and always knew his lines. He might be suffering from a hangover, he might be depressed or out of sorts and skulking gloomily in a corner. When, however, the call for action came he strode firmly under the merciless glare of the Kleig lights and smiled so bewitchingly, acted with such gaiety of heart and winning charm, that you would have thought him the happiest man on earth. Which, of course, is what he was supposed to be and why Paramount had invested a fortune in him.

At first he did not like the story they proposed. *Innocents of Paris* was a sentimental comedy in which he acted the part of a junk dealer who goes on the stage but renounces a theatrical career for love of the heroine Louise. The plot was feeble and the characterization lacking in bite. Paramount overcame his resistance by agreeing to let him include three numbers he had popularized in France, among them "Valentine" and "Les Ananas", which latter is in effect the French version of "Yes, We Have No Bananas". Another song he featured was to become as noteworthy as "Valentine". If, as he once reckoned, he sang "Valentine" some ten thousand times during his career, he must have performed "Louise" on almost as many occasions. The melody by Richard A. Whiting has a pleasing simpleness admirably suited to the breeze whispering "Louise" and the birds-in-the-trees-twittering "Louise". This touch of wistful pantheism gives the song memorability, and, when delivered in that roguish but tender French accent with a cunningly placed break in the voice at "Each little rose, Tells me it knows I love you", the effect is delicious. Louise and Valentine were the only girls to enter Chevalier's existence who never left it.

Shooting went smoothly except for the presence of a sly infant who played the heroine's nephew. He had a long and important scene in which Maurice comforted him when his mother threw herself into a river. Take One began with the child weeping tragically and Maurice attempting to soothe him. It was no good. Take Two fared no better. The Frenchman was puzzled. His director took him aside and explained. Did he not realize that the little fellow was playing the oldest trick in Hollywood and upstaging him? By placing himself so that Maurice had to turn round and talk to him, he ensured that he appeared full-face while his adult comforter displayed nothing more than the back of his neck. The child was rebuked, apologized profusely, and did the same thing in Take Three. They started a fourth time, Maurice now determined that three decades of stage experience were not to be defied by a mere six-year-old. The child began to shift round as the action proceeded but Maurice, exerting iron pressure, held him in place. By the end of the take, although his arm was being wrenched from its socket, he had managed to restrain the unscrupulous tot and to keep himself in profile on screen.

The "rushes", or "dailies" as they are now called, were competent enough. A preview of the film did not excite the audience until "Louise" won them over and evoked applause. Executives began to wonder if they had put their new star into a production unworthy of him. "The film's not up to much," said Adolphe Menjou kindly, "but never mind about that. You'll be the biggest hit a French actor's ever been over here." Chevalier swallowed hard and was grateful. With a few exceptions the Hollywood stars were young and beautiful. He, on the other hand, was forty years old with a pouting under-lip and a wart on his left cheek that even the most skilful make-up girl could not always conceal.

"You'll be crazy about him! Wait till you hear his thrilling voice, and see his flashing smile," burbled posters driven by their lyricism into iambic metres. The advertising offensive for the new "all-talking, all-singing picture" achieved happier results than had the doomed *White Birds* campaign. The *New York Times* agreed with Menjou, declaring that the star had won the hearts of the audience and saved an inferior film with his charm. Others spoke of his magnetic personality and compared him, for pathos and humour, with Chaplin. The *Los Angeles Examiner*, helpfully pointing out that his name was pronounced "Sha-val-yay", decided that *Innocents of Paris* was worth seeing for the presence of this "splendid artist" alone.

Paramount instantly offered to extend his contract for a year and guaranteed him over half a million dollars. Even Lasky and Zukor were pleasantly surprised at their new star's triumph. A wave of adulation swept the whole of the USA and, as *Innocents of Paris* gradually travelled along the distribution network, covered the whole world. "Louise" became the most popular international song of all. There were few places where the straw hat and the bow tie remained unknown, and few theatres or cabarets where imitation Maurice Chevaliers did not sing and skip.

In between films Maurice remembered his friend C.B. Dillingham, the impresario who had booked him in 1924 but had been forced to cancel because of his illness. For Dillingham, Maurice resolved, he wanted to do something special. He visualized a programme in two parts, the first with a jazz band which would, for the second, go down to the orchestra pit and accompany him. The band he chose was Duke Ellington's. This was an unusual, even daring move, for Ellington had never until then appeared outside Harlem. Pleased but a little wary, Ellington agreed to play in Times Square at the Fulton Theatre. The blend of Harlem and Paris on Broadway scored a double hit, and each night people were turned away at the box-office. Thus it was that a Parisian helped Ellington on his way to glory and also, in passing, himself, for the hour of songs and anecdotes which earned house-full notices gave him the idea which he later developed into "An Evening with Maurice Chevalier".

Florenz Ziegfeld put him into a late-night revue at the New Amsterdam Roof where the tradition of art deco luxury rivalled anything that Volterra and the Paris managers could show. The devious Flo was notorious for giving with one hand and taking away with the other, for although he launched many new names he was extremely reluctant to pay them, just as he baulked at settling accounts of any description. In Maurice he found a shrewd bargainer schooled by years of dealing with hard-faced managers and, now, a rather surprised but firm awareness of his much enhanced commercial value. This was proved in San Francisco where, at the Motor Show, a week of Maurice Chevalier cost far more than the two thousand dollars New York had been paying him a month or so previously.

Hollywood reclaimed him that year (it was 1929) for *The Love Parade*. This adaptation of a French boulevard comedy promised another "all-singing" picture, with the difference that the man in charge was Ernst Lubitsch. One is ready to believe that this stocky, round-faced little man was born with a cigar in his mouth, for he was never seen without a plump Havana screwed between his fleshy lips. He was a Berliner who trained under Max Reinhardt, whence his talent for composing big stage pictures and handling crowd scenes. As a gifted actor himself he had specialized in portrayals of comic Jewish businessmen, and it was probably this expert background which made him rehearse the players under his direction so thoroughly that they were left few chances of expressing their own individual talent. His supervision of the costumes was equally close and detailed, as Maurice found early on. Lubitsch took him to the costumiers and tried out every possible range of clothing – helmets, cloaks, uniforms, busbies, riding boots, epaulettes, jackets – which the hero, rather to Maurice's dismay a noble Prince, would conceivably wear. At last the director was satisfied with a Viennese dolman and an imposing shako. Photographers assembled and pictured him from every angle.

"Splendid, Maurice! Wonderful! You're a PRINCE!" exclaimed Lubitsch when he saw the results.

The Love Parade features the haughty queen of a mythical realm who marries one of her noblemen and treats him as a possession rather than as a husband. His masculine pride is outraged – was he not, before his marriage, the slickest Don Juan in Paris? – and the story tells how he brings her to heel and ensures that they live happily ever afterwards. Although the plot was originally French, the music which embroiders it closely follows the Viennese tradition and mingles Lehár with Victor Herbert. The composer, Victor Schertzinger, was also a film director, though his score for *The Love*

Parade appears to be the only durable monument he left in Hollywood. On the evidence of it he was a skilful musician who knew how to write a tune in the lush Viennese idiom. Any more definite judgement on his ability is hindered by the ominous fact that the orchestration was credited to Paramount's own music department, which, in common with other studios, employed European musicians who, at a moment's notice, could turn out effortless pastiche of Mahler, Wagner, Tchaikovsky or any other composer whose style was thought to fit the mood of a given scene.

The queen, whom Lubitsch discovered in Chicago, was a twenty-six-year-old singer and dancer called Jeanette MacDonald. His firm belief in her talent did not wholly convince executives at Paramount, and when his influence waned so did hers. Fifty years later her showing in *The Love Parade* seems to justify their scepticism. She had little acting ability. One of the most difficult actions on stage is to light and smoke a cigarette with naturalness. When done by a Guitry or a Gielgud the gestures are in themselves a model of grace. The Queen of Sylvania, in the person of Miss MacDonald, handles her cigarette so clumsily that one is fascinated by a morbid desire to see just how far she will go in bungling the operation. She lights up, fiddles with the object, does not know what to do next, and is entirely successful in killing the whole point of the scene. Neither was her voice all that accomplished. A shrill and piercing soprano, it lacked nuance or colour, and even the ruggedness of a sound-track half a century old cannot veil its strident deficiencies. She nonetheless pleased millions with her style of belting out songs during ten years or so of public favour.

Maurice thought of her as "a very sweet and very talented girl, about twelve years younger than I am, although she always professed to being even younger than that . . . I was not surprised when I later heard her referred to as 'The Iron Butterfly', although I was surprised to hear she found that amusing. I never thought she had much of a sense of humour." The "Iron Butterfly" did not enjoy his spicy stories. She came, like Menjou, from Pennsylvania, and her Puritan instinct warned that Chevalier was a man who could not keep his hands off women – though her chilly carapace would have been quite enough to repel a whole regiment of brutal and licentious soldiery.

With Lubitsch, however, Maurice's relations were easy. The director liked to work out every detail of script, costume and movement before an inch of film was exposed. So concerned was he with appearances that he even put on Jeanette MacDonald's clothes to demonstrate how she should wear them. Once he had prepared a scene down to the smallest item, he loosed off his actors on the set with a precise idea in their minds of what was wanted. There were those who argued that this method inhibited the cast and resulted in a bland uniformity. Maurice did not object and found, moreover, that at conferences Lubitsch was always ready to consider suggestions. Those he rejected usually proved unworkable in any case, and between the Berliner and the Parisian there grew up a mutual respect and liking.

Others working on the film included Ben Turpin, the hoary, cross-eyed veteran of silent farce, who put in a fleeting appearance as a lackey. Eugène Pallette, square-faced, square-bodied, with the familiar gravel voice and, in those days, a little more hair, played the Queen's Minister of War. An unexpected delight was the presence of Lupino Lane, descendant of Italian puppet-masters and comedians, who here impersonated the Prince's Figaroesque valet. He had, with Lillian Roth, an acrobatic dance number of superbly comic precision. The vigilant film-goer might also have spotted, as an extra in a box at the theatre, Jean Harlow of the platinum curls.

There were many examples of what, in the trade, became known as "the Lubitsch touch". Magnificent staircases abounded, and Ruritanian splendour and ornate boudoirs. When Maurice, discreetly fudging the high notes, sang "Paris, Stay the Same", a chorus of barking dogs completed the number for him. At his marriage to the domineering Queen, the officiating cleric pronounces them "wife and man". After he has affirmed his independence he walks through what seems mile after mile of palatial corridors to find the pyjamas he needs to pack for his going-away bag. The most striking achievement of the film is the way in which the director, so early in the sound era, blended music and dialogue with a natural smoothness.

The Love Parade came out in November 1929, and was everywhere praised. Its international success even outshone *Innocents of Paris*, an achievement quickly recognized by a new contract guaranteeing Maurice twenty thousand dollars a week plus travelling expenses for himself and Yvonne twice a year between America and France. On the train journey to New York there were fans at every station clamouring for his autograph. A broadcasting company installed an orchestra and equipment in his hotel room to record three songs and save him the trouble of moving, for which privilege they gave him five thousand dollars. He was very big business. A New York impresario offered him ten thousand a week – the same fee obtained by Paul Whiteman and a band of forty players – and his startled agent heard him demand twice that figure. He got it. No performer in America had ever been paid as much before, and he justified every cent by drawing houses of up to sixty thousand dollars. Tired out with giving three matinées and one evening performance each day, he refused to extend the engagement. They offered him thirty thousand dollars. When he still refused they thought him mad.

In Paris a shouting mob of admirers besieged the railway station to welcome him. He escaped to La Bocca and snatched a few weeks' rest on the hill overlooking the sea. His success began to terrify him. He knew that it was only too easy for one big film to be followed by disaster.

"It's more than my son deserves," remarked La Louque in her gentle tones.

"You're prejudiced!" he joked, and kissed her. Looking into her eyes he failed to see the expected flash of amusement, and he realized that she was growing very old, that her weariness of life had given her voice a strange far-off tone.

During his last weeks in France he appeared at the Empire music-hall. The short season was completely sold out, and each night thousands of people saluted him with noisy ovations. To reach the stage-door he forced his way through hundreds of men and women, who fought each other to touch his hand or sleeve or clamber into his car, as if by contact with him something of the magic and glamour would rub off on them.

This contact with a live audience again, hysterical though the moment was, reminded him of his original vocation. "You know, films are all very well," he told his friend Jacques Charles, "but you never have the public in front of you or with you. It's like a permanent rehearsal with never a first night. The cinema is a pretty woman: you only have dates with her on the telephone and you never hold her in your arms. And holding an audience, embracing it, hugging it to your heart, saying, 'Audience, I love you,' is so good, so wonderful, especially when it shouts back, 'We love you too, Maurice!' You never get that in the cinema. People don't clap at the end of the film, they've only one idea, to get out quickly. Who'd clap anyway, once the screen has gone black and dumb? In the cinema you can only gauge your success by a film's takings. Dollars are very nice. I prefer applause."

Yes, dollars were very nice, and so were the human pleasures they brought. Coming back on the *Île de France* he was touched by the modest bunch of flowers placed outside his cabin door each morning. They were put there, he learned, by a Negro cabin boy who had invested his small wage in a supply of cheap blooms and worried every day that they would not last out the crossing. At Le Havre Maurice bought him out of the service and engaged him for his own household. A century and a half earlier the great Dr Johnson had done the same for his African protégé Frank. Just as eighteenth-century ladies twittered their surprised delight at the novelty of a black face in his entourage, so did Parisian socialites at the presence of Maurice's new retainer. Yet for Maurice, as for Dr Johnson, the boy was to be cherished after a fashion as the son he never had.

iii

Marlene, Divorce, Exit La Louque

As *The Love Parade* began its triumphant international tour a cable arrived in Paris from Lubitsch. "You're on top of the world, Maurice," it said.

And so he was. Despite his misgivings about the cinema and his nostalgia for the flesh and blood of the theatre, he could not betray the place which had granted success and prestige in such overflowing quantity. Paramount tore up his old contract yet again and gave him an even more generous one. The studio's trademark, a mountain peak surrounded by a halo of stars, was highly appropriate to the next film he made, a sort of revue entitled *Paramount on Parade* featuring turns by all their leading actors and actresses. Clara Bow sang songs with a chorus of sailors, Clive Brook acted the part of

Sherlock Holmes with William Powell as Philo Vance, and Gary Cooper and Fay Wray appeared in a Technicolor sequence, a novelty for the time, about the American Civil War. There was someone called Harry Green chanting "I'm Isadore the Toreador" ("music from Bizet's *Carmen*", noted a straight-faced credit), and Maurice brought his own contributions to a grand finale with a Technicolor rendering of "Sweeping the Clouds away".

As soon as this forgettable entertainment was in the can he started on *The Big Pond* with Claudette Colbert. As Lily Cauchoin of Paris she had emigrated with her family at the age of six and, for her theatrical career, adopted the name of Louis XIV's most powerful minister. At her best she had a light touch, and although apt to flounder when a scene she played called for drama, in a romantic comedy like *The Big Pond* she acted with precision and wit. Some of the film's polish must have been due to the work of Preston Sturges, who helped write the dialogue, though his hour of celebrity was to come much later, in the nineteen-forties, as the director of inventive and freshly satirical comedies.

Claudette Colbert, Maurice remembered, was "dark-haired, delightful, gifted with charming talent as an actress and able to speak excellent English . . . very soon we realized that a new and attractive star was on the path to fame." They were together again in *The Smiling Lieutenant*, where Ernst Lubitsch worked his usual deft transformations on a subject which might have been made for him. It was based on *A Waltz Dream* by that old master of German operetta Oscar Straus, and the atmosphere of sentimental romance tinged with wry comedy was a sure sign of the Lubitsch manner. Critics who had detected a falling off in the standard of Maurice's pictures since *The Love Parade* welcomed the new film for a return to the quality of his début, "even", as a frank commentator observed, "when he does sing off-key". Amid the lilting waltzes and sweet tunes of Oscar Straus's music, who really cared?

On his annual visit to Europe in 1931 Maurice came over to London for a two-week appearance. Billed as "The highest-paid performer in the world", he arrived at Victoria Station to be protected by forty policemen from a raving crowd of twenty thousand fans. Although by now used to the high-pressure advertising methods of Hollywood, he still felt dubious of the raucous fanfare his impresario had organized. The slogan, said that ardent publicist, was brilliant.

He would be a terrific hit! It was all very well for him to talk, Maurice thought darkly – he did not have to go on the stage of the vast Dominion Theatre armed only with his personality, a straw hat and a dinner-jacket. After a chilly opening, his blend of English patter and French songs unleashed a wave of love, passion and admiration that rose from the audience and submerged the lone figure in the spotlight. There was nothing in films like this!

Half-way through the engagement his impresario came to him with unexpected news. None other than George Bernard Shaw had expressed a wish to see him. This was too much, said Maurice, really too much. Not to accept such an invitation, he was told, would be an affront to the whole country. Had he thought of that?

The interview was arranged, the gossip-columns chattered, and a reluctant Maurice called at the gloomy flat in Whitehall Court inhabited by the most famous dramatist of the time. Maurice knew of his reputation – who did not, throughout the civilized world? – but was familiar with none of his works. Given his daily routine of two performances, dozens of newspaper interviews and charity appearances, there was scarcely time for him to do the essential homework.

Tall, slim, straight-backed and white-bearded, the sage regarded him in silence. He broke the ice by declaring that he had read all the articles about Maurice and was interested to meet a man able to arouse normally cold English audiences to heights of excitement. Maurice thanked him awkwardly and stammered commonplaces as time dragged by with agonizing slowness.

A flash of mischief lit up Shaw's blue eyes.

"You seem to me a very congenial sort of fellow," he observed, preparing himself for a joke, "and so I'm going to speak frankly. I never go to the cinema and rarely to the theatre, and I know nothing whatever about you. I'm not even aware if you're a tenor, a baritone or a bass. But I'm a writer, and therefore curious to know a man capable of causing such a sensation in my country. And now, talk about yourself."

Relieved, amused, Maurice answered, "Your frankness has put me at ease. Now I can tell you that I haven't read a single one of your plays, either."

He returned to Paris and found that the long arm of Hollywood had stretched across the Atlantic to arrange a film for him at the Paramount studio there. The production was a two-reeler in Spanish and involved him with a trio of exotic beauties, all very popular in their own country – one of them, indeed, later finding distinction as mistress of the exiled King Alphonso. Once *El Cliente Seductor* was ready for the European circuit – the oddity still exists, it appears, and has been known to figure on Cinémathèque programmes – Maurice took ship for New York. The trappings of a first-class cabin, however luxurious, did not prevent him from beginning to experience the boredom of a regular commuter, and the distant sight of the Statue of Liberty gave him no more of a thrill than does the view of Waterloo signal box to the office-worker from Surbiton.

The Hollywood production line rolled smoothly on. *Playboy of Paris* came from a farce by Tristan Bernard, and so had the benefit of an intelligently constructed plot. Max Linder filmed it with happy results soon after the 1914–18 war, and Maurice, remembering this, persuaded Lasky to buy the rights to it. Lasky was not very keen on the idea since the Linder film had not done well in the USA, but in order to keep his top star happy he went ahead and bought it up. With songs by Richard A. Whiting, composer of "Louise", and a typically no-nonsense portrayal of a chef by Eugène Pallette, *Playboy of Paris* had some distinctive moments. Amongst them was a sequence where Maurice, who plays a waiter in the film, inspects the contents of a wine cellar, sips from each barrel, and appraises the casks as if they had been entrants in a beauty contest. At the climax he embraces a barrel of Burgundy which emits a glug of excitement. The story ends with a farcical duel and the union of true lovers.

It was Maurice who carried *Playboy of Paris* on the strength of his faultless comedy acting. The French version, according to critics, was even better than the American. Paramount often made dual-language versions of his films, and this one profited from the subtle art of the well-known actress Françoise Rosay, wife of the director Jacques Feyder. In the cast, too, was Yvonne Vallée, for whom Maurice had secured a part. He hoped that by introducing her to film work he might help to shore up their faltering marriage. The result was disappointing. A viewing of her performance showed only too clearly that she did not feel at home in the cinema, and when he optimistically suggested that she might go on to play other rôles, her only answer was to shake her head.

She never looked relaxed these days. The hectic life of filming and travelling great distances set up permanent strains. They no longer discussed their life together and he had given up confiding in her his fears and hopes. He realized that the link between them had weakened as his need for her support grew less and less, and that now, when he was in the Lubitsch phrase "on top of the world", she had little to offer him. It was not an irresistible love which united them in the first place but her compassion for him at a time when, without her solace, he would have gone under. The loss of their child sounded the knell of a relationship from which even mutual affection was soon to be excluded.

Other factors drove them still further apart. Hollywood, for such was the nature of its business, concentrated within its bounds the most potent assemblage of beauty and sexual allure anywhere in the world. In a place where physical perfection counted above all – "Remember, honey, you're just a piece of meat in a butcher's window," an executive once reminded a dazzling starlet who thought she had brains as well – awareness of sexuality was hypersensitive. The loveliest women and the handsomest men from every country in the world flocked there, some of them picked out by Hollywood and many others on their own pathetic initiative. Among the more exotic ones was Marlene Dietrich, who had been imported with her mentor Josef von Sternberg on the evidence of her German film *The Blue Angel*.

While shooting *Morocco* with Gary Cooper she had a dressing-room next to Maurice, who was busy with *Playboy of Paris*. Everyone was fascinated by her lazy walk and her distant, pre-occupied air – not least Maurice. She passed by his dressing-room without deigning to glance at him while he marvelled at her long, slim legs, her shapely hips and the disdainful, exquisitely sculpted contour of her profile. Her haughty manner annoyed but intrigued at the same time. The goddess of sex-appeal gave the impression of snapping her fingers at all the international celebrities around her. And that, of course, only served to inflame their curiosity.

The air of mystery and aloofness without doubt owed something to insecurity and even more to the fact that she did not wholly understand English nor speak it very well. Perhaps the fact that they were both aliens in a foreign land gave Maurice an advantage over home-grown rivals. He greeted her politely as she crossed his path. "Hello, Mr Chevalier" became "Hello, Maurice". They visited each other in their dressing-rooms and drank tea together. His native country, she said, she adored, and he told her how he had been moved by *The Blue Angel*, which he saw on his last trip to London, and how from that moment on he had longed to meet her. With Yvonne in hospital for an operation he felt, or at least he persuaded himself, that he was a free man for the time being.

Marlene amused him with her sharp conversation and her often unexpected little kindnesses. Hollywood buzzed with rumours about them, and to the anger of von Sternberg they dined often in restaurants where every gesture and every remark was faithfully noted by journalists. Soon they turned into what, in those euphemistic days, was described as "good friends". Their association reached a point where they appeared in public wearing identical clothes, Marlene in the same rig of white scarf and black suit that her companion wore. Von Sternberg, who saw himself as Pygmalion to her Galatea, was beside himself with fury.

So, too, was Yvonne. She had seen the photographs in the newspapers during her absence in hospital and had heard all the reports which kindly friends hastened to pass on. There was a confrontation. Bitter words were said, words that could never be taken back however much they were later regretted. He accepted her reproaches. After all, the situation had come to its logical end, since during the years of their honest attempt to live together they had not found a solution. Yvonne was still young, pretty and talented. A handsome financial settlement was made for her, and he hoped that she would find a partner more congenial than he had been. She retired into a dignified obscurity and ignored tempting offers to publish the intimate story of her marriage with one of the world's most famous stars. Forty years on she was to stand, alone and tearful, by his grave-side.

Since private lives in Hollywood evolved according to the rules of some uproarious game of musical chairs, it was not long before the nomadic Marlene found a partner elsewhere. No dramatic scene climaxed the end of her liaison with Maurice, for their relationship had been neither intense nor profound. A warm friendship remained, and in 1945 it was to inspire from her a gesture for which he was grateful.

Her place in his life was taken by Kay Francis. A dark, seductive woman, she made her name in romantic films of the nineteen-thirties, often appearing with the neatly moustached William Powell.

She was rather good, in dramatic terms that is, at sacrificing herself for a noble love, and her attractive manner of suffering emotional torment while preserving her elegance excited admiration. Her attractions caught Maurice on the rebound from Dietrich. His moods veered sharply between the exultant and the suicidal, and friends could easily guess at the latest stage in his involvement with her from the expression of happiness or despair which marked his features. She was something of an enigma, a baffling and elusive personality who, the moment he felt he possessed her, suddenly became remote. Perhaps he failed to realize that Kay Francis was not really interested in the marriage he proposed to her or, to tell the truth, in men at all. She was more fittingly absorbed in the young actresses whom, as she grew older, she took under her wing as protégées. Before long she drifted into making B-pictures and on one occasion was to know the ultimate insult of being mistaken for Cary Grant's mother.

Still under the enchantment of Kay Francis, he made it a condition of his next film that she should appear with him as the feminine lead. At the last minute she was committed to another production and he found himself yoked again to the indestructible Jeanette MacDonald, with whom, at least, he always knew where he stood. *One Hour With You*, jointly directed by Ernst Lubitsch and George Cukor, not always on the happiest of terms, went back to the music of Oscar Straus. It was a remake of a film Lubitsch once directed in silent days, and Maurice was dubious about the script, an amusing trifle that plays around not so much with a romantic triangle as with a pentagon. The novelty of the film lay in sequences where Maurice, in close-up, from time to time interrupted the action and spoke direct to the audience with confidential asides about the progress of his love affairs. Whether this was the idea of Lubitsch or Cukor is not known, but it certainly added flavour to an otherwise conventional plot.

Despite the smiling assurance and the fluent charm that pleased critics and filmgoers alike, he was dissatisfied with the way his career in Hollywood was developing. In each film he merely repeated earlier performances, and any attempt to vary the by now well established routine evoked horror from his Paramount employers. "You're hot box-office just as you are," they assured him. Why start tampering with a formula that drew packed houses in every corner of the world? To do so would be madness. But he was tired of the eternal label "cute". Since his earliest days with Mistinguett he had known that an artist should never be content to stay the same. He should seek always to renew himself – yet to experiment, in a Hollywood where enormous fortunes reposed on the manufacture of a safe and familiar product which had been thoroughly tried and tested, was a heresy that could not be allowed.

It became difficult for him to sleep at night, and one evening early in 1931 he only dropped off very late into a confusion of distorted images and threatening dreams. A knock at the door awoke him from his nightmares. A telegram was delivered, and with it a brutal shock: his mother had died. There was no final illness, no prolonged suffering, just a quiet departure as if a lamp had flickered and vanished into the night. He could not at first understand. A numbness crept over him, he felt dizzy and sick with a feeling that emptied him of strength. For days he wept helpless tears. When, through sheer exhaustion, the weeping stopped, the awful significance of the news hit him afresh and he began again to sob with despair. He was lost and wretched in a foreign land, cut off by death from the person who had meant everything to him. No friend, no other woman, could aspire to make up for the disappearance of La Louque.

He remembered the indefinable sadness that came over her when he said goodbye on his last visit to France. Never again would he feel the wrinkled hand stroking his hair, and never again would he know the comfort and strength this simple woman had given him. On the set he acted with his accustomed dash, and in front of the cameras no sign betrayed the misery that darkened his thoughts. Too many millions of dollars depended on his performance. In between takes, and throughout the sleepless nights, the tears still flowed.

La Louque was buried in a simple grave up on the heights of old Montmartre. If his native city now appeared to him as the loneliest place on earth, the streets, the houses, the trees and the sky nonetheless were closer to his heart than ever before and summoned him with an urgency to make him forget Hollywood. He stood beside her tomb up in the quiet cemetery of Saint Vincent and drew consolation from the presence of the woman who had never failed him. There was no need for him to have anything more inscribed on the stone than the golden letters which read: JOSÉPHINE CHEVALIER. Those two words summed it all up.

On stage at the London Coliseum in 1949

With Norma Shearer at the Théâtre des Champs-Elysées

Patachou and Chevalier welcome Gracie Fields to Paris

Chevalier and Margaret Lockwood at a reception at Drury Lane in 1948

An intimate moment with Patachou

The finale of "Plein Feu" at the Empire Theatre, Paris (1952), with Colette Marchand

Meeting the Queen at the Royal Command Performance at the London Palladium in 1952

Rehearsing a BBC TV show in his garden with Bob Hope in 1954

As Audrey Hepburn's father in *Love in the Afternoon* (1957)

At the races with Suzy Volterra, widow of his former impresario

CHAPTER SIX

"Momo"

> "The older I grow in this wonderful profession of which I
> have the honour to be a member, the more convinced I
> become that you can listen to waves on the shore of a brook
> in the forest, the wind in the trees, or the rain on the roof, but
> there is no more thrilling, no more exhilarating sound in all
> of nature than applause, and I never get enough of it."
>
> *Edward Everett Horton*

i

Love Me Tonight

France or America: which was it to be? Like a man torn between
two loves, he favoured sometimes the one and sometimes the other.
He was a Frenchman and Paris meant home. Yet whenever he
stayed in New York or California he sensed an electric thrill,
buoyant and supercharged, that made all other places seem a desert.

There were times, though, when he knew he could never be
anything else but a thoroughgoing Latin for whom Anglo-Saxon
attitudes would remain essentially alien. One of his closest friends
in Hollywood was Douglas Fairbanks. He admired "Doug's"
good fellowship, his joyous appetite for life and his kindly outlook.
Typical of the light-hearted Fairbanks circle was a film called *The
Stolen Jools*, which, made to raise money for charity, had a cast of
stars who joined in for the fun of the thing. It began with the theft of
Norma Shearer's jewellery, whereupon Wallace Beery as a police-
man interviewed the suspects, who included Maurice Chevalier,
Douglas Fairbanks junior, Gary Cooper, Barbara Stanwyck, Joan
Crawford, Laurel and Hardy, Buster Keaton, Edward G. Robin-
son, Loretta Young. . .

Such larks were understandable. Others Maurice found utterly
baffling. Every Sunday there was open house at Pickfair, the stately

home where Doug and his wife Mary Pickford lived as the royal family of Hollywood. After lunch and a siesta everyone went off to play tennis or to frolic in the vast swimming-pool, blue as the dazzling cerulean of the Californian sky. Fairbanks demonstrated his agility in spectacular leaps and rolls and dives, laughing with unconcealed pleasure at his gymnastic skill. Maurice, standing beside the pool in a smart grey-flannel suit, was suddenly grasped by a pair of muscular arms.

"What's the idea, Doug?"

He was picked up and thrown head first into the pool amid a storm of laughter. As he rose spluttering to the surface his expression, akin to that worn by the ghost of Hamlet's father, sent Fairbanks into uncontrollable bursts of mirth. His London-tailored suit was ruined and shrunk, his silk underwear muddied, his platinum watch broken, his buckskin shoes (McAfee of Dover Street) were soiled and stained. He did his best to join in the laughter but his smile was hollow. Out of the pool he scrambled like a wet dog, his clothes flapping sodden around a body trembling with cold and humiliation. Suppose pleurisy or bronchitis were to cut short his film career?

However hard he tried, he could not see the point of the joke. The poor slum child within him was outraged by the wanton destruction of good clothes. As a poverty-stricken urchin he had always longed for a watch, even of the simplest kind, and to hazard a platinum one for a laugh went beyond all comprehension.

When Fairbanks had recovered from his amusement he slapped Maurice on the back and chuckled, "You've no sense of humour, Maurice!"

He had, and he knew he had, but this was a point where French humour and American humour went on their very different ways. Once, however, he acknowledged the divide, he continued to regard Fairbanks as a close friend.

Other incidents reminded him of his Frenchness. At a dinner party he tried hard to make conversation with Greta Garbo, a person whose company he had never found easy. They were talking theatre when she suddenly asked him, "Do you like swimming, Monsieur Chevalier? In the ocean?"

He paused and nodded, taken off his guard.

"Very well then," she said peremptorily, "will you come into the water straight away?"

"Now?" he enquired, scarcely able to believe his ears. The Pacific, glacial at midnight, did not tempt him. Moreover, his feeling for the *convenances* was shocked. What place was this where females proposed to swim at so unaccustomed an hour? Garbo retired into her shell, distant, uncommunicative again.

Someone with whom he did eventually find a genuine rapport was Charles Boyer, yet another of the foreign actors Hollywood showered with gold and then allowed to idle for months, not quite knowing what to do about them. Boyer was a product of the Sorbonne, a prize-winning student at the Conservatoire, and had already made himself a respectable career on the French stage. The very distinguished Cécile Sorel, an ornament of the Comédie-Française, played Kate to his Petruchio in *The Taming of the Shrew*. They were both so carried away by the beauty of Shakespeare's verse that, long after the curtain fell, they remained in each other's arms. Cécile's jealous betrothed, the noble Comte de Ségur, leapt from behind the scenery where he had been watching and separated them with furious words.

Plucked out of his natural habitat and spirited away into a land where no one knew him, Boyer did not repine and set himself to learn English. One day he played a tiny part in a film as Jean Harlow's chauffeur. It lasted no more than a few seconds, but the graphic subtlety of his expression was enough to startle producers who knew about acting. They suddenly realized that for the past twelve months they had been harbouring in their midst one of the best French actors available. Soon he was the hero of romantic melodramas with Dietrich, Garbo, Hedy Lamarr, and all the glamorous leading ladies Hollywood could find to match him against. His brand of sultry romance was so distinctive that it won the compliment of innumerable parodies – and survived them all. As late as the nineteen-fifties his performance in Max Ophüls' *Madame De . . .* showed that, when necessary, he could still draw on a fertile talent. This cunning seducer on the screen was devoted to his English wife, and when she died he killed himself, shattered with grief at the age of seventy-nine, very soon afterwards in 1978.

Maurice was impressed by his new friend's social grace and the poise he retained throughout Hollywood parties and dinners that could be formidable when they were not boring. He, who had left school at the age of ten, marvelled at a culture and an education denied to him. Boyer encouraged him to read the classics. At night the middle-aged pupil buried himself in Montaigne and discovered that the old philosopher knew all about the problems of life, problems, in fact, which dated back even further than the time of the sixteenth century when he wrote. Bruised by his divorce and by the death of La Louque, Maurice began to find consolation in the writing of sages and thinkers whose names up to then he had never even known. He met and talked with Boyer often, at dinner and at long weekends. When they were separated he wrote him voluminous letters, often awkward and comically expressed but always trying hard to honour the intellectual standards of his mentor. The process of self-education which Boyer inspired with his amiable prompting was to last for the rest of Maurice's lifetime.

While his evenings were spent in the company of Montaigne, Voltaire and Jean-Jacques Rousseau, his days passed in the shooting of a new musical film called *Love Me Tonight*, which was released in 1932. The director was Rouben Mamoulian, a Russian from Tiflis who had studied at the Moscow Arts Theatre and directed stage plays in London before emigrating to Hollywood. During his time with Paramount he had been asked by Adolphe Zukor to make a film which would feature Maurice and Jeanette MacDonald, a prospect he found not all that inviting. Now Zukor, like Mayer, had a talent for the theatrical often as vivid as that of the actors whom he employed. The wily old Hungarian pleaded with Mamoulian in heart-rending terms. The studio, he declared, tears welling up in his eyes, would go bankrupt if it did not make the fullest use of these two great stars. Disaster threatened, failure was imminent, the whole towering structure of Paramount would crash to the ground without the aid of Mamoulian. Russian obstinacy gave way to Hungarian persuasiveness, and Mamoulian warmed to an idea which gave him the chance of combining music, dancing, singing, acting, lighting and décor in a fully integrated spectacle.

For his music and lyrics he went to Richard Rodgers and Lorenz Hart, a promising team whose later success proved the wisdom of his instinct. Everything was carefully planned in advance so that songs and words grew in a natural way from the action and kept the plot on the move. Only then were scriptwriters called in to write dialogue and bridge the gap between musical numbers. The technique recalls the old masters of French farce who would write their last scene first and work backwards in order to ensure that events leading up to the *dénouement* unrolled with flawless logic.

Maurice was a little disturbed by this method. Lubitsch had always included him in story conferences, and he felt ignored. The owlish, mop-haired Mamoulian gently explained that this was his way of working, that he was doing the production as a favour for Mr Zukor, and that he would in fact be greatly pleased if someone relieved him of the chore. The Frenchman subsided. He went to the grubby little cubicle where Rodgers and Hart toiled on their score. His blue jacket, blue shirt, blue scarf, blue trousers and blue shoes matched the sharp twinkling blue of his eyes. Geniality exuded from him in a compelling aura. How happy he was that they were writing the songs for his new film. Would they mind playing some?

They took it in turns to sing and play from the roughly scribbled manuscript. He heard them in silence, his face, usually so expressive, blank and inscrutable. At the end he rose from his chair and left without saying a word. They were appalled and fearful. Hollywood, until then, had not been the happiest of places for them, and in those years of the Depression they badly needed the salary it paid. Their sleep that night was haunted by visions of the sack, for if they could not please Chevalier they certainly would not please the front office. Next morning he appeared in the little room and filled it with radiance. He had been so excited by their wonderful songs, he explained, that he had not slept a wink all night. Neither, they thought wryly to themselves, had they, though for different reasons. His peasant caution, attuned over years of dealing with show-business people, had led him to the same conclusion as Talleyrand in the world of diplomacy: beware of your first impressions.

The nine songs written for the score included "Mimi", yet another young lady of an attractiveness to rival Valentine and Louise. He had put his right shoe on his left foot and his left shoe on his right, sings the lover, for Mimi's beauty threw him into such a tizz that he had also buttoned his trousers to his jacket. And one day, he adds, he would like to have a child by that "sunny little honey of a Mimi". The verse is written with elegant economy and the music with a crisp rhythm that suggests little Mimi herself trotting off down the street.

The plot, which need not be too closely examined, presents Maurice in the part of a tailor who masquerades as a baron in the ancestral home of one of his noble but heavily indebted customers.

A clever sequence opens in the tailor's shop where he progresses from rhyming dialogue to music. The song is taken up by his client, who hums it in the street and bequeaths it to a taxi-driver. The passenger in the cab, a composer en route for the railway station, overhears it and, later in his carriage, adds words to the music. A platoon of soldiers pick it up on the march, and they in turn pass it on to a gypsy camp, where it is repeated on swooning violins and is handed over to Jeanette MacDonald, a lovesick princess who that night is mooning over her balcony and waiting for her dream lover to appear. By this neat device hero and heroine are brought together, although he lives in Paris and she in a country house many miles away.

"Mimi" was not the only item made to measure for the leading man. He also had an "Apache" number in which, accompanied by a gigantic looming shadow, he thrilled the guests at a fancy-dress party. "Song of Paris", beginning on a close-up of his straw hat, opened the film with a bustling tour of the city as it awoke from sleep and even recalled for a moment the artistry of René Clair. Jeanette MacDonald showed an uncharacteristic turn of humour in "Lover" and, in the dramatic climax, remarkable skill as a horse-woman. She had to overtake a moving train and then make it halt by dismounting and standing on the rail. She scorned the aid of a double and justified once again her nickname of "The Iron Butterfly".

The most unlikely feature of *Love Me Tonight* was the presence of Sir C. Aubrey Smith, who not only played the part of a crusty French duke but also squawked the chorus of "Mimi" while tracing a few primitive dance-steps. This ancient monument to the British influence in Hollywood preserved the flavour of his acting in private life as the rugged captain of a cricket eleven which operated regularly on a strip of greensward shielded against the fierce Californian sun. His long-running impersonations of family solicitors, brave army officers and noble lords was given the accent and manner of a vanished England which Hollywood clutched eagerly to its bosom. Sir C. Aubrey had one string to his bow and he played it with dogged zest. It is not surprising that he distrusted writer fellows like Evelyn Waugh, who came across him on a trip to Hollywood and used him as an original for the mischievous portrait of "Sir Ambrose Abercrombie" in his masterpiece *The Loved One*.

From an artistic point of view *Love Me Tonight* was probably the most successful of all the Chevalier films made in Hollywood. An approach that was novel at the time is shown by revivals to have kept its freshness and ability to surprise. One reason for its satisfying wholeness is that Mamoulian pre-recorded the score in advance to achieve a perfect blend of the aural and the visual. He commissioned Richard Rodgers to provide the incidental music as well, a move which gave the score stylistic unity. Grateful to Maurice for his help in making the songs popular, Rodgers also paid their director a tribute from himself and his lyricist: "Is there any wonder that Larry and I were stimulated by a man as brilliant as Mamoulian?"

Maurice flitted through one more production before spending the summer of 1932 at La Bocca. This was *Make Me A Star*, a version of the novel *Merton of the Movies*, which has so fascinated Hollywood over the years that it has been turned into a film at least three times. The first adaptation was done in 1924 and the last, with Red Skelton, in 1947. The plot called for the hero to visit Paramount Studios and to see various players at work, among them Maurice, Gary Cooper, Tallulah Bankhead, Sylvia Sidney, and that endearing cross-eyed clown Ben Turpin. Once his little scene had been shot Maurice embarked for his native country. There he made a quick one-reel charity film called *Toboggan* (1932), where he was shown demonstrating his boxing skill in a gymnasium. After which he set off for La Bocca – and, to his alarm, a reunion with Mistinguett.

ii

Mist Again – The Merry Widow

Mist had reached her sixtieth birthday now but her vivacity was untouched by the passing years. In addition to her flat in Paris she had acquired a property at Bougival, once a village though gradually becoming a suburb on the outskirts of the capital. The eighteenth-century house had belonged to a larger mansion up on the hill owned by Madame Dubarry, and it was there, according to a tradition thoughtfully nurtured by Mist, who liked to identify herslf with glamour, however ancient, that the King's favourite had received her royal lover and spent her last days before mounting the scaffold. It would not be surprising to learn that Mist, ever acquisitive, had personally excavated the tree beneath which the unfortunate Dubarry was supposed to have buried her jewels.

Between revues Mist entertained there and received friends, among them her current stage partner Jean Sablon. The house had some twenty rooms and an all-pink salon designed by the fashionable painter Jean-Gabriel Domergue, a one-time master of the voguish fluffy portrait. The place resembled a zoo more than a home, with a hostess as bizarre as the animals that wandered freely through it. Fourteen dogs roamed about accompanied by a pig which, like a cockerel and a sheep nicknamed (mouton) Rothschild, was allowed excessive liberties. From banks of aquaria shoals of goldfish stared glassily at Mist's famous parrot. This talented bird, said wondering admirers, could sing "Mon Homme" in accents as plaintive as those of its mistress.

A mutual friend suggested bringing Maurice and Mist together again. Maurice temporized. When the subject was mentioned he thought it better not to try to revive the past. It was nearly a decade since they had met, and where was the point of digging up a relationship dead and buried? Gradually, in spite of himself, he began to feel curiosity. Would her fiery appeal have mellowed? Would her vibrant personality have acquired, with age, more understanding and tolerance?

One account of their reunion tells that they met at Bougival, walked beside the Seine, and returned happy and relaxed. Another relates that the meeting took place in Antibes, where she had a seaside home not far from La Bocca. Being almost neighbours they would probably have come across each other anyway in time. It was almost night when he arrived at her house. As he climbed out of the car he heard a door open. Mist stood before him, hands held out in welcome, her voice provocative still.

"So you found your way here at last, Cio?"

For a moment her smile wavered and her face paled.

"You haven't changed, Cio, and neither have I," she went on a little defiantly. "I'm still having the same success. Nothing's changed

at all, really." Was she trying to reassure herself? She had determined never to grow old and she ignored the passage of time.
Perpetual youth was what she demanded, and she closed her eyes to
reality.

"I've organized supper at a night-club in Cannes, Cio. You'll
know everyone there and they'll be thrilled to see you."

They danced together. Her body was soft, pliant, and he remembered the times when they had waltzed and tangoed in perfect
harmony. It was nice, he thought, to see her again, and he felt a
surge of affection.

Suddenly half a dozen photographers ambushed them with pop-
ping flashes. He stopped dancing and pulled her into a corner.

"What's the matter, Cio? Are you afraid of being photo-
graphed?"

"I don't want all the newspapers in Paris to show us dancing
together. Don't you see what they're getting at?"

"What does it matter?" She shrugged and went back to their
table.

A few weeks later the same thing happened. He had gone to see
her brother's granddaughter, and was playing with the child as Mist
stood beside him when a photographer appeared. No, Mist had not
changed, and neither had her gift for publicity.

Journalists interviewed him and enraged him by twisting his
words. "I was very saddened by that article yesterday," he wrote to
her after their meeting in Cannes. "It's just what I was afraid of and
it makes me look like a cad and a buffoon because, of course, I said
nothing like the things that are attributed to me. There are too many
traps for the friendship we want to show each other, and I'm sure
it's in our interest to beware of acquaintances who are too well
intentioned."

He signed himself, non-committally, "Your friend, always". She
wrote back with suggestions for appearing together at the Folies
Bergère. The present management was very sympathetic, she said,
and she knew they would do well at a theatre where they had had so
many triumphs in the past. The proposal fell on stony ground. He
was too involved with Hollywood and Broadway at the moment,
and the Folies Bergère must wait for the time being.

In October 1932 Mist was on tour in Geneva, despondent and
lonely, when the stage-door-keeper gave her a letter with familiar

handwriting on it. She had thought, after the Cannes incident and the newspaper stories, that Maurice would write no more – but here he was, telling her that she stood out above all other women of her generation and that he had never seen her equal anywhere else in the world: "I know very well it is those devilish gifts of yours that caused our estrangement and then the final break of what was the most beautiful thing in your life and in mine, and that the price we paid for those wonderful battles and those unrivalled successes has been the separation of two people made for each other. But what can one expect: it was our fate, the ransom that had to be paid. All one can do is think about it gently, kindly and with resignation. As for you, you have my admiration, my tenderness and my gratitude for as long as my brain is capable of thought." Was he coming back to her? Or was this just another brief exalted mood which, as he himself acknowledged, was as likely to be followed by one of depression?

She drafted her reply carefully, writing a rough sketch of it, crossing out, re-phrasing, more like a schoolgirl of fourteen preparing an essay than a sixty-year-old corresponding with a middle-aged man who had once been her lover.

"I was so sad when I left Juan-les-Pins," she wrote, "you'd hurt me so much. In an affection and friendship as solid as ours we shouldn't pay any attention to public opinion, which is always spiteful and jealous about other people's happiness. What could be more natural than that our meeting should have been one of the most upsetting moments in my life? I think about it every day. . . With all the strength of my unhappy heart I wish you *bon voyage* and hope for your good fortune and continuing success. You are a great artist and I love you."

Next month, from the Algonquin Hotel in New York, he told her that since his next film was not yet ready for shooting he had begun a month's tour of Paramount cinemas. "I'm singing four times a day and five on Saturdays and public holidays. It's a galley-slave's life, exhausting and absolutely deadly. I shan't sign any more contracts like this and can't wait for the final date in Chicago."

From Chicago he escaped to Hollywood and a new film called *Bedtime Story*. He was cast as a French nobleman whose romantic adventures are complicated by the discovery of a six-month-old baby in his car. This infant, known professionally as "Baby Leroy", starred in half a dozen more Paramount films before retiring at the ripe age of three and a half. His precocious ability to out-act and upstage older performers was notorious, and several actors refused to work with him. W.C. Fields had the misfortune to appear several times in productions featuring Baby Leroy, and once managed to make his hated co-star drunk. It was on this occasion that the celebrated misanthrope coined the epigram, "Any man who hates dogs and children can't be all bad." He added, with malicious afterthought, "The boy's no trouper. Anyone who can't hold his liquor shouldn't drink on the job."

Louella Parsons, who when not purveying gossip could be a shrewd critic, observed, "The charming Maurice Chevalier and a baby are all any woman needs to make her day complete." Maurice, unlike the peppery Fields, worshipped Baby Leroy, the child of separated parents, and wanted to adopt him, though nothing came of his ambition. They posed together between shots, the small boy wearing a miniature straw hat and doing his best to destroy the full-size article worn by Maurice.

Bedtime Story is worth another mention for the presence of Edward Everett Horton, one of those supporting players whose acting gladdened the heart in dozens of films. He was a stage-player who specialized in silly-ass Englishmen before going to Hollywood and dispensing his unique brand of dithering eccentricity. He never turned down a rôle, learned his lines more speedily than anyone else (his long stage experience had made him a "quick study"), and got his scene right first time with an efficiency that won him the nickname of "One-Take Horton". Although his flapping gestures and worried looks conveyed extremes of hysterical anxiety, the method behind it all was precise and miraculously timed.*

The atmosphere during the making of *Bedtime Story* was very agreeable. If W.C. Fields' bitter childhood had made him rancorous, Maurice's own youth, which was no less harsh, produced the opposite effect. He capitulated willingly to Baby Leroy, who was to know a life considerably more pleasant than either Fields or Maurice had experienced. *Bedtime Story*, he told Mist, was the film

---

* One of his films gave him a chance to show qualities far above those demanded by his usual sort of part. It was entitled *Summer Storm* and came from a Chekhov story. With George Sanders as the leading man, Horton played a decrepit Russian nobleman reduced to poverty. He did so with a genuinely moving blend of pathos and comedy.

"that has made me the happiest in my career. The public may not agree with me – but I'm satisfied with it, and that, in itself, is very rare. I don't know if I shall make the other film which I have to start in five or six weeks because things are going very badly out here at the moment and I'll try to get it put off until next autumn and go home to La Bocca after a short stay in London and Paris. . . I'm very pleased, Mist, that life has allowed us to renew our affectionate relationship, which is based on years of happiness and confidence and will enable us to look forward to many pleasant and enjoyable times in the future."

His comment that "things are going very badly" reflected the situation now confronting Paramount. Some of its biggest names had been tempted away by other, richer companies, and Maurice himself was on the point of accepting lures from Thalberg at MGM. The troubled firm went into liquidation, only to rise again almost immediately and to prosper anew thanks to the blessed Mae West and *She Done Him Wrong*. In the meantime, however, Maurice took his farewell of Paramount with a minor diversion called *The Way to Love*. It was made under troubled circumstances. The leading lady walked out, other members of the cast found pressing commitments elsewhere, and large quantities of film had to be thrown away. All that survived was a mild fable that Maurice worked hard to animate. Honours were divided between Edward Everett Horton as "Professor Gaston Bibi", a fortune-teller, and Mutt, a dog which regarded the camera with its liquid eyes and pert mongrel face and stole every scene.

Although Thalberg offered Maurice far better terms than Paramount could afford, it was his promise of the chance to experiment, to create a "new" Chevalier, that finally proved irresistible. All sorts of goodies were in store, promised Thalberg, including *The Chocolate Soldier* and a musical version of the play *The Last of Mrs Cheyney*. The first production was to be *The Merry Widow*, directed by Ernst Lubitsch. Maurice proposed the singer Grace Moore as his heroine. Her looks and her bright personality rather than her voice had taken her out of the opera house and brought her fame in the cinema. Thalberg frowned. She was too plump, he argued, and her films with MGM had so far been disappointing. What they needed, he enthused, was someone really outstanding, someone beautiful, someone who would be a revelation! A heavily advertised search for the ideal actress was begun, and after many months of anguished drum-beating the studio chose the lady who had been on their doorstep all the time: Jeanette MacDonald.

Maurice's heart sank. Her prim and disapproving manner grated on him, all the more so as he knew, and all Hollywood knew, of the wild affair she had been having with an agent. And she, for her part, returned his dislike. Her co-star was, she remarked acidly, "the biggest bottom-pincher in Hollywood".

They were both professionals, though, and on the screen they trilled and cooed with immaculate grace. *The Merry Widow*, as Maurice knew only too well, gave him the chance to redeem himself after a string of minor films. His professional conscience was more sensitive than usual, and in the middle of the night he would telephone his friends with anxious queries. "I've seen the rushes of my last scene," he agonized. "They've chosen Take One. Don't you think that my raised eyebrow in Take Three adds to the humour of the speech? Also, it seems to me that I was more amusing in Take Fifteen of the song than at Take Twelve." All this worried attention to the smallest detail ensured a performance in which the forty-six-year-old spoke, sang and danced with a gaiety and a youthfulness which were entirely convincing. In *The Merry Widow*, as in *The Love Parade*, his acting remains fresh and contemporary when the settings and all else around him have taken on an inevitably dated air. No matter that he loathed the heroine – his manner suggested a love for her that was sincere and wholehearted. As Sacha Guitry once observed, "To act is to tell lies with the aim of deceiving. Everything around one should tell lies. The good actor should say 'I love you' with greater conviction to an actress he doesn't love than to one whom he does. And he should convince the audience that he is eating on stage when in reality he is not. The refinement of refinements is to *appear* to be in love with an actress whom one does really love – it's like eating genuine chicken while making believe it's cardboard."

Lubitsch spent many thousands of dollars on recreating the atmosphere of a legendary Paris with its gilt-encrusted ballrooms and lavish restaurants. Champagne flowed headily and troupes of gorgeous girls manoeuvred in fascinating patterns. For all its knowingness, though, the tinselled spectacle he engineered seems oddly innocent beside the dark Freudian version which Erich von Stroheim filmed in 1925. Lubitsch brought in Lorenz Hart to rewrite the lyrics, and since wherever Hart went his composer partner Richard Rodgers went also, the two of them were credited with the words of Lehár's songs. It was, of course, impossible to improve on the "Merry Widow" waltz, the loveliest thing of its kind in all Viennese operetta. Hart was ill at ease with the assignment, which turned out to be far less rewarding than *Love Me Tonight*. He did not warm to the director's autocratic ways and his insistence on neatly typewritten sheets instead of the hastily scribbled bits of paper he offered. When their contract ended, Rodgers thought it only polite to take his leave of Thalberg. He found his way into a boardroom where the great man was presiding over a conference. Thalberg looked at him blankly. Rodgers explained that he was leaving and had come to say goodbye. Thalberg continued to stare without a gleam of recognition. He obviously did not know who the composer was. And that, decided Rodgers, was final deadening proof of the anonymous Hollywood factory system which looked on its employees, however talented, as mere cogs.

The Merry Widow took eighty-eight days to shoot, cost nearly two million dollars and eventually made a loss of a hundred and thirteen thousand. MGM was satisfied, nonetheless, and sketched out new plans for Maurice. Thalberg's mind turned to Grace Moore, who, since his rejection of her, had surprised everyone with her success in *One Night of Love*. She was, therefore, a hot property. "Columbia is ready to lend her to us. I've got an idea, and with the two of you we shall beat all records," he told Maurice.

A thoughtful silence followed. "There's just one detail to settle, Maurice. Columbia insists on Grace having top billing."

Maurice reacted angrily.

"The important thing is to make a good film," Thalberg pleaded. "And to make money. Don't you agree?"

"No, and I regret it. For more than twenty years I've always been top of the bill, and I'd prefer to be first at a little neighbourhood music-hall than second at the New York Palace."

The irony was painful. Grace Moore, whom Thalberg had refused when Maurice wanted her in *The Merry Widow*, had become a magnet for the crowds. Thalberg was in a delicate position. Business was business, and he needed her badly, despite the conditions imposed by the studio that owned her contract. Maurice realized how perilous existence could be in a Hollywood where even the satrap Thalberg was dominated, in the end, by the brute power of finance. He made his decision and revoked his contract.

"With three years of it still to run?" enquired Thalberg, astonished and perplexed.

Maurice was adamant. He bought himself out and left MGM in 1934.

"You'll come back to Hollywood one of these days," prophesied Thalberg after the dust had died down, "and you'll be greater than ever."

"Perhaps," replied Maurice as he shook hands, "though I doubt it at the moment."

Before his departure from Hollywood he made one last film. The company behind it was Twentieth Century, later to be transmuted under the flamboyant standard of Darryl F. Zanuck into Twentieth Century Fox. Zanuck was the last of the old-time dinosaurs, a long-lived survivor still operating in the nineteen-sixties who had entered the movies in the mid-nineteen-twenties as a writer of epics featuring the resourceful dog Rin Tin Tin. When Maurice knew him he had just reached the top of the greasy pole as head of production. Zanuck always gave an impression of being larger than life. The cigars he smoked were even more gigantic than those favoured by Lubitsch, and he had a massive appetite for hunting lions in Africa and beautiful women in Europe. On the way home to America from one such expedition he broke his journey in Paris and bought up rights to the words "Folies Bergère" as a film title. Two American night-clubs of the same name instantly took legal action against him, claiming infringement. It was pointed out, with unanswerable logic, that since there were two of them they would be better engaged in suing each other. They lost their case.

Having acquired a good title Zanuck, in the hallowed tradition, began looking around for a film to go with it. He offered the leading rôle to Charles Boyer. But Charles at that moment was deeply immersed in the whirlwind marriage he had just contracted. ("Charles Boyer has gone completely nuts," Maurice wrote to Mist, "and has married a little English girl, very pretty of course, whom he's only known for three weeks!") Boyer suggested Maurice, and Maurice it was who played the dual rôle of Fernand, Baron Cassini and Eugène Charlier, a Folies Bergère comedian. His leading ladies were the aristocratic Merle Oberon and the exuberant

Ann Sothern, who lavished her bouncing energy on "Rhythm in the Rain", a number which Maurice included in his French repertory as "La Romance de la pluie". A small but memorable part was taken by Eric Blore, another of those actors who, like Edward Everett Horton, lit up many a film with his cameo playing. His jowls were heavy and shook like the wattles of an outraged turkeycock, his mouth was wide and rubbery, and his big saucer eyes could at will express the darkest guile or the purest innocence. He made an excellent gentleman's gentleman, an ideal minor functionary, a perfect solicitor's clerk.* When he was not on screen to divert the audience there was Chevalier singing "Valentine" and dancing with Ann Sothern in a production number which involved both of them gyrating on top of a monster straw hat held in position by a ring of chorus-girls also wearing straw hats against a backdrop featuring a montage of yet more straw hats disappearing into infinity. As was the custom in those days, a separate French-language version was made of *Folies Bergère*. It had the advantage over the original, destined for the puritan Anglo-Saxon market, in that the chorus-girls neglected to veil their bosoms.

And that was that. Maurice walked for the last time around the place that had given him so much. He saw, from a distance, the vast hangar-like building containing the set where he had worked on his first production. The doors were shut and a red light warned that filming was in progress. Sadness overcame him, a feeling of regret that an episode in his life was over. Yet his decision had been the right one, he thought, and he had been wise to follow the dictates of heart and reason. Nothing now could make him change his mind.

"You'll never come back, Maurice, I'm sure of it," Kay Francis said to him at their last dinner in Hollywood. Who would be proved right in the end: she or Thalberg?

---

* Perhaps his best performance was as the shifty beachcomber Captain Nichols in the film of Somerset Maugham's *The Moon and Sixpence*.

Stage-fright

In New York he put up at the Hotel Astor in Times Square. The elegiac mood continued, for there he met again his old impresario C.B. Dillingham. They talked about Maurice's first visit to America with Mist and Earl Leslie, and a blur of nostalgia softened the memory of what had been in fact an uncomfortable occasion. In the crabbed, shaky handwriting of an aged man near death, the impresario added a postscript to the letter Maurice had just written to Mist: "Sweetheart, when times are bad I turn back the clock and think of the wonderful time you, Maurice, Atlantic City and I had. God loves you, but what is more important, I love you."

The flowers at La Bocca looked lovelier, the air was sweeter, the Mediterranean sparkled with a sharper brilliance. During the two months Maurice spent there on his annual holiday he made plans for a big new tour. He wanted to take things a little easier, and he felt he deserved a rest. It was too much for "le Père Maurice", as he jokingly described himself, to make films by day and appear on stage by night. Douglas Fairbanks, who had gone into partnership with Alexander Korda, spent a day at La Bocca discussing possible ideas. Mist had seen *The Private Life of Henry VIII* in Paris and reported favourably to Maurice. Korda, they decided, was a man to trust. A contract was drawn up and signed, although, like so many of the exciting illusions the Hungarian enchanter juggled with, the notion fell still-born to the ground.

For the time being Maurice knew that he would be content with footlights and a live audience. He wanted to hear the sound of laughter and applause, to see faces turned towards him, to be reunited with all the warm human feelings from which Hollywood had cut him off for so long. Although every gesture and every inflection was rehearsed precisely before he even set foot on a stage, it was only in contact with an audience that he was able to shape, from minute to minute, the definitive contours of his act, like a sculptor moulding from the living material.

In May 1935 he set off on a tour of the South that whisked him from Nice via Toulon and Marseilles to Paris. In the capital his welcome was not all that he had expected. The theatre where he sang, the big and rambling Châtelet, did not suit him, and the supporting bill was mediocre. It is difficult, even for a Chevalier, to wake up an audience which has been bored for over an hour by inferior turns, and although his reappearance was welcomed it did not amount to a triumph. After the years of absence he found his compatriots chilly by comparison with the Americans. While he had been away his rivals and his enemies had worked devotedly to undermine a reputation built up in the nineteen-twenties. His success abroad had inspired envy, and rather than take a patriotic pride in his achievement there were those who hated him for having earned so much money. "Nouveau riche!" they sneered, wishing, oh so desperately in their heart of hearts, that they could have done the same.

That evening at the Théâtre du Châtelet he experienced a stage-fright more anguished than anything he had known before. It was worse, even, than the feeling he had had when, as a boy of twelve, he had made his dédut at the old Café des Trois Lions. Then, he had known there would be other chances. Now, he had only one. Stage-fright is a permanent and incurable disease. So many things can go wrong on the stage that when a performer's subconscious allows itself for a moment to recognize the existence of one small anxiety alone, hundreds of others immediately start crowding upon him. While he plied his "five" and "nine" make-up sticks Maurice had all the usual symptoms: a heavy feeling that solidified at the pit of the stomach, a sensation of weight around the lungs and choking in the throat, a raging thirst on the tongue. His hands trembled and he smoked cigarette after cigarette, scarcely waiting to take a first puff before lighting up another. Once he made contact with the audience, however, he began to feel better. He acted and reacted, wooed and cajoled, alert always to strengthen the link that was growing between the solitary figure in the spotlight and the two thousand people who watched him in the darkness beyond. When he came off stage he was light-headed, his step springy with exhilaration where before it had been leaden and uncertain.

Charles Boyer was there in a box with his new young wife Pat Patterson. Afterwards they came round to see him.

"What do you plan to do now, Maurice?" asked Boyer.

"I'm going to *live*!" he declared, his face shining with sweat and jubilation.

The songs he had prepared for his return to France were carefully chosen. One of them, "Prosper", made a great stir, chiefly on account of a little trick he had worked out to fit between bars of the refrain: a flick of the legs and a shake of the foot at the yodelled words "Yop la boum!" The Prosper of the title, music by Vincent Scotto, is a pimp who transacts his "p'tit biz'ness" in a shady corner of the Place Pigalle. With his little green hat and thick, belted overcoat, Prosper is the darling of the peripatetic beauties whose operations he directs, a harem of night-girls who are mad about him. The song is a part of the romanticized Montmartre legend, a quaint and faded snapshot. Prosper today would be a cold-hearted murderer who kills as negligently as he lights a cigarette, a snuffer-out of bank cashiers and nightwatchmen.

For another of his songs Maurice relied on a team who in the mid-nineteen-thirties were revitalizing French popular music with a new and distinctive tone. They were Jean Nohain, son of the poet Franc-Nohain, who wrote the words, and the lady known as Mireille, who composed the music. Between them they produced over five hundred songs, wry, witty and often touched with a poetic irony. Mireille studied the piano at the Conservatoire, sang Cherubino in *The Marriage of Figaro* at the age of fourteen, played in operetta, and blossomed as an infinitely droll performer of her own numbers. She set Nohain's words to tunes that mingled elements of classical music with jazz, and on occasion dropped in a sly operatic allusion, as when she added a snatch from *Carmen* to a refrain. (Not that anyone took much notice – except for the outraged copyright-holders.) "Quand un vicomte", which she and Nohain wrote for Maurice, has an untranslatable wit. "Quand un vicomte rencontre un autre vicomte, Qu'est-ce qu'ils se racontent? Des histoires de vicomte!" it begins.* Then, on the same principle as Cole Porter's "Let's do it", the verses repeat the pattern but using different subjects. The emergence of the song provided another example of Maurician flair. Mireille had already composed the music to which Nohain, stuck for an idea, wrote the first words that came into his head, a sort of verbal doodle beginning "Quand un vicomte", etc. Maurice heard it, liked it, and was promised exclusive use of the number when they had polished it up. A week later they played him a final version with a different text. Maurice did not warm to it. "I much prefer the first one," he said. Nohain

---

* A limping translation might run: "When one viscount meets another viscount, what do they tell each other? Stories about viscounts!"

objected, pointing out that it had been nothing more than the result of an aimless association of words. Maurice prevailed. His judgement proved correct, and "Quand un vicomte" became a hit of 1935.

With numbers of this type, and making provision for sentimental interludes like "Donnez-moi la main, mam'zelle", Maurice put together an act that was varied and full of interest. After the battle of the Théâtre du Châtelet he returned in the spring to his home ground at the Casino de Paris, where Léon Volterra had been succeeded by Henri Varna, a jovial southerner. The latter changed his baptismal name of Vantard (it means "braggart", not unsuitable, one would have thought, for show-business), survived a Jesuit education to become an actor, and then took over the Casino in partnership with Oscar Dufrenne, who conveniently died and left the expansive Varna in control for the next forty years. The new management was as sympathetic as Volterra's had been, and Maurice regarded the Casino more and more as "his" theatre.

Those who feared that the American influence might have altered his individuality were reassured to find that, on the contrary, his Frenchness was, if anything, accentuated. He seemed to have acquired, moreover, a new and delicate sensibility which enabled him to introduce shades of meaning that in the old days would have been beyond him. His appeal ignored social divisions. He was as popular with the slum-dwellers of Ménilmontant, who loved him for his banter and the fact that he was one of their own, as with the middle classes, who liked his air of distinction and his avoidance of vulgarity. Even when he played a tramp, they felt, there was a suggestion of evening-dress beneath the rags.

At the Casino he began his act with a short spoken introduction. As time went on he expanded this until it became a veritable monologue interspersed with songs. The spoken sections gave him time to get his breath back, size up the audience, take them into his confidence and decide how to pace himself. With a few words he set the scene and created atmosphere. It was not just a matter of singing a handful of songs in front of a backcloth but of evoking an illusion into which the spectators could enter. Having persuaded them to join in this conspiracy with him, he would then present a gallery of "types" that were wholly believable, something he did without the aid of make-up or accessories but simply by altering his expression and physical stance.

Men, women, children, shop assistants and countesses, plumbers and stockbrokers, they all adored him. When they saw him in the street they would say, "Bonjour, Maurice." Women who telephoned him asked, "Is that you, Maurice?" rather than, "Is that Monsieur Chevalier's residence?" In earlier years people used surnames when they spoke of Mayol, Fragson and Dranem. They called Chevalier "Maurice". No other entertainer enjoyed such widespread affection. And this was only right because he combined within himself all the best qualities of those old performers whom he had seen, studied and absorbed, adding in the process a quality that remained inimitable. He was the embodiment of a tradition brought to its highest level. The heritage of the café-chantant, preserved and enriched over the generations, found its most perfect expression in the straw hat, the bow tie and the pouting lower lip of the man known everywhere as "Momo".

CHAPTER SEVEN

Grey Hair

"I know I earn more than a Prime Minister, but, after all, I do so much less harm, don't I?"

Little Tich

i

The Most Expensive Artist in the World

Where love and money are concerned nothing can be taken at its face value. Equally unbelievable are the Don Juan who boasts of his victories and the publicity man who trumpets the vast salaries of his clients, for inflated figures are an essential part of show-business mythology. Yet the London manager who in the mid-thirties billed Chevalier as "the most expensive artist in the world" was probably not far from the truth. Maurice had reached the top of his profession, both in France and abroad. His earnings were enormous, and, in addition, his share of the gross takings at theatres where he performed often amounted to as much as fifty per cent.

A story was told of an affair he had with a married woman. The moment her husband left the house it was arranged that the wife would throw a five-franc piece through the window as a signal to Maurice waiting below. The silver coin duly tinkled on the pavement, but no Maurice appeared. Time passed, and after half an hour or so the lady became impatient. When he finally entered she asked the reason for his delay. "Oh, I heard the coin fall, of course, but it was so dark out there that I had trouble picking it up," said he.

Had the lady been Mistinguett she would no doubt have joined him in the quest, for she shared with him an extreme carefulness about money – indeed, she would never in the first place have done anything so imprudent as to throw a coin out of the window. He was also one of those people who, when offered a cigarette, would thriftily put it away for future use and never return the compliment. The young Charles Aznavour once invited him out to dinner with Fernandel. The talk was marvellous, the company stimulating, but the fireworks that had scintillated before were as nothing compared to the brilliant withdrawal tactics carried out by the two older men when the bill was presented. It was Aznavour who paid.

Those who have not known poverty find it easy to laugh at such manic prudence. Maurice never forgot what it was like to starve as a child, nor how his mother drudged every working hour to keep a roof over their heads, and he did not find it amusing. The insecurity which craved the approval of audiences was deeply rooted. He looked on money as a charm which would save him from having to live again in the slums of his youth and to go hungry. Francs were for saving, not for throwing away on champagne and the high life. The careful husbanding of money was only another aspect of the well-ordered routine he had evolved for himself, a routine in which the day's tasks were allotted a strict timetable observed with rigorous punctuality. Appointments were kept sharp on the hour, and a minute lost or a minute gained was cause for annoyance. Discipline like this was essential to get him through a heavy and demanding list of professional engagements.

Paradoxically enough, the experience of being poor, which made him so close with his francs, inspired him to be extremely generous in other ways. At a time when no comprehensive scheme of social security existed, he endowed in the rue Réaumur a dispensary giving free medical aid to theatrical folk and others. Within two years the Dispensaire Maurice Chevalier had treated many thousands of patients. All this he paid for out of his own pocket, helped, involuntarily it is true, by society hostesses who, when they asked Maurice to sing for their guests, were invited to write a substantial cheque for "my Dispensary".

Awareness of past poverty and an uncertain future also made him a handsome benefactor of the home for old variety performers at Ris-Orangis outside Paris on the wooded banks of the Seine. He knew that his own good fortune was unique, and that for every Maurice Chevalier there were thousands of men and women who spent their last years in misery and need. The organization had been founded by Dranem, a firm believer in self-help, and a bust of him stands in the garden of the nineteenth-century mansion where elderly troupers live on their memories of past applause. Today a statue of Maurice is there too. In the nineteen-twenties a film was made of a match he fought with the boxer Eugène Criqui, and all the receipts went to the foundation. He sponsored many galas and benefit performances. A small "Maurice Chevalier Museum" there contains the straw hat and other souvenirs of the man who, for over thirty years, worked hard as Honorary President. Another body to profit from his open-handedness was the French performing right society (SACEM), to which he eventually gave the property at La Bocca, all of it, in perpetuity, as a home for music-hall artists. If he never returned a cigarette that was given him, he made up for such minor examples of avarice with deeds of impressive kindness.

However much he gave away there was one debt that could never be repaid. His mother's grave, now that he had settled in Paris again, became the object of frequent visits. It was only right, he thought, that a shrine should be approached on foot, and regularly he climbed up the steep rue Caulaincourt on his way to the Cimetière Saint Vincent. "Bonjour, Maurice!" cried an errand boy who spotted him, and the smile he received was tense. "Good Lord – how old he looks!" said a woman.

He remembered how La Louque used to make up her face when she knew he was coming to see her, and how she would dab on bits of rouge so as not to look pale for him. That face must have gone now, and those eyes crumbled into dust. Her grave was neat and simple with its gold lettering. "Bonjour, ma Louque," he whispered. How he longed to tell her his news and ask for her advice!

In the early days, and in fact as long as she lived under the same roof as him, she had always left her bedroom door ajar so that she would know he was safely back from the theatre. No matter how late it was, he would go in and sit on her bed to laugh with her and report the night's adventures. Even when he was no more than a gawky slum child she had supported him in what then had seemed a ridiculous ambition and ignored neighbours who criticized her for encouraging his "nonsense". There was still plenty of spite and ill-will about, he mused ruefully, both in and out of the theatre. Always be on your guard, she had told him – though it is better to be deceived than to deceive, she had added. He had been young and silly, and she could see in minutes what it took him thirty years to grasp. What would she have thought of his life in Hollywood? Could she have saved him from the traps he fell into over there?

He stroked the golden letters of her name and glanced around the deserted cemetery with a twinge of embarrassment. Then he stood up and made his way back down the hill of Montmartre. Behind the international star, behind "the most expensive artist in the world", there crouched a fearful little boy.

ii

The Cure for Smoking

Although he had re-conquered the French theatre, the attempt to carry on his film career was disappointing. Europe lacked the expertise of Hollywood and its genius for international appeal. He made three films in 1936, none of them today possessing much more than curiosity value. *L'Homme du jour* should have been a worthwhile production. For director it had the prolific Julien Duvivier, who, within the next three years, was to bring out such classics as *Pépé le Moko, Carnet de bal* and *La Fin du jour*. The leading lady was Elvire Popesco, a flamboyant *monstre sacrée* whose gurgling Romanian accent for years entranced Parisian theatregoers. The theme song, "Ma Pomme", had an easy-going lilt and a crazy flourish that Maurice delivered with insinuating humour. It did not save the film from a speedy disappearance, although Graham Greene, then film critic of the *Spectator*, decided that this "charming comedy" was "admirable *vin ordinaire*".

Avec le sourire was more substantial, being taken from a play by the smooth boulevard craftsman Louis Verneuil. It was a skilful black comedy about the adventures of a penniless confidence trickster who works his way up through plotting and blackmail, a sort of twentieth-century *Bel-Ami*, to become director of the Paris Opéra. It at least displayed an ironic bite that was entirely missing from his last film of 1936, *The Beloved Vagabond*, a romance based on a novel by W.J. Locke, fabricator of sentimental best-sellers long ago consigned to oblivion. The script called for Maurice, who wore a disgusting little moustache and a revolting pork pie hat, to fall in love with the beautiful young Margaret Lockwood.

Yet *The Beloved Vagabond* was a very important landmark for him: while staying at the Mayfair Hotel in London he managed to give up smoking. As a boy of fourteen he had begun with two cigarettes a day. Soon the score rose to five. When he obtained his first big contract he celebrated with a packet of "Three Castles", English cigarettes made of the light-coloured Virginia he preferred to the murky Caporal of French gaspers. Five a day became ten, then twenty. He lit up as soon as he woke in the morning. He smoked while eating his soup, cigarette in one hand, spoon in the other. It was impossible for him to go on stage without smoking up to the very moment when his foot touched the boards, and as soon as he made his exit he was smoking again. Every day he got through sixty cigarettes.

There had been isolated periods before when he had given up the habit. While a prisoner of war he had gone without for five weeks. At the time of *Dédé* and his nervous breakdown he denied himself in the hope of aiding a possible cure, but it did no good and he started again. On another occasion he abstained for three months, at the end of which he allowed himself just one cigarette. This led to a second, and a third, and before he realized it he was back to sixty Gold Flake a day.

This time, he decided, it would be for good, and to strengthen his resolve he made a solemn pact with a friend that they would both give up simultaneously, each keeping an eye on the other in case of backsliding. One Sunday evening he bade farewell to nicotine with a debauch of smoking so intense that he felt disgust. Next morning his dry throat clamoured pitifully for a cigarette. He ignored it. In his car on the way to the studio the desire prickled again, and again he repressed it. Every three minutes it came back. Over lunch, as he and his friend looked wistfully at each other, the urge flickered without respite. Their resolution did not falter. On the second day things were a little easier, though he was restless and fidgeted interminably. A third day dawned, and a fourth.

At the end of a week, in his room at the Mayfair, a sense of defeat overcame him. He could withstand the insidious pleading of his nerves no longer. Life was short! A bus might run him over tomorrow in any case! Why be so harsh with himself? In a shaking voice he telephoned for a packet of Gold Flake. Furtively he drew in the long, refreshing draught of smoke and inhaled to the pit of his stomach. Guilt flooded him. He rushed to the window, opened it and threw out the packet containing its nineteen temptations. It fell in the street among a group of surprised taxi-drivers. They looked up to see whence came this manna from heaven. He jumped back behind the curtain.

Every night the comedy was repeated: a quick call to room service, a hasty puffing, and then the packet less one cigarette tossed into the street. The taxi-drivers became so used to the routine that they gathered each evening to receive the benison, like seals with open mouths at feeding time.

The shame of it humiliated him, and in crestfallen tones he avowed the fall from grace to his partner in the struggle. The latter chuckled and condoled with him. Though he himself had not given way to secret indulgence, he said, he respected Maurice for having disclosed his weakness.

"I'm a coward, a traitor," Maurice lamented. "I swear an oath now, I tell you, that if ever I smoke a cigarette again you have the right to say that I'm done for, a man without strength or will-power. You can say I don't love my profession enough to make this sacrifice for it. You'll say how sad it is that an artist who can't overcome such a silly habit doesn't deserve the respect of the public."

He found dozens of arguments like this to fortify himself. They worked. Although the agony persisted, he managed to keep it at bay. At first he would think of smoking all the time. Then he found half an hour passed without the thought coming into his mind. Whole days elapsed, and gradually the prompting faded. The taxi-drivers waited outside, hopefully but in vain.

Total liberation came after a year. Singers, he thought, were of all people those who should not smoke. They had every reason to avoid the fumes that irritated vocal cords and roughed-up the throat. And what about the effect on heart and brain? Your memory was better, your mind clearer, when you lived without the constant assault of tobacco. Like all who have forsworn the habit, Saint Maurice glowed with a halo of piety and spiritual excellence. It was not, however, his lungs or his heart that did for him in the end – he preserved them against smoking only to be let down by his kidneys, which shows that you never can tell. But he was not to know this, and for the time being the feeling of moral superiority did him good.

In the heroic struggle to escape from nicotine it was as well that he had the support of a new companion. Yet another actress now shared his life and continued to do so for a long time from 1936 on. She called herself Nita Raya and had black Jewish eyes and long, slender legs. He always found it hard to resist brunettes of this type with short curly hair and child-like ways. A few years previously she had emigrated with her father and mother from her native Romania, and in Paris had started as a member of the chorus where her sharp good looks helped her to move up to small but worth-while rôles. Struck by the sincerity and ease of her playing, Maurice went backstage to congratulate her. He saw her again the next day, and within a short while Nita became a part of his household. She was nineteen years old, less than half his age.

In the theatre such disproportion of years raises few eyebrows. Actors do not grow old in the usual way. They have reserves of charm and adroitness which enable them to sustain the physical outrages of time with a skill not given to lawyers or accountants or shopkeepers. Their profession teaches them how to make the very best of their appearance and gives them just that little bit more agility and entertainment-value than the ordinary man. They can keep up their act as convincingly in life as they do on-stage, and the illusion is extraordinarily potent. Mademoiselle Raya surrendered to it, receiving in exchange for her youth the benefit of his older, world-lier affection.

She accompanied him everywhere on tours of Europe, Egypt, Morocco and South Africa. In 1938 they came to London, where he made a film with Jack Buchanan. The two men knew each other well, for Buchanan often appeared at the Casino de Paris during the nineteen-twenties. He found Maurice a tolerable dancer but was disappointed by Mistinguett, who, he complained, was "terrible. She had no idea of time or rhythm." A matinée idol of a sort now extinct, Buchanan had a style and polish achieved by hard work and a ceaseless urge for perfection. Alone in a deserted theatre, he would practise a single line over and over again, varying the emphasis in scores of different ways until he found the best method of delivery. He was also a daring businessman who risked everything he owned to build the theatre in Leicester Square which is now an important cinema. *Break the News*, for which he engaged Maurice as his co-star, was set up by his own film producing company. The original idea came from his friend René Clair, who had suggested remaking an earlier French film that contained a suitable rôle for him. Although Clair did not intend directing it himself, a tangled skein of contractual obligations eventually put him in charge of it.

Needless to say, *Break the News* is not vintage Clair. The genius who created *Sous les toits de Paris* and *A Nous la liberté* was not at ease with a project imposed from without, and there was little occasion for him to display his inimitable touch. The plot concerns two minor variety artists, Chevalier and Buchanan, who as a publicity stunt claim that one of them has been murdered. Buchanan, the supposed victim, hides away in an obscure Balkan country but is held up there by a revolution while Chevalier in England is sentenced for the murder. Only once is Clair's wit fully deployed, and that is when Buchanan saves his skin by perpetually changing hats, and therefore his supposed allegiance, to rescue himself from warring revolutionary groups. Buchanan's nonchalance had a perfect foil in Chevalier's light, quizzical humour. Both men admired each other, and on a photograph of them in a top hat and tails number Maurice wrote: "To Jack, hoping this is the start of something." To which he prudently added: "Please don't take this the wrong way – you know what I mean! Maurice."

That year, 1938, saw Momo back at the Casino in *Paris en joie* for a revue with new stage machinery to delight the heart of Henri Varna. The famous staircase was moved into position with an electrically operated crane and took less than a minute to set up. Plastic also invaded the Casino, and the back of the staircase was decked with artificial models of women so realistic that before the audience knew of the deception the mass of shapely forms vanished and was replaced by flesh-and-blood boys and girls. They formed up to salute the descent of Nita Raya, who, it must be said, came down the stairs with less aplomb than had her famous predecessors. But she was pretty and lithe, and there was always Momo to carry the evening with his version of "Ma Pomme" and his goodnatured imitations of current show-people.

Amours de Paris followed soon afterwards and showed yet again Varna's love of technical novelty. A system of "black" lighting tried out the year before at the Opéra provided him with a new toy that bathed his chorines with eerie luminosity. In addition, forty-five scenes pictured to Casino audiences an exhausting variety of themes, ranging from the love-life of the rose to the love-life of the *grande horizontale* Cora Pearl. The "Eight Exciting Skibine Ladies" were joined by what the programme described as "The Sixteen Red and Blonde Greasely Girls" in a frenzy of pirouettes and flashing legs. Chevalier made his entry by leaping out of a giant straw boater and carrying in his hand a top hat from which he drew flowers, flags and a bewildered dove. Nita Raya danced "The Lambeth Walk", an English import which for the next two years had French people jigging and waving their little fingers in the air. The finale presented Momo coming down the stairs in a white uniform, escorted by girls wearing blue military costumes and stamping out the rhythms of the grenadiers' march from *The Love Parade*. At the première Maurice picked out Marlene Dietrich and Grace Moore in the audience. He kissed them both. Mistinguett was there too, and he gave her a chaste handshake. Admirers protested and were not satisfied until he had kissed her as well.

Yes, life was marvellous. In the words of "Tout va très bien, Madame la Marquise", a song which kept its place for months in the hit parade, disaster might happen, tragedy might strike, but everything was absolutely OK. The audiences at *Amours de Paris* shook with laughter when Momo parodied a German love ballad in the screeching voice of Herr Hitler making one of his violent tirades. What a comedian Adolf was!

Next year (it was 1939) Maurice was busy by day at Joinville making a new film called *Pièges*. The plot turned on a series of personal advertisements in newspapers which lured young girls to their death. Erich von Stroheim, gloomy and secretive, played a mad dress designer, and Chevalier was the innocent night-club entertainer wrongly charged with the Landru-type murders. For a while, Graham Greene told his *Spectator* readers, it seemed as if the film was going to be another *Carnet de bal* with studies of the sad, the shy and the lonely, but it soon broadened out disappointingly on the lines of a conventional thriller.

Maurice never met von Stroheim while they were making the film as all their scenes were shot separately due to their schedules. Later the actor came to one of his revues and Maurice pointed him out to the audience, whereupon Erich had to mount the stage and acknowledge prolonged cheers. Curious, thought Maurice, that this man, who usually played unsympathetic rôles, villainous and sadistic more often than not, should enjoy affectionate popularity.

Within a year or so, however, Stroheim was to know genuine hatred. Nazi censors after the fall of France were ruthless in extirpating all trace of people on their blacklist, and Stroheim's episode in *Pièges* was brusquely amputated.

The summer of 1939 was cloudless. Maurice and Nita spent the sun-filled weeks at La Bocca and were happy. Politicians fluttered from capital to capital, bits of paper were signed, troops massed. On the last day of August, Maurice played golf with the Duke of Windsor. The atmosphere was bland, the coastline dozed in a veil of mist. A telephone rang, and while the Duke went to answer it someone switched on the radio. A shrill voice announced that German troops had invaded Poland and that Great Britain was committed to war. The Duke finished his telephone conversation. The call had been from his brother, George VI, in London.

"Monsieur Chevalier, I don't think we should play golf any longer. I'm sorry."

They dined in the garden. Servants came and went, chat round the dinner table flowed its polite and amiable course. No one spoke of impending disaster.

iii

Occupation

Maurice and Nita travelled from La Bocca to a Paris that was dark with confusion. Posters everywhere declared: "Because of the aggressive attitude of Hitlerian Germany, the Government of the Republic has had to order general mobilization. You must respond with courage, discipline and coolness to the appeal of the endangered country." Energy and patience were called for. France had one soul, and that soul was unconquerable, added the lyrical hand of the functionary who wrote this Cornelian exhortation.

Nita wrestled with her clammy, stifling gas mask when the sirens moaned for the first time. She and Maurice galloped down to the cellar, feeling idiotic in the masks which they obediently jammed over their heads. As they looked around them tension dissolved into laughter at the sight of their neighbours, who, with the black rubber attachments and staring goggles, resembled exiles from some grotesque picture by Max Ernst. They could stand it no longer and rushed upstairs to the open air.

There were no more raids. No poison gas came to swirl over the city, and the masks were forgotten. Life went on unchanged except for closed windows and drawn curtains at night. Perhaps "Tout va très bien, Madame la Marquise" was right. The *drôle de guerre*, the "phoney war", had begun its lulling existence.

Accompanied by Nita and Joséphine Baker, Maurice went on a tour of military outposts along the German frontier. Gracie Fields came over from England to do a charity concert, and Maurice flew to London on an RAF aeroplane for a London matinée, returning in time for the evening performance at the Casino. The lights were shining again and *Paris-London*, a new revue concocted in a fortnight, was packed out. After Joséphine Baker had monopolized the first half, Maurice came on to sing, hopefully, "Paris sera toujours Paris".

As winter dragged into spring, attendance at the Casino dwindled. Denmark and Norway were invaded. In May 1940, Belgium was infiltrated, and soon armoured columns were approaching Paris itself. Railway stations came under siege from desperate Parisians, and roads leading out of the capital were black with crowds of refugees wheeling prams, wheelbarrows and carts bearing their pathetic belongings.

At the end of May *Paris-London* played to a house of ten. The time had come to shut up and go. But where? La Bocca had been taken over by the French Air Force. One of the dancers owned a house in far-off Dordogne. Maurice and Nita decided to set off in their little Fiat and join her there, together with the rest of his entourage, which included Nita's parents and Félix Paquet, a comic singer who was with him in the current revue and who later became his secretary. All the stage costumes were left in Paris. The straw hat, the beret and a few other small items were stuffed into a little black bag. These, said Maurice, with the vocal scores of his songs would be enough to put on a show anywhere.

At nightfall they reached their distant objective, having passed on the way thousands of refugees who trudged on endless march over country roads. There was no coal or gas or electricity or even running water in the place, but they were infinitely thankful. It was almost like being on holiday. A few days later German troops occupied Paris.

Anxiety returned. Nita and her parents were Jewish, and the house was too small to hide the old people if troops came to investigate. Maurice found a nook in the village where they could be sure of concealment and braced himself for enquiries. With the announcement of the Armistice he began to think of moving on. The Germans divided France into two zones, the "occupied" and the "free", and since La Bocca was in the latter region he might just as well go there, as the Air Force which took it over had now withdrawn, indeed no longer existed.

With petrol scrounged from wherever they could find it, the little party made its toilsome way across France and went to ground at La Bocca. There, for a time, they felt safe, and the Raya parents were spirited away to a quiet corner of Nice while Chevalier and their daughter stayed in the house on the hill. Marshal Pétain installed his government at Vichy, also in the "free" zone, and received the thanks of a grateful nation. The aged Marshal was universally regarded not as a vain and mediocre figurehead but as the hero of Verdun, a wise and fatherly saviour who had preserved his country from ruin and made the best of appalling circumstances. While he intoned a bland gospel of religion, patriotism and family virtues, his Prime Minister, Laval, gleefully set about the demolition of the Third Republic and the launch of the new régime. From London, on 18 June 1940 (the anniversary of Waterloo, a date he would surely have avoided had he realized it at the time), General de Gaulle made his defiant broadcast appeal: "France has lost a battle but she has not lost the war!" History books piously record the event as one of importance, and there are touching anecdotes about listeners daring to tune in their sets at risk of death. In fact, very few people heard the speech at all. Relief at having avoided disaster was too widespread for the country to bother itself with an obscure dissident who was, into the bargain, not even a full general but only a *général de brigade*, or brigadier.

In the early days Maurice shared this relief and, like the majority of his compatriots, welcomed the Pétain government. Before long, however, his fears on behalf of Nita and her parents redoubled. In Paris an exhibition called "The Jew and France" attracted long queues of enthusiastic visitors. Photographs, maps and texts portrayed every misdeed committed by the people of Jehovah. Was it surprising, asked the Nazi organizers, that a Jewish creation such as the Third Republic should have crumbled into defeat? To help good citizens identify the evil in their midst, there were diagrams which listed the physical characteristics peculiar to these enemies of the human race. At about the same time over four thousand Jews were seized in the Popincourt district of Paris and taken away, no one knew where.

By contrast, the Propagandastaffel set in motion a campaign known as "Operation charm". Each week leading French personalities were invited to the German Embassy where flattering attentions and, much more important, scarce food and wines were served. In time an invitation of this sort came to be regarded as a certificate of "Parisianism", and the visitors' book reads like a directory of the most distinguished names in literature, the arts, business and affairs. Human memory is, often, conveniently short. After the war it was impossible to find anyone who could remember attending these functions.

Paris, ordained the Nazi authority, must recover its brilliance. The theatres and cinemas re-opened, subject, naturally, to purification of Jewish elements.* In a month when forty-eight hostages were shot as retaliation for the killing of a German soldier, the Casino de Paris took fifty thousand francs a day at the box-office. So great was the demand for entertainment that, while the Jewish population of France was being systematically reduced by a half, the Folies Bergère had to programme two matinées on Sundays. Mistinguett sang songs asking for food parcels only to receive, next day, five bags of coal and six legs of mutton, which she promptly sold at the highest black-market price she could get.

Maurice vowed above all to keep away from Paris. Things were difficult enough at La Bocca, with Gestapo agents prowling Antibes and Cannes in search of Jews. Occasionally he sneaked out on a provincial tour and once travelled as far as Switzerland. The press attacked him as decadent and frivolous. In Marseilles audiences demanded that he sing "Prosper", the ditty about the sympathetic

---

* When Sacha Guitry, prince of the boulevard theatre, brought a libel action against a newspaper for describing him as Jewish and won his case, Nazi bureaucracy stepped in and demanded cast-iron evidence of his Aryan respectability. It took him months of scrabbling through archives and public records.

pimp. He dared not, for the puritan censors of Vichy had already warned him of their displeasure at its flagrant "immorality".

For as long as he could he resisted every attempt to coax him from his southern retreat. A Paris newspaper reported, "Nearly all the famous names have returned to the capital except for Maurice Chevalier, who stays on the Côte d'Azur with his Jews." There were other, similar comments. At last he gave way and, in a curious fashion, did Henri Varna a good turn, for the Propagandastaffel were threatening to impose German productions on his beloved Casino if he did not mount a new revue. Called *Bonjour Paris* and launched in September 1941, it featured Momo in some of his most popular songs – "Ma Pomme", "Ça sent si bon la France", and the stirring hymn to his birthplace "La Marche de Ménilmontant". Jean Cocteau was there and wrote, "The empty stage contains only a piano to the right. Suddenly Monsieur Chevalier enters on the left. The moment he appears the stage is no longer empty. The criss-cross of limelight searches him out like an aeroplane. The play of shadows multiplies his famous profile. He comes in with his straw hat tipped forward over his eyes, and the straw hat masking him, and the way he walks, give him the bearing of a night reveller who's trying to get back into the house without being noticed. Alas! The walk and the hat only make him all the more recognizable. That hat! It's his other face. The walk arouses laughter. When he reaches the footlights our poor reveller finds himself confronted with the whole family gathered in the sitting-room. It only remains for him to exercise his charm. Monsieur Chevalier is an expert in this. . . A three-sided mirror combines the singer, the dancer and the acrobat." And when he sang "Ma Pomme", Cocteau added, "Beneath his greenish Daumier-like rags, he sculpts once and for all the character of the philosophical tramp."

Maurice did not go as far as Mistinguett and others who slipped into their performances veiled ruderies about the German Occupant. Instead, he played on feelings of nostalgic patriotism with a song like "Ça sent si bon la France", which evoked a simple and familiar picture of the French countryside – the church steeple in the rays of the setting sun, the flowery cornfields, the little gardens with their notices "Beware of the dog". The only topicality he allowed himself, and that harmless, was in a "Symphonie des semelles de bois" inspired by the wooden soles all the ladies wore now, due to the shortage of leather. When girls pattered over the cobblestones they sounded as if they were tap-dancing. By 1943 the "carpenters" of the French shoe industry were turning out twenty-four million wood-soled pairs a year.

His Paris flat was untouched and spick and span thanks to the guardianship of his faithful housekeeper, Madame Delpierre. For an hour or two he strolled from room to room, fingering his pictures, his books, his furniture. Life seemed normal again, and he could forget the German patrols outside in the street. Autumn approached, and when he returned at night from the Casino the unheated flat struck chill. He quickly went to bed, anxious for the oblivion of sleep, though his dreams were always of Nita and La Bocca.

In the autumn of 1941, towards the end of his engagement, came the invitation he had been dreading. A French government official called to ask him, on behalf of the Kommandant of Paris, if he would sing in Berlin. All the excuses he had used in countering past hints were dredged up: he was not well, his voice was failing, he had personal commitments in the South. . .

He was told to think about it. If Monsieur Chevalier went to Germany he could at the same time entertain French prisoners of war. An idea struck Maurice as he recalled his own wartime imprisonment.

"Is Alten Grabow still a prison camp? Are there Frenchmen there?"

It was and there were. The two men struck a bargain. He would sing at Alten Grabow on condition that the Germans released ten prisoners who came from his own boyhood district of Ménilmontant.

Twenty-five years after his own liberation he saw again the barbed wire of Alten Grabow. He recognized with a lump in his throat the heavy walk, the resigned expression of the men imprisoned there. On a makeshift stage he told them how he had spent more time in this very place than any of them, that he had almost given up hope, but that in the end he had survived and that freedom made life sweeter than ever before. The men brightened and he gave them song after song until he exhausted his repertoire.

He returned to Paris delighted and relieved to have mastered a situation that threatened to compromise him. A few afternoons later Madame Delpierre announced that a young man had called. In the drawing-room stood a bent, emaciated visitor.

"I've come back from Alten Grabow, Monsieur Chevalier. I heard you sing, and they told me we were set free because of you."

"You said 'we'. How many of you were there?"

"Nine others and me, Monsieur."

His accent had the umistakable tang of Ménilmontant.

Some time later newspapers picked up the scent. Facts were distorted, there was no mention of "his" prisoners, and the legend was created, to be readily believed by many, that he had toured Germany at the request of the Nazis. The Free French Radio in London named him as a collaborator and sentenced him to death. Another report told that he had already been shot by Resistants.

In fact, while at La Bocca, he had helped pass on information to the Resistance network in the area. The only blemishes on his record during the Occupation were small. The first was when, distraught on Nita's behalf, he forced himself to intercede with Henri Lafont. The sinister "Monsieur Henri", right-hand man to the Gestapo, directed from his grand "office" in the rue Lauriston the hunt for Jews, Gaullists and Resistants upon whom, when caught, he inflicted hideous torment in the cellar of the building. His immense power was based on fear and cruelty. Even the most important people asked favours of him, and Chevalier was not the only one to sue for his help, in this case to protect Nita.

The other fault Momo could have been reproached with was his behaviour during a radio broadcast in 1942. He had been engaged to sing four songs, among them "Ali Ben Baba", a comic number poking fun at North Africans. It so happened that on that very morning of 8 November Anglo-American forces had landed to invade Morocco and Algeria. The producers of the broadcast pointed out how very unsuitable "Ali Ben Baba" would be on this occasion. Maurice remained obdurate. He had been offered seventy-five thousand francs to do four numbers, and if one of them was dropped he would risk having his fee reduced. The song was cut, nevertheless, and he complained furiously to the management. He was told, in brutal terms, to hop it.*

* A report in 1951 even said that, as he opened the door to go, he protested: "Why did you stop me from speaking? I wanted to encourage our boys. We must help them resist American aggression and support them. We must tell them that in twenty-four hours German aerial divisions will be on the spot! We must help them stand firm!"

Chevalier's plea to the evil Lafont, coupled with what the historian Hervé de Boterf has described as his "liking for banknotes", does not justify the charge of collaboration which was levelled at the end of the war. During that savage period many old grudges were settled under the pretence of justice. Quite a lot of people turned into last-minute "Resistants" when they saw that their own record was vulnerable and that, in their own interest, attack was the best form of defence. Informing on your neighbour became a way of life and denunciations flowed in by the thousand. Men and women were accused not because they had collaborated but because their enemies had found a wonderful, a unique outlet for hatred and revenge. "Black lists" proliferated of those thought to have worked with the enemy. The world of the theatre, so rich in malice and fertile in jealousy, produced a crop of notable suspects which included Arletty, Yvonne Printemps, Edith Piaf, Tino Rossi and Sacha Guitry, to name but a few.

Maurice was arrested and taken before one of those ruffians who gloried in brief authority as a Resistance "Captain".

"Two months ago," spluttered the Captain, scarcely able to hide his angry disappointment, "we'd have had the pleasure of shooting you on sight. You know, don't you, Monsieur Chevalier, that you were condemned to death? But today we can't shoot on sight, especially with someone as internationally famous as you. We have to render account and wait for the decision of the National Resistance Committee before killing such famous traitors. . ."

A declaration was signed in which Maurice testified that he had gone to Germany only to obtain the release of "his" prisoners, that he had never taken part in events of a political nature, and that throughout the Occupation he had refused to make films.

The Captain glowered. Where, Maurice, thought to himself, had he seen before such cruelty in a man's eyes? He remembered: one day in Cannes at the railway station when a German Gestapo agent swooped on a Jew trying to escape by train.

He still had to appear at one of those Purification Committees which were set up in every sphere of activity. The one dealing with the theatre engendered, as may be expected, a number of piquant moments. Unsuccessful dramatists clamoured for the death of playwrights whose work had been seen on stage during the Occupation. Failures, who in times of peace would never have been heard of, were noisy with denunciations. "Why, Madame," the chairman of one such committee asked Arletty, "did you sleep with a Wehrmacht colonel?" "Because," she replied, "he was a good looker and gave me a far better time than you ever could, Mister Chairman." She went on to make one of the famous witticisms of liberated Paris: "My heart is French but my—is international."

At Momo's hearing four anonymous letters were presented accusing him of collaboration. They were easily disproved. As he left the building he heard that Mistinguett had been summoned to appear. He would, he thought, give quite a sum for the privilege of being a fly on the wall during her interrogation. She later came to lunch with him. The garrulous Mist never stopped repeating how she bravely defended him against his detractors. Finally he lost patience and, exasperated, told her that, if he had had to let her know each time she had been criticized in his presence, he would not have stopped talking for a quarter of a century.

iv

Silence is Golden

Paris was herself again. From the aeroplane soon to touch down at Le Bourget, Maurice saw his contemporary, the Eiffel Tower, and the familiar streets and avenues radiating out like the spokes of a wheel. Autumn had already touched the leaves of the plane trees with gold, and even the outlines of bullet-holed walls were losing their harshness in the softer air. At home in his flat he made a short film for Paramount newsreels telling the story of his expedition to Alten Grabow. Then he took part in the march to celebrate the liberation of Paris.

Nita looked round the flat. "I hadn't remembered it was so small here after four years, Maurice. There's no room to rehearse. How can I learn new songs if I've nowhere to work on them?"

A decade had passed since he first saw her on stage, a marvel of youth and grace. He felt he had lived through too much, seen too many things.

An unexpected visit woke him from his reverie. Marlene Dietrich embraced him, chic and svelte in a glamorous military uniform that would have looked magnificent in a grand climax at the Folies Bergère.

"Noël Coward and I are singing in Paris at the Stage Door Canteen. It's time you got back to work too. Why not join us?" He was grateful to her for an invitation that no one yet had offered him.*

The Stage Door Canteen was followed by appearances at the giant ABC music-hall and then the Casino de Paris. He was back, as popular as ever, although his hair showed streaks of grey, his face had taken on a comfortable plumpness, and there was a cautious glint in his eye whenever he shook hands with anyone.

René Clair, fresh from exile in America, asked him to take the leading rôle in a new film. *Le Silence est d'or* (1945) was an affectionate backward look at the age of silent filming, that happy period when the Lumière brothers astonished matinée audiences with realistic pictures of a train roaring into a station and leaping, so it seemed, into the very midst of a terrified audience. Those were the days when Georges Méliès, conjurer turned film-maker, depicted miraculous journeys to the moon and wonders from the *Arabian Nights*, in which his overflowing genius anticipated every trick of the modern cinema. Amid a décor of Paris in the nineteen-hundreds, Clair told the tale of an enterprise that flourished on hand-cranked cameras, painted back-drops and, most of all, the imagination of dauntless pioneers.

As with other Clair films, not the smallest episode could have been elided without damaging the whole, so exquisitely balanced were the proportions. On the first day of shooting, Georges van Parys, composer of the incidental music, visited the set to find Maurice quietly sitting in a corner.

"You look like a well-behaved little boy," he joked.

"That's what I am," Maurice replied gravely. "It's a privilege for me to make this film with René Clair, and a great opportunity for me." He cupped his hands at the side of his eyes. "I've put on my blinkers. And I shall only do what he tells me to, like a child."

With Maurice were members of the Clair repertory company – those vintage actors who continually reappeared in Clair's films

---

* Some of the minor French performers on the bill had urged that Momo the "collaborator" should be banned. Whereupon Dietrich and Coward refused to appear unless he, too, was with them.

over some twenty years. From *Les Deux Timides, A Nous la liberté*
and *Quatorze juillet* came well-known faces. The cameraman was
the fiercely moustached Gaston Modot. The props man turned out
to be the round-featured Raymond Cordy. And the embattled
cashier, perpetually aghast, a wispy beard fluttering in the breeze,
was Paul Olivier of the anxious, darting glance.

Momo's part was that of Emile, a middle-aged film director who
takes under his wing a pretty girl. She is the daughter of a woman he
once loved in his youth, and, though a skilled seducer, he is afflicted,
in this instance, by a severe attack of morality. The crew of the film
set are instructed to leave her alone on pain of immediate dismissal,
and he yields up his bedroom to her while sleeping chastely on a
sofa. His protégé, a young actor played by the sympathetic François
Périer, falls in love with her. And now begins the irony, for Emile
has given him many a light-hearted lesson in conquering women, to
the extent of indicating what lines to use and on what occasions.
The young man shows himself an excellent pupil and the girl
returns his love. Neither man is aware that they have both fallen for
the same person, and Emile happily continues to lavish worldly
advice on his young friend. When the situation is resolved he stands
aside and makes way for youth. His eye roves elsewhere and finds
an attractive companion next to him at a cinema. "Do you like
happy endings, Mademoiselle?" he enquires as he slips a comforting arm around her. "So do I."

The irony of the narrative is beautifully sustained. Themes are
introduced and developed as in a piece of skilled counterpoint: the
café where Emile and his protégé both in turn entertain the girl; the
serenade that's played to them there; the dialogue that recurs in
identical situations. Even the happy ending is conveyed with
subtlety as Emile directs the young couple in an episode from his
current film which reflects their love story itself. The jokes are
lightly but wittily planted, and throughout the whole film the
atmosphere, indulgent and civilized, recalls the humour of Molière
and *L'Ecole des femmes*, with Momo as a latter-day Arnolphe.

Clair's method of using artificial sets rather than actual streets for
backgrounds is sometimes thought retrograde, and his preference
for understatement is confused with lack of purpose. Worse still, in
these grim days he is accused of making comedies instead of
dramas. Yet there is quite as much feeling for human brotherhood
in *A Nous la liberté* as there is in Renoir's highly praised but over-

blown *La Grande illusion.* "Tears, even obtained by vulgar tricks,"
observed Clair when speaking of *Le Silence est d'or,* "seem nobler
than laughs inspired by delicate means. The spectator, who'd never
think of saying 'How beautiful!' at the end of Charlie Chaplin's best
film, will do so after a melodrama. Doesn't it seem as if an audience
is proud of the tears it sheds and, as it were, embarrassed by the
laughter snatched from it? Like nations which forget the peaceful
kings who've ensured happy times but which respectfully build
statues of those who led them to slaughter, the public, through the
same masochism, is grudging towards those who make it laugh and
grateful to those who make it weep. Yet, without going as far as
Paul Léautaud, who claimed that the only good theatre was comic
theatre, one may argue that those who believe in the tragic mood
are living under a delusion. *Serious plays* are put on a higher level
while their authors are still alive, but the comic theatre sometimes
takes its revenge under the test of time. Molière is nearer to us today
than Corneille and even Racine."

Comedy and tragedy were, however, mingled in the shooting of
Le Silence est d'or. Clair's mother died suddenly after work on the
film had begun, and a mass was said at the little church in Neuilly
where she lived. She was followed, within a very short space of
time, by his father. François Périer telephoned the studio to find out
about the funeral ceremony. "It's being held in the little church at
Neuilly," he was told "*as usual.*" The line might almost have come
from one of Clair's own scripts.

Silence, indeed, was golden – did the title imply a longing for the
freer days of the silent film and the greater artistic challenge it presented? – and *Le Silence est d'or* won a number of critical prizes. As for
Maurice, it gave him a perfect way of re-entering the cinema. He
was fifty-eight and at a point where age could no longer be resisted
without unseemliness. Even as the hero of *The Love Parade* he had
relied on professional skill rather than on looks to create a semblance of youth. In the words of Ronald Firbank, a certain peace
descends when there is no more room for another wrinkle. Of
course, healthy living and the art of the dentist were invaluable in
keeping up a decent façade, and he still preserved a fresh com-
plexion and a springy step. Yet it was unwise to claim a juvenility he
did not possess.

The rôle of Emile was one that he began increasingly to play in real life. Nita's ambition flowered anew after the war and she was impatient to take up her career again. He used his friendships in the theatre to get her relaunched. Then, he said, he would find a flat for her parents and install her with them.

"So I shan't be living with you any longer?"

"It's better like that, I think. We could still see each other as often as we liked, but I wouldn't need to bother you with my personal problems."

Only on stage, where everyone remarked on his incredible energy and enthusiasm, did he really feel at home. Light, an audience, music, and above all the sound of applause were what he needed to bring him alive. Then he truly existed. Everything else was unimportant, and he had difficulty in relating to what went on outside the theatre. The stage invaded life and he lost sight of where illusion ended and reality began. No one could blame him since it is a problem which has exercised philosophers since the world began. It happened that the enigma presented itself in unusually stark terms.

If the truth were told he rather enjoyed playing his final scene with Nita. The gentle tone, the avuncular eye, the air of noble renunciation, they all came over with perfect timing and mellow sincerity. She was young, he murmured, she had her life ahead of her, if she needed his help he would be there, and they must remain friends, good friends. Nita wept and played her part very well, too. Though she spoilt the effect by marrying, soon after this touching incident, a very rich man who was already courting her with ardour.

Henceforward, Maurice vowed, he would live alone. And then, like Sacha Guitry in a comparable situation, he began to wonder: with whom? The answer came quickly. He happened to be at a film festival where *Le Silence est d'or* won him a prize. At dinner afterwards an actor friend he had known for years shook his head in despair and said, "We all have to grow old, but even that can't stop Maurice winning prizes. There's no justice!"

Maurice laughed. An unknown girl sitting beside him challenged the actor, "Whether you're young, old or middle-aged, what prizes have *you* won, then?"

Later they danced together and he thanked her for coming to his defence. "I didn't," she replied sharply. "As for growing old, let him speak for himself. You only *acted* the rôle – *he* lives it." Her name was Françoise, and the Jesuitical finesse of her compliment earned her the place in his life which Nita had but recently vacated.

CHAPTER EIGHT

Discoveries

"I am an open sort of person, whereas Chevalier was a
secretive man. I like to see old and new faces around me:
Chevalier didn't care for people walking into his life. He
was, I would say, in every sense the contrary of Piaf, who
loved mankind."

Charles Aznavour

i

Utrillo, Matisse and Colette

His life was a perpetual source of astonishment to him. The story of
his rise from the slums of Ménilmontant to international fame and
riches enthralled him, and he never ceased to contemplate it with
renewed wonder. In 1946 he published an autobiography. It owed a
great deal to the help of a ghost-writer, but even so he felt an
exquisite pride at the sight of his name on the cover of a book. His
entry into the mysterious world of authorship pleased and excited
him. In the theatre you know immediately whether you have
scored success or failure. A book, on the other hand, takes months,
years, to make its way around. Long after it has appeared, when you
have almost forgotten it, a letter arrives from some unknown reader
to show that the printed page is still continuing the silent, subter-
ranean work. His book, put out by one of the leading French publishers, was so successful that eleven other volumes of reminis-
cences followed it over the years.

He dedicated this first venture to "Charles Boyer, who taught me
how to read properly". Having read books and now become the
author of one, he started to teach himself about painting. A post-
war exhibition of pictures rescued from German hands awakened
his curiosity about Goya, Fragonard, Monet and Rembrandt. He

haunted museums and galleries. For a Christmas present to himself he commissioned from Utrillo a picture of the church square in Ménilmontant. Together they went and looked at the place, Utrillo studying shades and textures and committing them to memory. Though sunk in the last stages of alcoholism, the artist gazed intently at the church and then back at the photograph Maurice had taken, comparing, analysing, transforming. The ruined face became expressive and mobile, then relapsed into blankness once he had seen everything he needed. His everlasting thirst sent him to a little bistro in the rue Ménilmontant, and there, among the plasterers and lorry drivers at the zinc-lined counter, he knocked off with a shaky hand glass upon glass of rough red wine.

A short car-ride away from La Bocca, Matisse was still alive at Cimiez on the heights overlooking Nice. His home was a flat in a vast converted hotel full of white marble and containing a lift big enough to hold ten people. A friend took Maurice up to the second floor and through a hall piled with books into a bedroom where the aged painter, crippled by illness, worked at a collapsible table. His manner was grave but not melancholy. It was, he said, a pleasure for him to chat with Momo, whom he remembered seeing often in the old days at the Eldorado music-hall. He only granted interviews to those he really wanted to see: journalists and admirers were kept at bay with a whole repertory of white lies to preserve his valuable working time. All around him on the walls were sketches he drew by manipulating from his bed long sticks tipped with charcoal.

Three years had just been spent ignoring lucrative commissions for the sake of designing the windows and Stations of the Cross in a little chapel at Vence. "My good fortune has been to love work above all else and to find in it my happiness and my reward," he remarked. "Ten years ago I nearly died after an operation. Then one of the nuns refused to give up. She went on praying for me. You never know, she said. I came through and since then I've lived on an extra allowance of time."

The work at Vence was still unfinished. He stroked his pencils and his brushes, the instruments of happiness. "When I paint a good picture," he went on, "it's not me but God who holds my hand. I have a feeling that once my chapel is completed I shall go down like a pricked balloon . . . ssss. . ."

In the summer of 1947 Maurice called on another aged celebrity, the writer Colette, whom he had known briefly during his provincial tours in the early nineteen-hundreds. He was flattered that she used him for one of the characters in *La Vagabonde*, and he told her how, dazzled by her beauty, he had not found the courage to approach her.

She looked at him sympathetically. Her once lovely form was distorted with arthritis. "How silly, Maurice. You ought to have told me. What a pity I'm old and fat now and it's too late!"

On that radiant sunny day they talked about their work. "It's so painful to write and fill page after page," she sighed, "but it's such happiness, too, that I can't stop. And neither can you, Maurice."

"No, as long as I'm still on my feet," he answered.

"How long will your next tour last?"

"More than six months."

"And after that?"

"The world's so big, Colette, and the future's so inviting," he shrugged.

He saw that she was tired and he made as if to leave when he noticed a book on the table.

"Have you read it, Maurice? I wrote it during the war."

He shook his head, not knowing, in the cloud of nostalgia which enveloped them both, that he had just fingered a book destined to change his life. The title on the spine was *Gigi*.

New links were forged and old ones renewed. In 1947, after an absence of nine years, he returned to London. Wartime bombs had done little to alter the face of Paris, but the English capital he had explored with Mistinguett was now scarred with ruins. The pre-war brilliance of window displays in Bond Street and St James's had gone and a feeling of austerity prevailed. Even the celebrated Mr Lock had no hats to show. Yet the atmosphere of good humour was inspiring.

Jack Hylton, an impresario Maurice had known in the Thirties as a dance-band leader, presented him at His Majesty's Theatre. C.B. Cochran entertained him, and Hannen Swaffer (he was, thought Momo, "the wittiest of English critics") laid down the law, coughing cigarette ash over the preposterous bow tie he habitually wore.* Sid Field, a short-lived comic genius, was on show at the Prince of Wales Theatre and struck Maurice, in spite of a strange resemblance

* I once described Swaffer as "witty and irrepressible". The editor of the newspaper to which Swaffer contributed riposted, "I don't know about witty, but he's bloody irrepressible!"

to Jean Gabin, as being "in the great tradition of English pantomime comedians with much more simplicity and truth than the old ones". He closed the chapter on George Robey and Leslie Henson, Maurice decided, and there was no one at all comparable in France.

On a stage empty except for his pianist, Maurice told stories, danced a little, tried a few impersonations and sang songs. It does not seem a very substantial evening's entertainment, yet for two hours, sometimes three, his audience listened and watched in fascination. Many hours of rehearsal had gone into what appeared to be an easy and spontaneous performance. The little monologues flowed so effortlessly that it seemed as if he were telling them for the first time, whereas, of course, each phrase, each word, had been carefully studied for intonation and placing. As for the songs, every verse was analysed and broken down into its various "points" before he tried it with an accompanist. Then came the working-out of gestures and the matching of them to his voice and expression. The flick of a finger, the wave of an arm, could change entirely the significance of a word. Like Yvonne Arnaud, who for years delighted her English followers with an accent that waxed yet more Gallic as her career developed, he cultivated his Parisian brogue, though not so much that it hindered clarity of diction. Charles Boyer once remarked, "I can say 'wiz the' or I can say 'with ze'. But 'with the' is impossible!" Maurice knew, with Boyer, that this apparent disability gave him a shining advantage as far as Anglo-Saxon audiences were concerned. They thought it charming and were pleased that a foreigner should take the trouble to entertain them in their own language. It even gave them a feeling of superiority, which made them all the more vulnerable. Momo was only too aware of this and played on it with cunning skill.

London approved of his one-man show. Would New York? A monstrous regiment of photographers clustered around him as he disembarked from the *Queen Elizabeth* in March 1947, and he drove through Manhattan feeling that he had come home again. He had all the superstitions of the theatre: under no circumstances would he leave a hat on a bed, or walk under a ladder, or whistle in his dressing-room, or open an umbrella on stage. As a young man he had given La Louque a tiny diamond ring, and since her death he had worn it always and kissed it for good luck before each performance. Four days prior to his appearance at the Henry Miller

Theatre he thought he needed a hair-cut. His pianist was horrified. Did he not know that to have one's hair cut before a première meant the worst possible bad luck?

At night, in his hotel bedroom, he heard muffled noises from the street below, the hiss of cars, the wail of an ambulance, the thud of buses running down Fifth Avenue. It was like the heart-beat of a giant – a giant he was to confront next evening, alone and unassisted. He decided against a hair-cut.

That night he slept little. On the way to the theatre his blood ran faster and his nerves pricked and jangled. Luckily the Henry Miller was small and intimate. The bijou proportions made him feel that orchestra and balcony were within arm's reach, and this was important because for his type of act he needed an audience at close quarters. Reassured by the surroundings he ambled lazily under the spotlight and, from that moment on, was at one with the spectators. "When are you coming back to Hollywood to put on your *tour de force* there?" asked Charles Boyer after the performance.

It was a tempting idea. Boston, Philadelphia and the major Canadian cities had been booked for his tour, but not the place where he had distinguished himself ten or so years ago. His present visit was intended to furbish up his reputation on stage, not on film. Nonetheless, Irving Thalberg had predicted that he would return one day. It was necessary, he thought, that when he eventually presented himself in Hollywood he should have a solid new triumph to his credit.

He was back on the tightrope again, successful, yes, but knowing how difficult it was to stay there. Audiences were quick to notice any slip. The moment you made a mistake their reaction was immediate and you sensed it, however imperceptible. Only self-discipline and watchfulness could save you. There was no room for indulgence. The beaming figure on stage who invited his listeners not to worry, who told them to let themselves go and to forget their troubles, lived a private life as austere as it was regular. Having given up smoking he now cut his drinking and limited himself to a fixed modest intake. He had the down-to-earth common sense of the French *bourgeois*, and believed that prudence in looking after oneself physically as well as financially was the greatest of all virtues. If the girls who flitted in and out of his life grew younger as he himself grew older, he did not allow himself the luxury of passion. It was agreeable to look at youth and to bask in its admiration. Experience, he had learned, was more successful than good looks, and he found no problem in surrounding himself with attractive company – indeed, the difficulty lay in making a choice among all the beauties who eagerly submitted themselves, who crept shyly into his dressing-room, who waylaid him at the stage door. In his youth he had been dominated by women. Now, older and more deeply versed in the ways of the human heart, he knew how to conduct a relationship with the subtlety that enabled him to hold an audience in his hand. More important still, he knew how to end an affair with a gracefulness that touched his partner so that she remembered him afterwards with affection and gratitude. Kind Maurice! Infinitely wise Maurice! He was such a gentleman, and he said goodbye in tender tones that you never forgot for the rest of your life.

ii

Patachou, Aznavour and Piaf

He loved anniversaries and celebrations. For his sixtieth birthday in 1949 he booked a table at the Lido night-club and invited twelve friends. The huge cake, a-glitter with sixty candles, towered before them. With one powerful breath, a sure sign of physical fitness, he extinguished the flames amid cheers. He had had nearly fifty years on the stage, he thought to himself, and it was time he slowed down. Why not relax at La Bocca for seven months of the year and spend the other five making films, broadcasting here and there and trying out the new medium of television? No one took the idea seriously, least of all himself, and within days he had committed himself to new engagements that took him to England, Germany, Italy, Sweden, Spain, Switzerland, Canada, South America, the Lebanon and Egypt.

Although his address book contained hundreds of names from all over the world – social figures, theatrical celebrities, the people he met and mingled with on terms of hollow intimacy at first nights and gala occasions – his circle of real friends was very small. The dearest of them was Paul, who had always been his favourite brother. When Paul's wife died he came to live permanently with Maurice at La Bocca. They were both approaching the autumn of life and the years brought them closer together. Paul resembled La Louque with his practical sense and warm personality, and that alone would have endeared him to his younger brother. At La Bocca he pottered about doing odd jobs and small repairs, happy to be reunited with Maurice and to recall their early days, so grim then, so moving in retrospect, when as "The Chevalier Brothers" they dreamed of going on the stage. They sat by the fire, talking away the hours about La Louque, about their boyhood in Ménilmontant, about Paul's life as an engraver. Not the least of the pleasures his good fortune had brought him, Maurice reflected, was that of being able to have Paul beside him and to shelter him from material worries.

Other members of his inner circle included the modest entourage that accompanied him on his ceaseless tours. There were three of them: his pianist, his administrator François Vals, and Madame Vals. As a young man François Vals was a passionate admirer of Momo and compiled weighty scrapbooks, photographs, pictures, documents, cuttings, everything he could find about his idol. His father commented drily, "We're very fond of Maurice Chevalier in this house, but all the same you'll have to think seriously about getting a job, because, if you'll allow me to say so, you can't live on Maurice Chevalier alone." This was one of the few mistakes made by the normally shrewd Vals *père*.

When Maurice came to Bordeaux where Vals lived at the time the young man asked him to autograph his scrapbooks. They talked for half an hour. "Come and see me again," said Maurice. Vals went off on his military service and afterwards took a job at the Laines du Pingouin, the big firm owned by Jean Prouvost, the magnate who at that time also included *Paris-Match* and *Figaro* in his empire. Vals *père*, who had spent a lifetime in the wool business, approved. François became engaged to a beautiful girl called Madeleine. He remembered Maurice's invitation and made contact with him again. The result was an offer to work as Chevalier's administrator. What about the lady shortly to be his wife? There would be a lot of travelling involved and he did not relish leaving her behind for long absences. "Bring her along to meet me," said Maurice. When he had taken a quick but expert look he added, "Ah, I'll find a job for her later." François and Madeleine, efficient, resourceful, unruffled by the last-minute crises that invariably upset the smoothest planning, remained with him for twenty-two years until his death. And for twenty-two years he looked on them as his children.

One of his oldest friends, Mistinguett, continued to battle on. He still exchanged letters regularly with her for old times' sake, bantering, affectionate, addressing her sometimes in nonsense syllables as "Très chère Mikelouillaninalillenette". She was seventy-eight when a heart attack on stage drove her into the wings shedding tears of angry frustration. Thereafter she held court in her flat above the Boulevard des Capucines amid her nineteen-thirties glory. Deliberately she forgot the names of younger stars. "Who's that plain little undersized woman with a voice too big for her body?" she would ask disdainfully, and everyone would know she referred to Piaf. The last of her partners, Jean Sablon, called one evening to escort her to a film première. It had taken her three hours to rig herself out in a taffeta dress too large for her and to smother it with every jewel she possessed: rings, pearl necklaces, diamond chains fixed with safety pins, her arms loaded from shoulder to wrist in gold bracelets and coins, emeralds and rubies. An old white fox fur smelling of mothballs and yellowed with age crowned an ensemble which pathetically recalled her great days. Clanking and shuffling – her knee played her up a lot and often gave way – she leaned heavily on Sablon's arm as they got out of the car. Searchlights flickered in the sky and crowds strained against barriers to cheer new arrivals. When the shouts of "Bravo, Mist!" thundered out she straightened her back, forgot her bad knee, and strode firmly over the red carpet flashing her broadest grin. Once inside the cinema she nestled down in her seat and dozed off throughout most of the film.

Curiously enough, at this moment in her one-time protégé's career, the Mistinguett/Chevalier pattern was being repeated, though in a much diluted form. He had been very impressed by a new singer who called herself "Patachou" (*pâté à chou*, cabbage pie). Her real name was Henriette Ragon and she had worked as a typist before marrying the owner of a cake-shop and bakery in the place du Tertre up in Montmartre. Henriette was ambitious and put on a cabaret nearby. After customers had dined she would invite them to join her in chanting old French songs, most often of the barrack-room type favoured in the days of the Chat Noir. One evening she came across a diner who refused to sing.

"If you don't sing I'll cut off your tie!" she threatened.

"I bet you won't!" he dared her.

The scissors swooped and she waved the fragment in triumph. She had discovered her formula, and business prospered each night Chez Patachou, where the tables were crammed with guests happily prepared to hear the raucous female insult them and to wave their ties at her ruthless scissors. That she was more than a passing fashion was borne out by the years that followed. Georges Brassens made his début Chez Patachou, and the hostess herself began to show talent as a *diseuse*.

Momo saw Patachou as the successor to Madame Angot, that legendary figure dating from Napoleonic times, an outspoken women of the people who queened it with rousing songs and the gale-like force of her vulgarity. Patachou was plump and well rounded. Her blue eyes and sensual mouth imposed a dangerous authority which tamed the liveliest reveller. Hers was a personality made for the music-hall. Alas that she had a husband and a baby child! Her origins lay in Momo's own home district of Ménilmontant, she spoke the same language as he did, and like him she had the authentic qualities of the Parisian street urchin. He advised on her songs and helped to shape her act. She made her first appearance at the ABC music-hall, where he introduced her, then stood aside and watched, gratified, her ascent to stardom.

People gossiped about his relationship with the baker's wife. When he joined her and the family on weekends at Deauville onlookers chuckled knowingly at what they took for a very "Parisian" ménage. Yet although he so much admired her talent and her personality, he restricted himself to sharing in her success and giving her counsel. It was pleasure enough for him to be in her company and to enjoy a sentimental friendship with a woman thirty years his junior. Once he had seen her fame established in Paris he wanted to show London his discovery, and at the Embassy Club in Bond Street he exhibited her with pride. All fears that such a Gallic vintage might not travel well dispersed when, brandishing her scissors, "Lady" Patachou exploded Anglo-Saxon reserve and mesmerized staid Englishmen into bawling choruses as heartily as she did.

Other new talents caught his eye. Charles Aznavourian, alias

Charles Aznavour, the son of Armenian immigrants, had admired him for years and had, indeed, been inspired by his example to take up a music-hall career. At the age of nine Aznavour had heard a gramophone record of Momo singing "Donnez-moi la main, Mam'zelle", and decided there and then to become another Chevalier. When he told his little sister of the magic voice he had just heard she sneered: "Like Joan of Arc!"

During the war most Parisians travelled on the Métro – it was, apart from bicycles and home-made rickshaws, about the only public transport left – and there Aznavour met Chevalier for the first time. He boldly gave him one of the early songs he had written and suggested that he sing it. Momo took the manuscript. Aznavour heard nothing for another twenty years or so. The reason was that he had forgotten to include his address, and Momo, always correct, would never have performed a song without the author's agreement.

This rather old-fashioned correctitude, Aznavour found, was allied to a reserve that bordered on secretiveness. Much later he visited Chevalier at home to show him a new song. Momo asked him to leave the room while he tried it out, and the accompanist was ordered to keep his eyes strictly on the keyboard. As Rodgers and Hart already knew, Momo would never allow anyone to see him working on new material. Like a cat preferring to give birth in deliberate seclusion, he did not relish the presence of outsiders to witness his nervous fumbling.

In the end he decided against the song, but was interested by the talent it showed. There were certain things, he told Aznavour, that could not be said in songs, and the words needed changing. When Aznavour disagreed Momo told him, in the friendliest manner, that he was being pretentious. What the older man did not realize was that there were too many years between them. Yet although they belonged to different generations and Momo's stubborn nature prevented him from sympathizing with the new fashion, their relationship did not suffer. He knew the business well enough not to underrate the value of something he did not quite comprehend, and he limited his advice to helping Aznavour place his songs.

The young singer made a triumphant first appearance Chez Patachou. Momo was there, warm in his compliments and full, as usual, of suggestions about what titles to sing and what to leave out. Though a little bored by this grandmotherly fussing, Aznavour endured it with grace. Later, on one of his American tours, he happened to be in Hollywood at the same time as Maurice. The latter introduced him on stage in fulsome terms. To show his gratitude Aznavour wrote a song, "Môme de mon quartier", and offered it to him.

"I don't sing love songs any more," sighed Maurice. "At my age it's too late for love songs."

Aznavour played it to him, nonetheless, and Momo wept. He was very touched, not only that the younger man should pay him the compliment but also because no one, now, ever bothered to write songs specially for him as they had done in the past. However, and despite the friendship that united them, Aznavour knew that he could not penetrate too deeply into the reserve he was allowed, as a privilege, to broach. Age, Maurice had discovered, was a valuable weapon in preserving his intimacy.

Edith Piaf he had known since before the war. Her world of brutal légionnaires, of manly sailors, of forlorn sweethearts, of squalid hotels, of shabby dance-halls and of tearful partings on misty quaysides was entirely different from the cynical but light-hearted atmosphere that he himself purveyed. For that reason he appreciated her all the more. When he first heard her, round about 1935, he stared at the gaunt, skinny little creature, so unlike the popular women singers of the day with their ample forms and dominating presence, and he declared, "She's got what it takes. She's a natural."

Their background was identical, though her early years had been even ghastlier than his own. She was born, by an accident, under a lamp-post in the slums of Belleville. She went blind at the age of four but recovered her sight after a pilgrimage to Lisieux. The incident gave her a belief in religion that survived the wretched youth she struggled through. "You are a poet of the streets," said Jean Cocteau, who adored her and put her into his play *Le Bel Indifférent*.*

"Maurice Chevalier and Edith Piaf are the only people who can sing off key and still fall on their feet," commented a songwriter. They both had a stage personality which overcame flaws that in lesser characters would have meant failure. They were, otherwise,

---

* "It's unbelievable," she once said about Cocteau. "When I listen to this man I understand everything he says, but when I read him I can't understand a word." She was by no means the first to remark on this quirk of authors, especially poets.

completely unlike. Edith once reflected on what character she would most like to have been in history. "I can't have been anyone but Marie Antoinette. That woman had my character absolutely. I'd have thrown cake around like that, too. They complained because she spent so much. Well, so what? It's not worth being a queen if you have to count your pennies like everyone else."

And throw it around she did, in a way that horrified Maurice. The virile lovers who flitted in and out of her bed were showered with gold cigarette lighters, diamond cuff-links, expensive suits and crocodile-skin shoes. In night-clubs she treated everyone present to champagne. When she went out to dinner she gathered around her, like a pied piper, a crowd of hungry camp-followers who turned the meal into a banquet for which she paid. She gave money away as if possessed, and total strangers with a hard-luck story could always rely on her, not for loans but for gifts of many thousands. The whim took her to buy a weekend farm outside Paris for fifteen million francs. Another ten million were spent to make it habitable. She visited it three times during her five years of ownership and then got rid of the place for six million. Momo shook his head over such profligacy. He agonized both at the waste of money and of a talent he prized. Why did she not exercise more prudence? Could she not see the abyss that loomed before her? Edith heard of his disapproval and snorted, "Well, if he has enough to pay for a gold coffin, I've no doubt it'll help him on his way. When my time comes a simple pine box will do for me."

She had always said that she wanted to die young. Her wish was granted. Edith was forty-eight and soaked in alcohol and morphine when death came to her in 1963 – on the same day, by an ironic chance, as it took her friend Jean Cocteau.

Greeting his beloved brother Paul on returning from America in 1958

Showing off his roses to Monsieur Jollet, Director of Paris Parks, who designed his gardens

Gigi (1958), with Louis Jourdan and Leslie Caron

Deborah Kerr cuts his birthday cake on the set of *Count Your Blessings* (1959)

With Charles Boyer in *Fanny* (1961)

Can-Can (1960) with Frank Sinatra

Squiring Marlene Dietrich and Ingrid Bergman in 1963

"Boxing" with Georges Carpentier, the former world light-heavyweight champion, in 1969

At home beneath a portrait of "Lá Louque"

In his sitting-room at Marnes-la-Coquette

Chevalier's last stage performance in October 1968

June 1971, in his eighty-third year

iii

Momo the Red

Bouncy, indestructible, he opened a new season of one-man shows in 1950 at the Théâtre des Variétés and played over a hundred and thirty consecutive performances. The printed programme contained a flattering testimonial from Sacha Guitry. "You have known how to please women – while not displeasing men – and I think that must be unique," wrote Sacha. "You were acclaimed at your entry on stage, and – a very rare privilege! – the ovation you received at your exit was no less enthusiastic." He referred to all the distinguished actors and actresses who had appeared at the famous old theatre. Maurice was now their equal. He who had been their pupil had become himself a master.

Once Momo took a taxi to the theatre. When he arrived, he asked the driver what he owed him.

"Nothing at all, Monsieur Maurice," replied the man in a heavy Russian accent. (In the nineteen-fifties there were still Parisian taxi-drivers who had taken up the business thirty years earlier as emigrants from the Revolution.)

"What do you mean?"

The driver explained that having been told by his doctor to give up smoking he had tried very hard but found it impossible. Then he had heard of Momo's victorious battle to conquer the habit, and this had helped him succeed.

"But business is business. . ."

"No thank you, Monsieur Maurice. It's the least I can do!"

However many Aznavours and Piafs might come on the scene, the public's loyalty to Momo remained staunch. If Paris regarded him with affection, London rejoiced in him. He was always careful, before an English audience, to tone down the spicy material he offered his compatriots. The Command Performances he appeared at were doubly dangerous. Each performer was allowed a bare six minutes in which to make his mark while at the same time respecting protocol. Once, daringly, he sang "Valentine". He had done so years ago for King Alphonso of Spain, and throughout the song had worried that the mildly *risqué* lines might give offence. They had

167

not. But the monarchs of Great Britain were different. Or were they? When he had finished they laughed as heartily as anyone else.

At the 1950 Command Performance he lined up to be presented to the Queen Mother beside "Monsewer" Eddie Gray. Now the "Monsewer" was the most anarchic member of that anarchic troupe The Crazy Gang, a tall, bony apparition with a monstrous handle-bar moustache and granny glasses, who specialized in a surrealist variety of fractured French. When the Queen Mother started talking to Momo in the language Eddie noisily interrupted. "There's no need to chat *him* up," he complained. "One can *parlez-vous français avec moi*, if one likes."

"I'm afraid I don't speak your kind of French, Mr Gray," came the Royal reply.

Eddie stroked his moustache. "Oh well," he said haughtily. "Please yourself."

Momo's post-war seasons in London were regularly sold out. During the day he went on long walks through the city. One evening he mingled with the crowds outside Buckingham Palace. "Look," said a voice, "it's Maurice Chevalier!" Instantly a mob of autograph-hunters surged round him. Two policemen came to his assistance and held them off. "You've been coming here for over thirty years now, Mr Chevalier, and we must keep you fit for another thirty!" Later he talked with his old friend Ronald Kennedy, who had taught him English when they were prisoners of war together. Kennedy was on the point of retirement and looking forward to cultivating his garden.

"I've had enough of work. Haven't you, Maurice?"

The question startled him. He made his way slowly through a dense fog that had suddenly come down over London. Clouds of mist invaded the Hippodrome and swirled over stage and audience. Weird shapes danced and dissolved in the beam of the spotlights, and the raw air pricked at his throat. Afterwards he sat and pondered in front of the make-up mirror, where he did so much of his thinking. Should he retire and give up the constant challenge and satisfaction of his job? The answer came quickly: never!

He had returned to films and was making *Le Roi* in 1946, a version of the classic boulevard play by Flers and Caillavet that wittily satirizes international diplomacy. It did not reach the standard set by a 1936 film which had Raimu in the leading part – that of a

French senator whose wife and mistress are seduced by a foreign king on a state visit in return for the signing of a vital treaty. Still, Momo was a devilish charming monarch, and when he awarded the obliging senator a decoration for services rendered his smile had an irresistible innocence. Then, descending as it were from riches to rags, he made a film in 1950 called *Ma Pomme*, built up around his famous song. Once again, in the decrepit garb he had worn so often on stage, he incarnated an easy-going tramp who gives up a legacy for the sake of his freedom to trudge the roads. "Ma Pomme, c'est moi," he sang, happy to chalk his drinks on a slate at friendly taverns and to live a life in which he had only himself to please.

Ma Pomme gave a small role to a character actress noted for her playing of vulgar old women. Maurice detected something familiar about her. When she smiled at him they exchanged looks of vague but sympathetic embarrassment. He sorted through his memories of time past. Among them, a long way back, was a vision of a furnished room in the Place Pigalle and of a young, attractive singer who initiated an even younger music-hall artist, no more than a boy still, into the pleasures of love. She had been his first, and now she was a wrinkled seventy-year-old. As they acted their little scene together and she picked up her cues with professional skill, he caught a spark of reminiscent tenderness in her faded, grey eyes.

On the last day of shooting – appropriately enough in the Place Stalingrad – the camera crew asked him to join them in signing a petition against the atomic bomb. Work had finished, the atmosphere was relaxed, and everyone felt pleased at having got the film safely in the can.

"There's nothing political about it?" enquired Momo cautiously.

"Not a bit of it. Simply a matter of personal opinion."

He added his signature and thought no more about it. After all, who wants to be fried alive?

There were other much more interesting things to preoccupy him. That year of 1950 marked his jubilee, and to honour half a century on the stage the champagne firm of Moët et Chandon organized a charity event in their cellars at Epernay. A special train brought nine hundred guests from Paris to dine by candle-light and drink vintage champagne served by a small army of attendants under the command of the head waiter at Maxim's. It was, for Momo, the pleasantest surprise of the year.

Then the Hollywood producer Billy Wilder invited him to make a film about his life. What better occasion could there be for his return to the world's film capital? Ever since the war had ended he had been seeking a chance to resume his Hollywood career, and this at last was the perfect opportunity. A long and complicated itinerary was drawn up that would take him on a series of recitals through the USA and Canada. With him travelled Patachou, who had also been booked for engagements on the tour. Every day her attractiveness became more desirable to him, and every day he nobly resisted temptation. "We're so lucky," he thought complacently, "at being able to achieve the loveliest possible romance that can unite a young married woman, and a mother, with a fellow who means no harm because he's reached the point where his mind can dominate his instincts." He had, for the moment, quite overlooked Françoise and Nicole and the procession of all the other young beauties who took turns to console his whitening hairs.

His party went via London to embark at Liverpool for Montreal. At the Palladium they saw Judy Garland, and Momo looked in vain for the winning little girl he had known: instead he beheld a plump matron. When, though, she sang and attacked the audience with the full blast of her talent he forgot her puffy features and swollen body. "She's like a little female Al Jolson," he said in wonderment. "The same strength, the same punch and the same emotions whirling around in that powerful voice."

They set sail on the *Empress of Canada*. As the boat neared Montreal the captain asked Maurice into his cabin and showed him a radio message that had just arrived. An announcement from Washington declared that a visa would not be granted to Maurice Chevalier because of his alleged Communist sympathies. The fact that he had signed, in the company of other well-meaning dupes, what became known as the Stockholm Peace Appeal against the atomic bomb was enough to damn him in the eyes of a State Department hypersensitive to left-wing movement.

In vain he protested. "I'm an artist and nothing more. I've never belonged, and never shall belong, to any political party. I'm neither for nor against anyone else in my country. . . Yes, I did sign it, and in good faith, believe me. Millions of Frenchmen have signed it. Someone came around asking if I was against the atomic bomb no matter who used it and, well – nobody likes the atom bomb, so I signed. . ."

His naïveté did not impress Washington and he had to cancel his contract with Billy Wilder. Instead of visiting Hollywood he started an extensive tour of Canada and South America. Montreal refused to believe he was a subversive influence and fêted both him and Patachou. They sang in small towns as well as big ones. At Joliette a girl came up to him as he walked along with his pianist Fred Freed and the latter's wife, a fair-haired Dutchwoman. "You are as *joliette* as your town," said the gallant Maurice, bestowing the required autograph on her. She turned delightedly to Mrs Freed. "Would Madame Mistinguett be kind enough to sign my book too?"

Ottawa and Toronto welcomed him ecstatically. By contrast an unbearably hot night found him at Windsor singing to an open-air audience of six thousand through a defective microphone that echoed and clattered over the vast spaces. It was after nights like this that he sat alone in his hotel room and gave way to depression. Singing for two hours was a great enough ordeal, but what about matinée days when he had to sustain double that period of tension in front of an audience? They were four hours of nervous expenditure during which it was vital not to lose contact for a second. It was not surprising that he felt an overwhelming tiredness, that his ageing body was starting to protest. But in Quebec soon afterwards the riotous cheers of an adoring audience made him forget his passing fatigue and he jubilated once more with a full heart in the profession that was his life, his happiness and his reason for being.

The Chevalier group flew from Canada over the distant night lights of Miami in an America forbidden to him and landed at Caracas in July 1951. No one knew them, no one spoke French or English, and for an hour and a half they wallowed unhappily in a bleak customs shed. Despite the enormous distance he covered Momo never thought of himself as a good traveller. It was hard for him to adapt to the many different towns he passed through, and at the lavish dinners organized in his honour by local celebrities he politely stifled yawns and thought longingly of his bed. The only thing that truly possessed him was his work, and if that went well he was happy and cared about nothing else. "Don't worry if the audience doesn't applaud much," kindly Venezuelans told him. "They're very cold but very nice, all the same."

He took plane for Rio de Janeiro and struggled hard to warm up an elegant but frigid audience in the Copacabana Theatre, where the intrusive hum of faulty neon lights disturbed a contact which was fragile at best. In that city he appeared for the first time on television. The cold inhumanity of it frightened him. The atmosphere was even more soulless than that of a film studio, and, performing as if in a vacuum, he felt nonplussed by the absence of any personal reaction. He had, he thought, a duty to keep up with progress, but television was a medium to be handled with the utmost wariness and prudence. When he viewed the broadcast his opinion was confirmed. Much more than in a film studio, where you act a rôle with the aid of a script and the cameraman uses all his skill to present you at your best, on television you are yourself and yourself alone. You are defenceless.

Before going on to Buenos Aires and Montevideo he visited the notorious Bom Retiro district of Sao Paulo. He had known the red-light streets of the Vieux Port in Marseilles and of Bordeaux and Toulon, but Sao Paulo outdid them all. At the entrance to the street policemen searched pockets that might contain guns. Once past the barrier droves of men wandered up and down between the lighted windows where girls displayed their faded charms. Whites, half-castes and plump Negresses lolled there, pock-faced and weary. Momo was quickly recognized and his name shouted from window to window. He stopped beside one of them and saw a French woman about forty years old.

"Oh! Monsieur Maurice, I heard you last night on the radio. Do you like Sao Paulo? Are you pleased with your success here?"

"Have you been here long, Madame?"

"Twenty-four years, Monsieur Maurice. I was brought here when I was sixteen."

"Have you always been in the profession?"

"Oh no, not in France. I came from a respectable family."

"And since then you've been in Brazil?"

"Yes, I've always worked."

"For twenty-four years?"

"Yes, Monsieur Maurice."

"How many times a day on average?"

"Between twenty and thirty, sometimes more, sometimes less."

CHAPTER NINE

Uncle Momo

"The best and most commendable lives, and best pleasing
men are (in my conceit) those which with order are fitted,
and with *decorum* are ranged to the common mould and
humane model: but without wonder and extravagancy.
Now hath old age need to be handled more tenderly. Let us
recommend it unto that God, who is the protector of health,
and fountaine of all wisedome: but blithe and sociall. . ."

Montaigne "Of Experience",
(Trans. Florio)

i

Marnes-la-Coquette

Early in 1952 he made over his property at La Bocca to SACEM, the
French performing right society, as a home for elderly stage performers. He had owned it some twenty-five years, this haven, this
shelter where he could take refuge in the still, quiet sunshine, could
breathe the cleaner air of the Mediterranean and could escape the
stress of his punishing routine. "La Louque" became "Le Village
Maurice Chevalier", and the entrance gates faced a road that was
soon christened the "Avenue Maurice Chevalier".

The name "La Louque" was, however, to be perpetuated. He
wanted a home near Paris and found what he sought in the little
village of Marnes-la-Coquette, which on one side is bounded by the
Parc de Saint-Cloud and on the other by a wood. It is trim (*coquette*)
and pretty, with a residential quarter built on land that once
belonged to Marie Antoinette.

The house Momo bought was ancient, rambling and dilapidated.
Majestic old trees and lawns surrounded it, and there were acres of

potentially beautiful garden. Much building work needed to be done. In between tours of Spain, Portugal, Switzerland, Germany and Belgium, he anxiously scrutinized builders' estimates, worried over the cost of roofing, wondered if he could really afford new support walls and floors, and tended guiltily to ignore his accountant's eye.

By July the house, newly restored, was ready for him to move in his treasures. Tall windows shining in the sun reflected a smooth sweep of greenery and the sturdy shapes of trees hundreds of years old. Beyond the close-shaved grass lay beds of flowers in bloom and sanded paths that skirted feathery saplings. Sometimes, as he lay awake at night, Momo shuddered at the thought of all the money he had spent and of how deeply, too deeply, he had drawn on his reserves. When morning came and he looked out from his study at "his" grounds and "his" trees, he forgot the monstrous sums the place had engulfed and comforted himself with the thought that all this beauty was the just reward of half a century's toil.

A string of lorries brought all his possessions from Cannes, and for months every second he could spare was devoted to hanging pictures, arranging furniture, deciding on the best layout of carpets. Looking down on him at his work table was the portrait of La Louque. To his left, within arm's reach, hung a townscape by Utrillo and a flattering profile of Mayol, sprucely quiffed and beaming. There were pictures of Mistinguett, young and beautiful still, and everywhere lay scattered reminders of a career unique in the theatre. On the foundations of an old lodge in the gardens he built an open-air stage. Here, he planned, he would present in the summer entertainments for his friends, would give promising young actors and actresses their first chance, and would engage the most famous international artists. As a New Year present to himself and his brother Paul he commissioned a bust of their mother. Working from photographs alone the sculptor produced an amazingly faithful likeness. As he moulded the soft clay Momo and Paul guided him with their comments – perhaps the cheeks should be a little rounder? The nose a bit more pointed? The cheekbones they had lovingly stroked a shade less prominent? Her features gradually emerged, rejuvenated, to show her as she had been at the age of fifty in all the beauty and gentleness and purity they had known and never forgotten. He built a monument to her in the garden beside a shady tree, and put next to it, on flagstones criss-crossed with grass, a bench where he could sit and meditate.

One of his first tasks in the new home was to teach himself to read and write music. Apart from the handful of lessons he had had as a boy he knew nothing of the art and mystery of notating sounds. Flair alone had sustained him, and he thought it was time he learned more. With the same doggedness he had shown in his attempts at self-education under Charles Boyer he took up the puzzling challenge of keys and crotchets. A professor from the Paris Conservatoire was engaged to help with expert tuition. At a touch of Momo's finger a device he carried in his pocket sounded the note of C and enabled him to "place" in his mind's ear the other steps in the scale. His head filled with thoughts of white keys and black, of quavers and semi-quavers. He dreamed of the time when he would be practised enough to note down on paper the melodic lines that trotted through his brain from time to time. The aim was to write both words and music so that in future what he sang would be entirely his own. Thus he aspired to the ideal put forward by Jean Cocteau that the artist should be responsible for every aspect of what he created. But however learned Momo might have become, however adept at modulations and harmony, his native gift remained his strongest asset. No amount of erudition could have taught him how to sing "Valentine" or "Louise" with an originality that others merely imitated. Once he started analysing the techniques of his art, you felt, he risked ending up in the dilemma of the centipede. A malicious friend once asked the insect how it contrived to walk on so many feet at the same time. The centipede, which had never given the matter a thought until then, started trying to explain and tumbled on its back in a ditch.

In the high-windowed dining-room at Marnes-la-Coquette he gave elaborate luncheon parties where his butler served dishes prepared by Maria, a cook of near genius. Here came close friends like the writer Louise de Vilmorin, the actress Michèle Morgan, and once the shy and withdrawn Georges Brassens, whom Momo had charmed out of his determined seclusion. As time went on younger people such as Antoine and Mireille Mathieu, singers in whose careers he took a benevolent interest, joined him round the polished table sparkling with cut glass and fresh flowers from his garden. Ambassadors, editors, film directors, television producers and authors drove out from Paris to accept hospitality at the big white house. He was happier as host than as guest, for he never felt at ease in high society and preferred to choose the people with whom he mixed. At Marnes he was surrounded by a small entourage of old and trusted friends. They were his brother Paul, François Vals and his wife, and Félix and Maryse Paquet. Paquet had been a successful comedian and singer who, in the nineteen-twenties, displayed a remarkable gift for winning over audiences and persuading them to join in his nonsense songs. A certain diffidence, a want of energy, caused him to leave the stage, and for years afterwards he devoted himself as Momo's secretary. He was, said Chevalier, an exemplary companion and "my best audience too".

As soon as the new house was complete Momo took up his engagements once more. He opened a "Maurice Chevalier" wing at the Ris-Orangis retirement home and inaugurated a plaque there in 1952. Around him gathered many of the old familiar faces, elderly actors he had known in the old days of trekking from agent to agent when the girls, now wrinkled and withered from years of slapping on stage make-up, had been fresh and pretty, and the men, their voices hoarse from bawling in noisy music-halls the length of France, had been smart and upright. They put on a concert and sang in quavering voices all the old hits of the nineteen-hundreds.

"There, but for the grace of God. . ." he must have thought to himself as he prepared for his next tour. Some of the folk at Ris-Orangis were not much older than he was, and little physical deficiencies that began to occur more frequently reminded him of the fact. His greatest fear was of losing his voice. In San Francisco his left ear started to block up when he sang. It gave him the disagreeable experience of hearing his voice resound in his ear, and although the sensation would vanish in time, it often returned when he swallowed. Specialists muttered about the Eustachian tube and advised treatment that did not last. While he was on tour in the South of France later that year his voice disappeared and he could not speak. For the first time in his life he cancelled a performance. He stuffed himself with penicillin and started off in a tiny shred of voice, about a tenth of his usual volume. Even this quickly faded. In desperation he explained to the audience what had happened and for the rest of the evening depended wholly upon the microphone which, up to then, he had always avoided where possible, whispering his songs into the despised instrument and holding the lifeless metal close to his mouth. His old friend Louis Armstrong was in the town and gave him a private remedy, an arcane mixture of honey and glycerine. It worked, and thereafter Momo took the magic elixir with him to every performance. Each time he religiously dosed himself with it he chuckled at the thought of Armstrong's own rusty voice and wondered what it could possibly be like without the softening influence of glycerine and honey.

He toured Europe. His pianist Fred Freed, who had once lived in Berlin, showed him around the devastated city, pointing out in the ruins, "Look, that's where Marlene Dietrich and her family used to live," and then, indicating an imaginary fourth-floor in the air, "That's the flat I had with my wife." After Berlin he came on one of his frequent visits to London. The city was preparing for the Coronation of 1953 and his four-week season at the Hippodrome sold out completely. He appeared in a Command Performance at the Palladium and, at a reception given by Douglas Fairbanks junior, inveigled the Queen into clapping the rhythm of "Louise". The ageless troubadour popped up in Bristol and Leicester. He looked over the Mappin and Webb factory in Sheffield. His reception in that town was much jollier than the one given years ago to Marie Lloyd. "So *this* is where you make your knives and forks, is it?" she had hissed at an unfriendly audience. "Well, you know what you can do with them." She added, as a clinching shot, "*And* your circular saws, too!"

The neat homely countryside and the placid English atmosphere relaxed nerves tautened by so much travelling and performing. But peace was shattered when he landed at Dublin to be met by angry pickets of the Musicians' Union, which had come out on strike. What had it all to do with him, he wondered, bemused, as demonstrators waved threatening banners at his hotel window?

Scotland was more congenial. In Glasgow a member of the audience, primed on whisky, shouted in Gaelic for Momo to sing the songs of Harry Lauder. It was all very good humoured, and later there was a visit to the Lauder home just outside Glasgow which the great little Scot, as careful with his bawbees as Momo with his francs, had built on the proceeds of his international career. The Gorbals, *"faubourg populaire"*, reminded the French sightseer of his native Ménilmontant, and he drank in a pub where days previously a man had been murdered. From what he was told it appeared that the toughs of the Gorbals were, in fact, handier with the razor and the bicycle chain than even his Ménilmontais compatriots.

Edinburgh he loved most of all with its prospect of the castle, the handsome shops in Prince's Street, and even the cemetery of St John's Church, a "village of the dead" beautiful in its austerity. Momo's native country has ancient links with Scotland, and he made a point of visiting "little France", the area so named by Marie Stuart because it reminded her of the French landscape. Another similarity struck him on the way to Abbotsford as he drove through a scene of mountains and forests that recalled the craggy Dordogne. Here he toured Sir Walter Scott's grandiose mansion, noting with approval a self-made man like himself who had built a dream home on money earned from a lifetime of hard work.

He crossed the border again with regret and ended his two-month engagement at the Opera House in Manchester, "a town of simple and distrustful folk" whose cold reserve gave him a few initial qualms before he was able, by exercising every ounce of stagecraft, to win them over. London was to see much of him in Coronation year, and he crossed the Channel often for appearances at the Savoy Hotel and the Café de Paris. On BBC Television in April 1953 he did a complete forty-minute solo turn, relayed to eight million viewers in Europe as well as in Britain. Wryly he thought of the time fifty years ago at the Casino in Malo-les-Bains when, a youthful tyro, he had played to an audience of one man who, into the bargain, read a newspaper throughout the whole act. He no longer feared television quite so much and was coming to grips with the special technique it demanded. All the same, he recognized the danger of doing too much: television was a monster that ate up material and personalities more ruthlessly even than films or radio.

Despite the ceaseless round of travel and international success old memories kept coming back. In Marseilles he played again for the manager Franck, who in 1906, a lively and energetic young man, had given him early encouragement and, in 1924, the chance of a comeback after his nervous breakdown. Franck was seventy-four and tortured with a rheumatism so crippling that he needed two chairs to accommodate his twisted body as he sat watchfully in the wings. During an engagement in Tunis in August 1953, Momo sang at a luxury cinema recently constructed, they told him, on the site of a building called the Palmarium, which he would not have known. But he did! He had performed there forty-seven years ago.

After Nice, where he spent seven weeks making a film called *J'Avais Sept Filles* and acted the rôle which so became him these days of an elderly but graceful Papa, he had a meeting with the most formidable ghost of all from his past. Mistinguett, a shaky octogenarian with a tiny voice, stood in shadow at the entrance to his dressing-room.

"Cio," she said with a shaky laugh, "I haven't got any photographers hidden up my sleeve. Can I come in?"

He took her in his arms and saw that time at last had finished its bitter work on her. Great bags trembled under her eyes, a pendulous double chin hung over a scrawny throat, her hands were spotted with keratosis. She was thin, worn, fragile.

"Are you well, Mist?" he enquired anxiously.

"Don't I look it?" she snapped defiantly. "The proof is that I've come to see you this evening. And I shall be here next time too."

As she walked slowly away she stopped a moment and clutched at the door for support. He felt he had seen her for the last time.

ii

Thank Heaven for Little Girls

In 1955 the American government decided that he was no longer a threat to security and allowed him the entry visa he had petitioned for over the years. Immediately he launched a six-week show at the Lyceum Theatre and, late each night, a turn at the Waldorf Astoria. "Has there, indeed, ever been anyone more indomitable?" asked the *New York Times*. Momo was the sensation of Broadway. "He entertains, but he does not trifle," wrote another critic. "He is intent on giving value for value; there is respect and civility in everything he does, and though he may occasionally be indecent, he is not even brushed by the wing of vulgarity."

With all flags flying he plunged into rehearsals for a ninety-minute television spectacular amid a tangle of cameras, blinding lights, worried technicians and dancers trying out final steps. In those days few studio productions were filmed in advance: they went out live and nerves were, accordingly, at their highest pitch. An assistant waved for silence, the red bulb of Camera One glowed into life, and the programme began. During each minute of the hour and a half ordeal there was the danger of a misspoken word, an ill-timed gesture or a thoughtless grimace being picked up by the merciless eye of the lens and revealed to fifty million viewers across America. When, at the end, the credit titles rolled up on the screen Momo's versatility had assured a flawless presentation. His first experience of television in Rio de Janeiro had warned him of the pitfalls. America taught him, at the age of sixty-seven, that it was just another challenge to be overcome, another medium to be conquered with the sincerity and naturalness he showed on stage cunningly reduced to the intimate proportions of the drawing-room.

His television exploit brought him an engagement at the Dunes Hotel in Las Vegas. Danny Kaye, once cast to play him in a biographical film that never materialized, introduced him to an audience of hardened gamblers who, as it were, dared him to amuse them. Las Vegas was a difficult date. If the fees were astronomical the risks were equally high. Yet the performer who had tamed the hooligans of Marseilles in far rougher circumstances had no trouble in the strange dream-like surroundings of Nevada. He did not take Marlene Dietrich's advice to revise his orchestrations, he ignored Sophie Tucker's hint to change the position of the band, he refused Danny Kaye's tip to wear make-up, and, as a result, he charmed Las Vegas in his own way. After the performance each night he marched through the gambling rooms and looked neither to right nor to left. Bourgeois caution told him that if he once began to play the machines he would never be able to stop.

On one such evening he went back to his apartment, steadfastly ignoring the one-armed bandits that clicked and clattered invitingly on each side of him. In his room he switched on the late-night news. The name of Mistinguett was spoken. She had had a stroke and was not expected to live. The vivid days of his youth returned: he thought of their first kiss in the carpet number, of the fight with his rival, of his return from the war and their reunion. She had been, despite the bitterness that came between them and her ridiculous character, the greatest love he had ever known. Next morning he heard that she was dead. Later, in Paris, he went to a requiem mass.

Winter struck cold on the ancient stones of the Madeleine as solemn chants echoed eerily through vaulted aisles. Of course she was no longer young, she would have had no peace in old age, she had been spared a great deal . . . but she was one of those people you had always thought of as being immortal. "You were my wife, my mistress, my greatest friend," he said in a valediction.

He kept in touch with the family. To her niece Fraisette he wrote of his success at the Greek Theatre in Los Angeles where, for three weeks, he played to standing-room only. The "Maurice Chevalier Show" on NBC-TV kept his image green among the new generation he had won with his earlier television programme, and thereafter he appeared often on the small screen: with Bing Crosby, with Diahann Carroll, with Sophie Tucker. In 1956 he compèred the award ceremony of the sesquipedalian Academy of Motion Picture Arts and Sciences. Gradually, ever so gradually, he was edging back towards Hollywood. And, not long afterwards, the summons came.

Billy Wilder, the Viennese-born director, asked him to take part in a film he planned called *Love in the Afternoon*. It was a comedy about a private detective assigned by a jealous husband to shadow a rich playboy in Paris. The detective has a beautiful young daughter who falls in love with the playboy, whence the mild complication to which no less than two hours of film are devoted. With no songs to sing Momo at first experienced a sharp bout of stage-fright and worried over his accent. At an early run-through he and the other members of a cast which included Audrey Hepburn and Gary Cooper trembled like leaves. Billy Wilder soon put them at their ease, and working with him, Momo found, was as pleasant as it had been in the old days with Ernst Lubitsch.

Wide-eyed and beautiful in the nineteen-fifties manner, Audrey Hepburn frothed vivaciously through her scenes with Papa Chevalier. Gary Cooper played his usual wooden-faced self, though for once the expressionless features showed a tragic melancholy which had never coloured them in earlier rôles: the illness that killed him only a few years later was already giving premonitory signs. The liveliest fellow on set was Momo, whose high spirits overflowed in a characterization as humorous as it was mellow. He really deserved better for his return to Hollywood. The film was long, much too long for the little anecdote it related, and the stretches of tedium were exaggerated by incessant repetition of

Marchetti's little tune "Fascination", a melody that seemed to have obsessed Billy Wilder, so often did it keep coming back. Yet *Love in the Afternoon* was generally accounted successful both in America and elsewhere.

A short while later Momo's Hollywood agent cabled him: "MGM want you for musical version of *Gigi* based on Colette. Good part. Good songs for you. Await reply." He thought of his visit to the ageing Colette and of how he had fingered the copy of her novel before leaving. It was a trifling thing, a mere sketch about a grandmother and a great aunt who, from the depths of their worldly experience, groom their little Gigi as the mistress of a handsome young heir to a fortune, and are nonplussed when he falls so much in love with her that he proposes a respectable marriage. Where was the part for Momo in this slender tale?

The answer came from Alan Jay Lerner. He and his collaborator Frederick Loewe had had a great success with *My Fair Lady* and now intended to do for Colette what they did for Shaw. In *Gigi* there are several mentions of the hero's uncle, and Lerner built up this very minor personage as a character for Chevalier, whom he had always highly regarded. The uncle expanded into what is known in boulevard plays as a *raisonneur*, a commentator on the action, a guide, philosopher and friend. Lerner and Loewe flew to Belgium where Momo was doing a season at a night-club in Le Zout. After the show they went backstage, expecting to do no more than pay their respects as he would probably be tired. But no: he was, after more than an hour on stage, fresh and adroit. "At getting on for seventy," he told them, "I'm too old for women, too old for that extra glass of wine, too old for sport. All I have left is the audience, but I've found it's quite enough." Some time later these words came back to Lerner and inspired him with the song "I'm glad I'm not young any more".

Momo showed enthusiasm. They met again at "La Louque" and the same ritual occurred as with Rodgers and Hart: he listened politely to the songs they tried out for him, "Thank Heaven for little girls" and "I'm glad I'm not young any more", picked up the music, and departed in silence. Next day he rang to make another appointment. Like Richard Rodgers, the two writers wondered apprehensively what had gone wrong. Punctual to the stroke, he reappeared beaming. He liked the songs so much, he announced, that he had worked on them all night. However, would Alan be kind enough to sing the middle section of "Thank Heaven"? Alan could phrase it better than he did. Flattered yet feeling utterly absurd, Lerner duly croaked the lines to his friend's accompaniment. Momo listened intently, offered grave, profuse thanks, and vanished into the dull Parisian afternoon.

At a party in Maxim's the night before shooting started each member of the cast was given his script. While everyone else put aside their copies for the next day, Momo took his into a quiet corner and began studying it. He was the only one who, the following morning, rang Lerner to say how much he liked it.

Location filming began at seven on an August morning of 1958 in the Bois de Boulogne. Fashionable carriages rolled back and forth, elegant *cocottes* waved from their barouches, hundreds of *Belle Epoque* strollers massed in a sea of top hats and crinolines. A frock-coated Momo, splendid with gold watch-chain and silver-headed walking-stick, greeted the passers-by. Something went wrong and the scene was re-taken. Carriages and strollers went into action once more. Momo flashed his smile. Still it was no good. By the end of the day the take had been shot dozens of times. Momo's smile did not falter as he greeted old friends in the Bois and simulated pleasure over and over again with the same winning spontaneity. At the end of the day clouds threatened and a heavy shower of rain sent everyone hurrying beneath the trees. The scene was not yet perfect. Twelve hours later Momo was there, still beaming with all the sincerity in the world for the camera.

The settings and dresses which were so opulent a feature of *Gigi* had been designed by Cecil Beaton. Hundreds of drawings were dashed off to recreate the gilded life in Paris and Deauville of the nineteen hundreds. Certain shades proved dangerous. Grey, Beaton was disconcerted to find, had a tendency to become Prussian blue. Technicolor made chartreuse yellow into Jaffa orange, and bright red showed a distressing urge to melt into a sort of claret. And although costumes and décor are rarely observed full-length in the cinema, most scenes being viewed at eye level, no detail of ornamentation could be scamped for fear of the omnipresent camera's eye. When the shooting moved to Hollywood, Beaton spent happy days in the studio warehouses, great hangars crammed with furniture of every period, glass, china and props of a beauty to ravish the imagination. Here he found Sèvres porcelain and tables and chairs made by the craftsmen of Louis XV. All had been plundered from Europe to deck out Norma Shearer's *Marie Antoinette*.

The heroine of *Gigi* was Leslie Caron, herself a French girl, whose wistful beauty illuminated the part with a gauche tenderness. Her lover took the shape of Louis Jourdan, French too, handsome, dark, the essence of Latin charm. Among the old folk Momo was partnered by Hermione Gingold as the grandmother and Isabel Jeans, another English veteran, as the aunt. With Hermione, benevolent gargoyle of pinched smile and viper eye, Momo sang "I remember it well". In a haze of romantic memories he looked back on their flirtation many years ago . . . and got it all wrong: it was not April, it was June; it was not a Friday, it was Monday; she did not wear a gold dress, it was blue. At every reminiscence his ancient one-time love interrupted him with an acid correction. Yet the very tartness of her precision betrayed how much the memory meant to her. From this witty duet Gingold and Momo distilled an affection as touching as it was humorous.

On his own, and with a conviction he had no difficulty in expressing, for the lyric summarized his own deepest feeling, Momo sang "I'm glad I'm not young any more". What joy it was to be free of youthful entanglements, to be racked by passionate affairs no longer, to be shot of star-crossed involvements. He had never felt so comfortable in his life before. The autumnal character he played in *Le Silence est d'or* was rounded off and given a lasting gloss in *Gigi*. But, just to show that the old man's eye was as sharp as ever, that he had by no means reached the edge of the grave yet, he offered up a "Thank Heaven for little girls". For little girls get bigger every day, and without them what would little boys do? Because:

> Those little eyes so helpless and appealing
> One day will flash
> And send you crashing through the ceiling!*

Momo was reminded of how little boys can grow up when the *Gigi* company arrived in Hollywood to shoot the final scenes. On the beach at Santa Monica, which stood in for turn-of-the-century

---

* This verse cost Lerner hours of agony. "You can't crash through the ceiling," he moaned to Loewe. "You crash through the floor." "Who says so?" retorted Loewe. "It's your lyric and if you want to crash through the ceiling, crash through the ceiling." It was six o'clock in the morning and Lerner could battle no more.

Deauville, he was approached by a tall, rugged, deeply tanned swimming instructor.

"Mr Chevalier? I just wanted to say hello to you. I'm Baby Leroy," said the young man.

Baby Leroy! Twenty-odd years ago Momo and his director had visited an orphanage to select a child for the film *Bedtime Story*. They had found Baby Leroy, a gurgling chuckling infant who was perfect, so endearing, in fact, that Maurice had wanted to adopt him. Once the filming was over a number of scenes had to be re-shot, by which time Baby Leroy had grown two teeth. Thus, in the finished production, a scene showed him with bare gums. The next one presented him flashing his tiny molars. A few seconds later he was toothless again.

"Very well, Monsieur Leroy," said Momo, sizing up the giant who now confronted him. "Come and sit on my lap!"

MGM threw a party to celebrate his seventieth birthday in September 1958. His old antagonist Jeanette MacDonald came along and, perhaps believing it was safe to do so now, kissed him sweetly. The news of his birthday was reported in the papers and hundreds of letters poured in, among them one from an English actress. He had known her while touring Lyons in 1906, and she told him how she had loved him then, reminded him of their long walks together, and spoke of how her irate father, the manager of the troupe, had parted them. Certainly he remembered their doomed affair! Her next letter recounted worldwide travels and a loveless marriage undertaken in the hope of forgetting the French boy she had loved. His heart beat a little faster, even after the passage of so many years. They dined together, and he saw a white-haired woman, charming, dignified, a credit to a beautiful memory. The scene was *Gigi* brought to life, and he resolved that he, too, would grow old gracefully in the time still remaining to him.

Many talents went into the creation of *Gigi*. Lerner's pungent verse and Loewe's exhilarating music were enhanced by the pixie features of Leslie Caron, the dash of Louis Jourdan, the sly comedy of Hermione Gingold and the exquisite designs of Cecil Beaton. There were, however, those who thought "the old master showman Maurice" had stolen the film completely and was himself the heart and soul of the production. With ease and insouciance he blended his old verve of the nineteen-thirties with a natural quality that was somehow very modern. He was buoyant, suave, the incarnation of worldly benevolence. His attraction seemed everlasting.

Gigi won nine Academy Awards. In addition, Momo was given a special Oscar "for his contribution to the world of entertainment for more than half a century". On the day of the award ceremony he had signed a contract to make a film with Sophia Loren, and that voluptuous beauty accompanied him amid an inferno of flashlights and jostling crowds. As she undulated beside him his eye strayed to her dramatic décolletage, and he needed to remind himself sternly of the paternal role he was to enact opposite her.

More beauties surrounded him as he sang "Thank Heaven for little girls", and then Rosalind Russell came forward to hand over the statuette that symbolized the honour granted him. It was an evening thick with emotion. At the banquet in the Beverly Hilton among hundreds of famous faces, he kept telling himself that this was the greatest night of his life. Afterwards, on the plane back to Chicago, he could not sleep – not because sleep evaded him but because he wanted to savour and treasure every remembered moment.

Love in the Afternoon and *Gigi* had made him the idol of a whole new generation that he could not have reached with his songs alone. He seemed to them like a favourite uncle of a type that perhaps did not exist within their own family circle. More and more young people started coming to his recitals, and among the theatre audiences he attracted the nostalgic middle-aged were often outnumbered by eighteen-year-olds in jeans and blouses. Although his career had by no means faltered up to then, he sensed a novel, invigorating stimulus. Discipline became yet more imperative. Having given up cigarettes years ago, he now forswore drinking entirely. Renunciation was hard, but he managed it.

After *Gigi* he was to make a dozen or so films. *Count Your Blessings*, inspired by Nancy Mitford's novel *The Blessing*, missed the subtlety of the original but gave him and his partner Deborah Kerr the chance of deploying a feather-light technique, he as a ducal *raisonneur* and she as the English wife of a philandering Frenchman. The Anglo-German Ronald Squire acted as a counterweight to Momo. It must have been one of the last appearances of this superbly polished actor whose ripe tones and impeccable style graced over the years so many West End comedies. After shooting on location in France and

England Momo waited around for weeks in Hollywood to complete his scenes. The interlude was more or less a paid holiday, and his strict scruples made him uneasy about taking cash for doing nothing. It also reminded him, and this caused a twinge, of the relative smallness of his part.

He had more scope in *A Breath of Scandal* and even a little song to sing, though the quality of the script and direction was mediocre. The film had been set up by Carlo Ponti as a vehicle for his wife Sophia Loren, yet the sensuality of the star was outrivalled by the splendour of location shots in and around Vienna. From Austria Momo went back the same year to Hollywood for *Can-Can*, a version of the Cole Porter musical in which he played an elderly but sympathetic judge of the *Belle Epoque*. There was much excitement on set in autumn 1959 when the Russian Prime Minister Nikita Kruschev visited Twentieth Century Fox studios on a tour to acquaint himself at first hand with the decadence of capitalism. Momo predicted, alas only too correctly: "American politicians can learn an important lesson from this occasion. Before too long the candidate seeking office who shows an interest in the performing arts, and can perform himself – especially on television – will be the one who is most successful. Inevitably, of course, all political campaigns will be exercises in acting with the best performer getting the most votes. It has already begun, you know, because even now any good politician is an actor."

The lion's share of the songs in the score fell, of course, to the big stars Frank Sinatra and Shirley MacLaine. Momo was granted a skittish number with Louis Jourdan, "Live and let live" ("I like Offenbach, you do not, so what, so what"), that helped flesh out his portrayal, so smooth and second nature to him now, of the tolerant, disabused elder. Yet the point of the characterization, and what gave it extra spice, was the underlying hint of vitality, the suggestion of fires only banked, not extinguished. "This cat's really a gasser," enthused Sinatra. "He's got the market cornered in youth."

While *Can-Can* was being made he rented a house in Beverly Hills that had belonged to Elsie Janis. It was she who, years before when he was trying to break away from the domination of Mistinguett, had been kind to him and given much-needed support at his London début. She had been a great star in those days, and now the former apprentice, an even more celebrated name than his mentor, was living in the rooms that once echoed to her famous voice. With him were, as always, François and Madeleine Vals, the young pair whose simple vivacity complemented his own. This, he thought, was contentment.

For his next film he returned in 1961 to France and the blinding sunshine of the Marseilles waterfront. Someone, somewhere, had had the unwise idea of bringing to the screen a Broadway play which, entitled *Fanny*, was inspired by the trilogy of films Marcel Pagnol wrote in the nineteen-thirties. Pagnol does not enjoy favour with intellectuals at the moment. They speak haughtily of his "popular" appeal and his "tinned theatre". This is to forget that no work of art can be truly universal without depicting the basic emotions that are common to humankind. Pagnol's films have a Dickensian vigour that has kept them gloriously alive for close on fifty years. He is concerned with elemental things: family, love, marriage, birth, death. The characters are his fellow-Provençaux, men and women who live life with robust intensity and who experience the dramas that fall to everyone's lot. You can almost smell the garlic and the bouillabaisse.

Around him Pagnol had gathered a cast of memorable players. Raimu, whom we have met earlier in his music-hall days, gave one of his finest performance as César, the Marseilles worthy who dominates a group of cronies including the round-visaged Panisse (Charpin) and the skinny pince-nez'd Brun (Vattier). Pierre Fresnay took the part of César's son Marius, and Orane Demazis was the heroine Fanny. In the Hollywood film it was Momo who inherited the role of Panisse, a well-off elderly shopkeeper who marries the pregnant Fanny when she is deserted by young Marius. Charles Boyer appeared as César, Horst Buchholtz as Marius, and Leslie Caron as Fanny. Momo's friend Boyer had, like him, matured into a character actor. His playing of César would have been an effective cameo-study had it not shrivelled into eclipse under memories of the tempestuous Raimu. Horst Buchholtz displayed a pretty face but gave little hint of the struggle between love and the call of the sea which Pierre Fresnay expressed with such anguish. And somehow Leslie Caron's pert *gaminerie* failed to convey the tragic, womanly essence of Fanny.

Only Momo came anywhere near the spirit of Pagnol. For years he had been careful about his figure, holding himself upright to reduce the tiny paunch that threatened to destroy his slim outline. Now, in the cause of art, he could let himself go, for Panisse, the well-rounded burgess, enjoyed his food. Momo gave him a genuinely sympathetic flavour. One believed in this ageing man, whose decrepit exterior hid a fundamental decency and sweet nature. It was a skilful piece of acting, the best in the film, and perhaps an even greater technical achievement than his work for *Gigi*.

The rôles he played in subsequent films made few demands on his talent. He was an amiable old village priest in *Jessica* (1962), a film star on the decline in *Panic Button* (1964), and a maundering grandfather in *I'd Rather Be Rich* (1964). A Walt Disney film, *In Search of the Castaways*, enabled him to visit London again in 1962 and to combine studio work with theatre appearances. He was always glad to see London, the foreign city he had known best and frequented most in his youth. All the comedians he had appreciated and learned from, the Robeys, the Hensons, the Grossmiths, were dead now. But London continued to throw up valuable talents. *Beyond The Fringe*, which displayed the unique and hilarious gifts of four young English amateurs, was a revelation. "Their names are Alan Bennett, Jonathan Miller, Peter Cook and Dudley Moore," he wrote. "Remember those names. You'll hear them again." His taste for novelty remained keen despite his seventy-four years. An evening at *Stop The World, I Want To Get Off* impressed him with the performance of Anthony Newley and his Pierrot make-up, his mime routines inspired by Chaplin and Marceau, his frail but arrogant singing voice. Even though he missed the point of the fast, idiomatic dialogue, Momo could grasp the originality of what he saw. London, in fact, was an exhilarating kaleidoscope of old and new, for there he renewed acquaintance with Suzy Volterra, wife of his late impresario at the Casino de Paris. She had carried on the racing triumphs of her husband and was in England to see her horse, the favourite, run in the St Leger. If there are sons of great men who occasionally managed to become famous in their own right, she was one of the very rare widows who had added prestige to a name that already belonged to a Parisian legend.

Once more he sang at a Command Performance, this time, in 1962, with Jack Benny and Sammy Davis Junior. Afterwards the Queen Mother told him of how tears came to her eyes during his act at the memory of hearing him in Paris when she had been there on the 1937 State Visit with George VI.

He went from the Palladium to Pinewood studios and filmed *In Search of the Castaways*. The Jules Verne story provided all sorts of excitement: an earthquake, an attack by a giant condor, terrible floods, an avalanche and an erupting volcano. Momo was an eccentric scientist who goes on a worldwide expedition in the company of an English lord (Wilfred Hyde-White) and an ingenious child heroine (Hayley Mills). There was also a Ben Gunn-type character, all beard and splutter, impersonated by Wilfrid Brambell. Later to be known as the senior partner of *Steptoe and Son*, Brambell had for years enriched films and plays with artful studies in dottiness. He took to Momo's unaffected ways and his total modesty. Once he visited him back-stage and was flattered to the point of embarrassment when the Frenchman spoke all the time of "Wilfrid's" work and never mentioned his own, presenting him, at the end, with a book inscribed "To Wilfrid Brambell, fine artist, fine chap". They shared a youthful spirit which marvelled at the spectacular adventures shown by *In Search of the Castaways* – all of them, incidentally, created by Disney's special effects group at Pinewood studios. It was one of the two films Brambell ever saw right through as a member of the audience. The other was Douglas Fairbanks' *Robin Hood*, which as a boy he sat through nine times. On the ninth occasion he was so carried away by one of his favourite scenes that he grabbed the knee of the woman sitting next to him, squeezed it ecstatically, and remarked, "This is my favourite bit!" An ear-splitting scream burst forth and the house lights were turned on. Did he ever tell this story to Momo? The latter would have adored it.

iii

Around the World in Eighty Years

He was very rich. Long, long ago he had passed the stage that
Austin Dobson characterized as:

    . . . the coming of the crows' feet,

    And the backward turn of beaux' feet,

yet he went on working, his hair snow-white, his face etched with
benevolent wrinkles. There was no need for him to do so. Most
people at his age would have been happy to vegetate in the peace-
able house at Marnes-la-Coquette, surrounded by the little group of
close friends and helpers and served by a devoted staff. Yet the
septuagenarian gladly condemned himself to a treadmill of blank
hotel rooms, aeroplane cabins and railway compartments on journeys that took him everywhere throughout the world except
beyond the Iron Curtain.

Was it greed for money? All conceptions of wealth are relative, and,
rich though he was, Momo would have judged himself a poor man
compared with a Getty or a Gulbenkian. His parsimony was
notorious, and in Hollywood the story was often told that, rather
than pay ten cents for parking his car outside the Paramount
studios, he would leave it five blocks away at a meter that only cost
five and then walk back. At that time he earned twenty thousand
dollars a week (£14,400) in nineteen-thirty values.

Avarice alone would not have driven him so obsessively in a
routine of two-hour performances each night and twice on
matinée-days in theatres from Bordeaux to Seattle, from Manchester to Rio de Janeiro. The habit of a lifetime's discipline was too
ingrained, too hard to break, and his response to the challenge of an
audience lost none of its compulsion however long his tale of years.
For Momo, as for any performer, wherever two or three people
were gathered together there was an audience to be amused, thrilled
and moved. Like a general without an army or a prime minister
without office, Momo without an audience did not exist. No
woman, no form of sensual pleasure, could equal the joy and
satisfaction of making two thousand people rock with laughter and
tremble with emotion under the spell he wove around them.

He enjoyed the best of both worlds. On days when he was not
travelling he would be driven into Paris and kept himself up to date

with the latest plays and films. At home he lived a quiet, contented existence, admiring his Utrillos and his Cézannes or rehearsing a new song or polishing a routine he had just worked out with his accompanist Fred Freed. Although the essays of Montaigne were his permanent bedside companions, he read all the important new books, both fiction and non-fiction, as they came out. Often he found himself admiring the talent of young writers but deploring the existentialist despair of their message. He had lived long enough to know that if, in Johnson's phrase, human life was everywhere a state in which much was to be endured and little to be enjoyed, there were nonetheless unexpected compensations.

An author whose work appealed to him was, oddly enough, Marcel Jouhandeau. He read *Réflexions sur la vie et le bonheur*, published in 1956, and these thoughts on life and happiness made him eager to know the personality of the writer who had expressed them. Jouhandeau was then only a little younger than Momo. He was over ninety when he eventually died and had written more than a hundred books – not quite novels, not essays, but a unique mixture of self-confession and scandalous revelation. A devout Catholic who sinned with regular enjoyment, a Puritan of unbridled fleshly impulse, Jouhandeau had, in the late nineteen-twenties, been persuaded by Jean Cocteau to marry an eccentric dancer by the name of Elise. This disastrous union, which locked two antipathetic characters in warring bondage, was a piece of luck for Jouhandeau the writer. It gave him the material for many books in which he described, with feline humour and lucid prose, the tragi-comedies of an uproarious marital existence.

Again and again Momo underlined passages in Jouhandeau's book that impressed him with their truth and clarity. Here was a man who had confronted the problem of old age and discovered how to endure it happily. In real life Jouhandeau was a sly charmer, an inexhaustible source of anecdotes comic, revealing and indiscreet. Momo went to lunch with him expecting to find a precious dandy. Instead he discovered an alert and wiry child-ancient, bubbling with animation, simple and natural. Their combined ages totalled a century and a half. Their talk had a vivacity that would have outdone people much younger.

Jouhandeau in turn appeared at "La Louque" flashing the big opal ring he wore on his third finger and delighting the lunch table with his sallies. "It's better to deserve a decoration and not to get it than not to deserve one and to receive it," he chuckled. Momo, who had been promoted to the rank of Commandeur in the Légion d'honneur in September 1956, hastened to note the witticism as soon as his guest departed. No two men could have belonged to spheres so utterly different. Jouhandeau was a cult writer with a following that did not amount to more than a few thousand, while Momo the popular entertainer counted his admirers in millions. Despite which they had one characteristic overwhelmingly in common: they knew the secret of eternal youth.

On a l'âge de son coeur, says the French proverb, and Momo confirmed it with an appetite for life that refused to stale. In 1967, when he was seventy-nine, he went to Canada for the big international exhibition held at Montreal. He filled the rôle of unofficial ambassador to "Expo '67" and took the lead in one of the main events called *Flying Colours*, a music-hall revue presented in an open-air stadium seating twenty-five thousand people. The designer of the spectacle was Erté, an old acquaintance from the Folies Bergère days and himself an example of irrepressible longevity: in his eighties he was still creating sets and dresses for opera productions. Three big stages were arranged so that everyone in the colossal audience could see what was going on. In the middle towered an immense rock garden which Erté peopled with exotic birds and flamboyant plants brought from the Caribbean Islands. Momo was to make his entrance by climbing a flight of steps to the rock garden–cum–platform. Would they be too much for an elderly man? Erté asked himself. His worry proved baseless. Momo ran up them like a youngster.

Early on the opening night a fine drizzle began. It developed into a raging storm and the audience fled like scurrying ants. At the second evening a deluge again held up the show. It stopped abruptly as it began, and Momo scampered up the steps to open his turn. The searing gleam of the spotlights was so harsh that it blinded him and he had to gauge audience reaction by the sound of laughter and applause alone. The buzz of jet aeroplanes overhead and the clatter of trains shunting in a nearby yard challenged his piping voice with a stubborn susurration. He simply gave up all attempt at subtlety and bellowed his songs into a twanging microphone. Although his act was timed to last half an hour the audience made him sing for at least forty-five minutes. "His vitality," said Erté, "was fantastic."

By the time his three weeks in Montreal ended he had perfected the art of communicating with twenty-five thousand people while at the same time staying inside the limits of the Chevalier style. It was an effort, but his vocal chords, usually so fragile, seemed to thrive on the cutting breezes and the assault of rain, from which he was protected only by his straw hat. Each day he spent an hour practising with Fred Freed, smoothing out problems that had arisen the night before and correcting the occasional slip that tended to creep in: the misplaced accent, the punch line that came an instant too soon, the word that always gave him trouble in pronunciation.

In August that year he began to think of retirement. His mind and body were in perfect shape. Montreal had proved that he could still adapt to the most difficult situations and that his skill was untouched. Could he be sure that physical health would continue into his eighties? When Mistinguett refused to give up she was eventually forced off the stage by a humiliating breakdown in public. The ageing Mayol went on giving "final appearances" for years until he ended up with the lowest billing on circus programmes among clowns and performing dogs. How Momo sympathized! For as long as he remembered he had fought and suffered for that one glorious moment when he took the stage and felt the current of affectionate excitement quiver into life between himself and the audience. What a terrible deprivation to forgo it. On the other hand, surely it was best to leave with dignity before he had outstayed his welcome.

He started preparing for an eightieth birthday tour across the world in August 1968. At Orly Airport he was presented with an enormous cake moulded in the shape of a straw hat. Mireille Mathieu helped him cut it, and then, accompanied by Fred Freed and François and Madeleine Vals, he flew off on a voyage that was to cover twenty-two American cities in two months. He opened in Kansas City to house-full notices. Before he travelled on to California he visited the Grand Old Man of Missouri, ex-President Harry S. Truman. Did he, enquired Momo respectfully, speak French as well as his daughter? "Nope," replied he. "To tell the truth, I don't even speak good English."

Los Angeles, New York and Washington gave him ovation after standing ovation. In Pittsburgh he began to feel the strain, was so tired that he could not move or see straight. Galas, banquets and receptions only reminded him that in surroundings other than "La Louque"and the theatre he was a fish out of water.The genial mask, he put on hid an awkward peasant who longed for the homeliness of Marnes-la-Coquette. But, like an old war horse that scents battle, the moment he heard the rustle of an expectant audience and the warning bell for curtain-rise, he became himself again. Ottawa turned out in force to greet him, but Toronto was disappointing. So were a few of the Canadian provincial cities where memories of him were fading and people had begun to seek their entertainment elsewhere. On the whole, though, he had reason to be satisfied. "Thank Heaven for Chevalier," said newspaper headlines, and the feeling was as sincere as it was general.

He settled back thankfully in "La Louque". The heavy snow that fell in Vermont while he was there had given him a nagging cold. He had difficulties in adjusting to the time difference between America and France, and at night he could not sleep for more than two or three hours. The next stage of his farewell tour through England and Scandinavia loomed over him and he dreaded it. A few days' rest at home gave him new strength, however, and even a whirling snowstorm that greeted him in Helsinki failed to quench his spirit. In a Stockholm theatre a group of trumpeters heralded the presentation to him of gifts, flowers and official medals. He had not known such an effusive show of affection anywhere else in the world.

By way of Göteborg and Copenhagen he travelled to Vienna and, at the Hotel Imperial, luxuriated in a suite that resembled the sort of thing Ernst Lubitsch would have built for him in *The Love Parade* forty years before. After Amsterdam he landed in Manchester. The Mancunians, as usual, were slow to warm up, and it took him four songs to get them moving. A snowbound Glasgow immersed him in a wave of loving enthusiasm. Coventry loyally refused to believe that this was his swan-song. London, he told himself, was the final test. Here he had to confront the city of Beatlemania and miniskirts, the foggy town which had given him inspiration in his youth and more triumph than failure. On the evening before his appearance he looked over the Palladium and made arrangements for his act. It was an easier theatre to play than many others he knew. The tiers went up very high, and there, he thought, remembering the fiasco of *White Birds* in 1925, was where any trouble would come from. In the event there was none. On the contrary, London said farewell to him with regret.

Someone asked him how he felt at his age. "Not bad," he responded drily, "considering the alternative." The veteran packed his bags again for the penultimate phase of his marathon tour. He passed through Hollywood and did not like what he saw: the place looked done for, out of date, and the people there had a distinctly old-fashioned appearance. In New York in September 1968 he received a special "Tony" award at the hands of Audrey Hepburn as a recognition of his long career. Next morning he awoke with a strange feeling of sadness, for he realized he had made his last appearance on Broadway.

South America followed, and Mexico and Quebec. He returned to Paris in time for the great event, his eightieth birthday itself on 12 September 1968. All the leading names in the Paris theatre and music-hall came to his party at the Lido night-club, an occasion of vintage champagne and quite the biggest cake anyone had ever seen. Noël Coward sat to one side of him and on the other was Claudette Colbert, his partner in the film *The Smiling Lieutenant* nearly forty years before. Charles Aznavour gave an emotional little speech. "You are," he said, "the greatest master of the *chanson* – the Eiffel Tower of the *chanson*."

The television network showed programmes about him. An exhibition featured the story of his career. The item that most touched him was a yellowing photograph of a singer called Fréhel. She is unknown in England and scarcely remembered by her own country. In 1907, the date of the picture, she must have been twenty or so and was very beautiful. She had loved Momo then, and after a brief affair, when he deserted her with youthful callousness, had ruined herself in a twilight round of drugs and dissipation. He always thought she could have been among the great singers of the time. Whenever he came across a reminder of past times like this he felt sentimental – and also relieved that the old flame was no longer there to recall the venom that had flowed at their moment of parting. He shrugged his shoulders and brought his odyssey to an end by touring sixty towns in Spain and Italy.

It was fitting that he should give his last recital of all in Paris, where he had begun as a red-nosed comic and where, as generation succeeded generation, he had matured into a symbol, a national monument. A gala audience of blasé, steely-eyed Parisians awaited him at the Théâtre des Champs-Elysées, the atmosphere strict with first-night tension and the clinging perfume of women. He made his entrance and, before he could say a word, everyone stood and cheered. For five minutes, an eternity, they applauded him while he gasped and swallowed. He gave them "Valentine", "Prosper", "Ma Pomme" and "Paris je t'aime". No matter that the songs were old-fashioned and that no one else would have dared sing them. He even persuaded that sophisticated audience to join in the choruses. When it was over they clapped him for ten minutes more, and his dressing-room was invaded by a mass of celebrities anxious to congratulate him. The same thing happened at each of his performances during the three weeks that followed. At the nineteenth, on 20 October 1968, he announced; "You have just seen the last recital I'll do anywhere." And he left the stage for ever.

"Au Revoir" was the name of a song he had sung at the Théâtre des Champs-Elysées. It was not quite right. "Adieu" would have been a better choice, but since no one had written such a number for him it had to stand. Perhaps, though, "Au Revoir" was, after all, appropriate, for he lived on in the memory of people everywhere in the world. Sixty-eight years of entertaining the public were not so easily forgotten, and he had made his final bow with all the grace and dignity he had hoped for.

iv

Easeful Death

"I am retired leisure," wrote Charles Lamb. "I am to be met with in trim gardens. I am already come to be known by my vacant face and careless gesture, perambulating at no fixed pace, nor with any settled purpose. I walk about; not to and from. They tell me, a certain *cum dignitate* air, that has been buried so long with my other good parts, has begun to shoot forth in my person. I grow into gentility perceptibly."

For the international star, as for the old clerk of Southsea House, retirement at first meant confusion and emptiness. Momo felt strangest round about four o'clock in the afternoon, the time when normally he would begin to experience the early twinges of stage-fright at thought of the evening's performance. Sometimes, at night, he would panic: surely he ought to be at the theatre? Then he remembered and a gentle melancholy descended upon him. Very gradually he evolved a different style of living. It had compensations. He was able to take up drinking again, though moderately, for an affliction called Menière's disease had attacked his inner ear, and if he allowed himself more than one glass of champagne bouts of dizziness were sure to follow.

People invited him out a lot. He dined with his friends the Duke and Duchess of Windsor, and he went often to the races with Suzy Volterra. At receptions he tried hard to make small-talk with the Pompidous, the Artur Rubinsteins, the Salvador Dalis, and was a little hurt when the imperious Brigitte Bardot gave him no more than a cold acknowledgement. He crept back to the comfort of "La Louque", where he could please himself about the company he kept. He entertained friends to lunch and waved them goodbye afterwards, all the more relaxed in that he did not have an evening performance to worry about now. A cup of tea late in the afternoon, some reading, a plain supper in front of television, and the host of "La Louque" was ready for bed at half-past nine.

He knew Montaigne very well now. Ever since Charles Boyer introduced him to the Sieur d'Eyquem he had been reading and re-reading the essays, each time discovering something fresh, something that lit up his own acquaintance with life. He became aware that to philosophize is to learn how to die, and that no man's happiness can be judged until after his death. Even a music-hall performer could appreciate that men are tormented by the opinions they have of things and not by things themselves. (A theatre, says the pessimist, is half-empty. The optimist would argue it was half-full.) These days Momo came back more and more to the last essay, the one entitled "Experience". If, says Montaigne, you have been able to think out and shape your life, you have achieved the hardest task of all. "It is our duty to set certain standards for ourselves. Our greatest and most glorious accomplishment is to live in accordance with them. Everything else, be it building cities, reigning, or earning a fortune, amounts to nothing more than added quibbles and details."

Momo looked back on his career and saw there a shape formed and standards achieved. When people asked him the secret of his durability, he replied, "You must love what you are doing." That he had done with a passion whole-hearted and unstinting. The stage was a jealous god, and he sacrificed to it however hard the effort, however poignant the denial. In the theatre he found his home, and in the public his family. Was he a truly happy man? Only after death, as Montaigne pointed out, could that be decided. Perhaps the light-hearted singer of "Dans la vie faut pas s'en faire" cannot have tasted the ultimate in happiness, because he was a perfectionist, and the perfectionist is never satisfied.

From what source did his mysterious power of attraction come? The words of his songs were commonplace enough, and yet they inscribed themselves on everyone's memory. Much of his repertoire was obvious and sentimental, but flavoured with a streak of cynicism that prevented it from cloying. You might call it limited, though life itself is limited. It was the irresistible blend of qualities that made him unique: naturalness constantly refreshed, sympathy evoked by his lowly origin and straightforward appeal, optimism distilled by the warmth of his voice and the charm of his smile, and the very French aspect of a personality which, straw hat tilted forward with cunning negligence, recalled the boulevard of earlier days. All these things combined to give his image a seamless continuity that resisted every change of fashion. The audience, lured by his confidential wink, turned into his accomplice.

As the days rolled smoothly by at "La Louque" he mused on his sixty-eight years in the profession and drew up a personal balance-sheet. What had he done best? In spite of the golden disc he had been awarded he did not think much of his records: his voice was not good enough. For the same reason he felt that his broadcasts were no more than adequate. Television had proved a technique which, once mastered, served merely to project a style created elsewhere. No, what he was proudest of he had done on stage and in the cinema. Those old films of Lubitsch, now they were good, and so was the film he had made for René Clair, *Le Silence est d'or*. Best of all, he thought, was his "one-man show". Without a band, or partner or scenery, the one-man show, consisting of himself and a pianist on a bare stage, was the purest essence of his craft. That was what he would like to be remembered by.

Impresarios kept trying to woo him out of retirement by offering fabulous sums. He refused them all except Walt Disney. It amused him to sing the title song of *The Aristocats*, for by doing so he could claim to have worked in every type of film: silent and sound, feature and short, black and white and colour, drama and comedy, romance and thriller, fact and fiction, musical and straight, and now cartoons.

Towards the end of 1969 he broadcast on "Radioscopie", a long-running French programme which, five times a week, carries interviews with notable people. His voice, firm and youthful, belied his eighty-one years. In the light accent of Ménilmontant he spoke with easy eloquence about himself and the "electric" Mistinguett. He was a contented man, he declared, and believed that he had been born under a lucky star. Noël Coward, asked what his ideal of the perfect life would be, succinctly replied, "Mine". That, one feels, would have been Momo's answer.

Two new faces appeared at "La Louque". He had met Odette Meslier, blonde ex-actress, forty-year-old widow, and taken to her. She was the mother of a small handicapped daughter. He invited them both to live with him at Marnes-la-Coquette, and they became, with other members of his circle there, the companions of his old age. He was fond of the widow. He doted on the child. One day he made his will. After bequests to nephews, staff and many charities, he left to mother and daughter the house they lived in together. It stands there today, in the garden where Momo loved to sit beside his mother's memorial and where the kindly features of La Louque peer out across the lawns still.

But the idyllic atmosphere soon clouded over. He missed, more than ever, the audience which had been his life, and when he went to the theatre nowadays he longed to be up on the stage rather than fretting in obscurity among the other spectators. Visitors to "La Louque" came away with a queer sense of unease. There were signs that Momo's old comrade Félix Paquet was trying to dominate an octogenarian whose mind was not always very clear, and that the one-time faithful friend had his eye fixed on an estate worth several million pounds. Momo could bear it no longer. The suicidal depression he had known years ago came back to engulf him once more, and one night he yielded to it by swallowing a mouthful of sleeping tablets and slashing his wrist with a razor. Early next morning he was found, alive still and wallowing in bloodied sheets. After a week in hospital he was restored to an existence which had neither joy nor meaning for him.

The summer of 1971 was a fine one. He watched it pass into autumn as the ancient trees outside turned yellow and shed their leaves for the hundredth time. Sometimes a spasm of pain clouded his sharp blue eyes, for he had begun to have trouble with his kidneys – nothing much, just enough for discomfort. But it did not improve and in fact gradually worsened until, in December, he was advised to have an operation.

The day the ambulance called on its way to the Hôpital Necker in Paris he spoke urgently with François Vals. "In the left-hand drawer of my desk you'll find envelopes for the New Year presents I want to give everyone in my little household," he said. "I've written the greeting cards. Will you put the various sums of money into the envelopes?" He paused. *"Do this, whatever happens."*

The surgeons operated, and in his room afterwards he felt well enough to sit up in a chair and eat. The rally proved deceptive. He was eighty-three years old and his body could not take an artificial kidney. Within a short while came the first heart attack and, on New Year's Day 1972, he died as quietly and gently as had La Louque. The funeral procession wound through Montmartre and up the familiar hill to the cemetery where La Louque was buried. They·laid him beside his mother. The circle had completed itself, and in his end was his beginning.

The Films of Maurice Chevalier

Silent

1908   TROP CRÉDULE (France). One reel.
    Director: Jean Durand
    Cast: Maurice Chevalier; Joaquin Renez

1911   UNE MARIÉE QUI SE FAIT ATTENDRE (France). One reel.
    Director: Louis Gasnier
    Cast: Max Linder; Maurice Chevalier

1911   UNE MARIÉE RÉCALCITRANTE (France). One reel.
    Director: Louis Gasnier
    Cast: Max Linder; Maurice Chevalier

1911   PAR HABITUDE (France). One reel.
    Director: Max Linder
    Cast: Max Linder; Maurice Chevalier

1914   LA VALSE RENVERSANTE (France). One reel.
    Director: ?
    Cast: Mistinguett; Maurice Chevalier

1917   UNE SOIRÉE MONDAINE (France). One reel.
    Director: Henri Diamant-Berger
    Cast: Mistinguett; Maurice Chevalier

1921   LE MAUVAIS GARÇON (France). Five reels.
    Director: Henri Diamant-Berger
    Cast: Edouard de Max; Pierre de Guingand; Marguerite Moreno; Maurice Chevalier

1922   LE MATCH CRIQUI–LEDOUX (France). One reel.
    Director: Henri Diamant-Berger
    Cast: Maurice Chevalier

1923   GONZAGUE (France). Three reels.
    Director: Henri Diamant-Berger
    Cast: Marguerite Moreno; Albert Préjean; Maurice Chevalier

1923   L'AFFAIRE DE LA RUE LOURCINE (France). Three reels.
       Director: Henri Diamant-Berger
       Cast: Odette Florelle; Marcel Vallée; Maurice Chevalier

1924   PAR HABITUDE (France). Three reels.
       Director: Henri Diamant-Berger
       Cast: Georges Milton; Pauline Carton; Maurice Chevalier

1924   JIM BOUGNE BOXEUR (France). Three reels.
       Director: Henri Diamant-Berger
       Cast: Georges Milton; Odette Florelle; Martinelli; Maurice
       Chevalier

Sound

1928   BONJOUR NEW YORK! (USA). Three reels.
       Director: Robert Florey
       Cast: Maurice Chevalier; Yvonne Vallée

1929   INNOCENTS OF PARIS (USA). 78 minutes.
       Producer: Jesse L. Lasky
       Director: Richard Wallace
       Script: Ethel Doherty, Ernest Vajda, based on the story "Flea
           Market" by Charles E. Andrews.
       Photography: Charles Lang
       Music: Richard A. Whiting
       Cast: Maurice Marney – Maurice Chevalier; Louise Leval –
           Sylvia Beecher

1929   THE LOVE PARADE (USA). 100 minutes.
       Producer/Director: Ernst Lubitsch
       Script: Ernest Vajda, Guy Bolton, after the play *The Prince
           Consort* by Léon Xanrof and Jules Chancel.
       Photography: Victor Milner
       Art direction: Hans Dreier
       Music: Victor Schertzinger
       Costumes: Travis Banton
       Cast: Count Alfred – Maurice Chevalier; Queen Louise –
           Jeanette MacDonald; Jacques – Lupino Lane; Lulu – Lillian
           Roth

1930   PARAMOUNT ON PARADE (USA). 128 minutes.
       Two guest appearances.

1930   THE BIG POND (USA). 85 minutes.
      Producer: Monta Bell
      Director: Hobart Henley
      Script: Robert Presnell, Garrett Fort, after the play *The Big Pond*
          by George Middleton and A.E. Thomas.
      Photography: George Folsey
      Cast: Pierre Mirande – Maurice Chevalier; Barbara Billings –
          Claudette Colbert

1930   PLAYBOY OF PARIS (USA). 79 minutes.
      Director/Producer: Ludwig Berger
      Scripts: Percy Heath, after the play *Le Petit Café* by Tristan
          Bernard.
      Photography: Henry Gerrard
      Art direction: Hans Dreier
      Music and lyrics: Richard A. Whiting

1931   EL CLIENTE SEDUCTOR (France). Two reels.
      Directors: Richard Blumenthal, Florian Rey
      Cast: Imperio Argentina; Rosita Diaz Gimeno; Charles
          Martinez Baena; Carmen Navascués; Maurice
          Chevalier

1931   THE STOLEN JOOLS (THE SLIPPERY PEARLS) (USA). Two reels.
      Director: William McGann
      Guest appearance

1931   THE SMILING LIEUTENANT (USA). 88 minutes.
      Producer/Director: Ernst Lubitsch
      Script: Ernest Vajda, Samson Raphaelson, based on operetta "A
          Waltz Dream".
      Photography: George Folsey
    Music: Oscar Straus
    Cast: Niki – Maurice Chevalier; Princess Anna – Claudette Colbert;
          Max – Charles Ruggles

1932   TOBOGGAN (BATTLING GEORGES) (France) One reel. (Made for
    charity.)
      Director: Henri Decoin
      Cast: Arlette Marchal; Raymond Cordy; Paul Amiot; Sophie
          Duval; François Deschamps; John Anderson; Maurice
          Chevalier

1932   ONE HOUR WITH YOU (USA). 80 minutes.
      Producer/Director: Ernst Lubitsch (also George Cukor)
      Script: Samson Raphaelson, based on the play *Nur ein Traum* by
          Lother Schmidt.

Photography: Victor Milner
Art direction: Hans Dreier
Music and lyrics: Oscar Straus, Richard A. Whiting, Leo Robin
Cast: Dr André Bertier – Maurice Chevalier; Colette Bertier – Jeanette MacDonald; Pitzi Olivier – Genevieve Tobin; Professor Olivier – Charles Ruggles

1932 MAKE ME A STAR (USA). 83 minutes.
Guest appearance.

1932 LOVE ME TONIGHT (USA). 105 minutes.
Producer/Director: Rouben Mamoulian
Script: Hoffenstein, Young, Marion, based on the play *Tailor in the Château* by Leopold Marchand and Paul Armont.
Photography: Victor Milner
Art direction: Hans Dreier
Music and lyrics: Richard Rodgers, Lorenz Hart
Cast: Maurice Courtelin – Maurice Chevalier; Princess Jeanette – Jeanette MacDonald; Gilbert, Vicomte de Varèze – Charles Ruggles; Count de Savignac – Charles Butterworth; Countess Valentine – Myrna Loy; The Duke of Artelines – C. Aubrey Smith

1933 BEDTIME STORY (USA). 85 minutes.
Director: Norman Taurog
Script: Waldemar Young, based on the novel *Bellamy the Magnificent* by Roy Horniman.
Photography: Charles Lang
Music and lyrics: Ralph Rainger, Leo Robin
Cast: René, Vicomte de St Denis – Maurice Chevalier; Sally – Helen Twelvetrees; Victor – Edward Everett Horton; "Monsieur" – Baby Leroy

1933 THE WAY TO LOVE (USA). 80 minutes.
Director: Norman Taurog
Script: Gene Fowler, Benjamin Glazer, based on own story "Laughing Man".
Photography: Charles Lang
Music and lyrics: Ralph Rainger, Leo Robin
Art direction: Hans Dreier
Cast: François – Maurice Chevalier; Madeleine – Ann Dvorak; Professor Gaston Bibi – Edward Everett Horton

1934 THE MERRY WIDOW (USA). 110 minutes.
Producer: Irving Thalberg
Associate Producer/Director: Ernst Lubitsch

Script: Ernest Vajda, Samson Raphaelson, based on the operetta
     by Franz Lehar.
Art direction: Cedric Gibbons
Music and lyrics: Franz Lehàr, Richard Rodgers, Lorenz Hart,
     Gus Kahn
Cast: Danilo – Maurice Chevalier; Sonia – Jeanette MacDonald;
     Ambassador – Edward Everett Horton;
     Queen – Una Merkel

1935   FOLIES BERGÈRE (USA). 83 minutes.
     Producer: Darryl F. Zanuck
     Director: Roy del Ruth
     Script: Bess Meredyth, Hall Long, based on the play *The Red Cat*
          by Rudolph Lothar and Hans Adler.
     Photography: Barney McGill, Peverell Marley
     Art direction: William Darling
     Cast: Eugène Charlier and Fernand, Baron Cassini – Maurice
          Chevalier; Baroness Cassini – Merle Oberon; Mimi – Ann
          Sothern; René – Walter Byron

1936   L'HOMME DU JOUR (France). 93 minutes.
     Producer/Director: Julien Duvivier
     Script: Charles Vidiac, Charles Spaak, Maurice Chevalier
     Music and lyrics: Borel-Clerc, Michel Emer, Vincent Scotto
     Cast: Alfred Boulard – Maurice Chevalier; Mona Talia – Elvire
          Popesco; Suzanne Petit – Josette Day; Cormier de la
          Creuse – Alerme

1936   AVEC LE SOURIRE (France). 90 minutes.
     Producer/Director: Maurice Tourneur
     Script: Louis Verneuil, based on his play *Avec le Sourire*.
     Photography: Thiraud and Nee
     Music and lyrics: Marcel Lattès and Borel-Clerc
     Cast: Victor Larnois – Maurice Chevalier; Gisèle – Marie Glory;
          Villary – André Lefaur

1936   THE BELOVED VAGABOND (England). 68 minutes.
     Director: Kurt Bernhardt
     Script: Hugh Mills, Walter Creighton, Arthur Wimperis, based
          on the novel *The Beloved Vagabond* by William J. Locke.
     Photography: Franz Planer
     Music and lyrics: Milhaud, Mireille, Heymann
     Cast: Paragot – Maurice Chevalier; Joanna – Betty Stockfield;
          Blanquette – Margaret Lockwood; Asticot – Desmond
          Tester; Comte de Verneuil – Austin Trevor

1938   BREAK THE NEWS (England). 72 minutes.
     Producer/Director: René Clair
     Script: Geoffrey Kerr, based on the novel *La Mort en fuite* by Lois
       le Guriade.
     Photography: Phil Tannura
     Music and lyrics: Cole Porter, Van Phillips, Jack Buchanan
     Cast: François Verrier – Maurice Chevalier; Teddy – Jack
       Buchanan; Grace Gatwick – June Knight

1939   PIÈGES (France). 100 minutes.
     Director: Robert Siodmak
     Script: Jacques Companeez, Ernest Neuville
     Photography: R. Voinquel
     Art direction: Wakevitch and Colasson
     Music and lyrics: Michel Michelet, Reville, Vander, Gardoni,
       Chavoit, Willemetz
     Cast: Robert Fleury – Maurice Chevalier; Pears – Erich von
       Stroheim;   Bremontière – Pierre Renoir;   Adrienne –
       Marie Déa

1945   LE SILENCE EST D'OR (France). 106 minutes.
     Producer/Director: René Clair
     Script: René Clair
     Photography: Armand Thirard
     Music: Georges van Parys
     Art direction : Léon Barsacq
     Costumes: Christian Dior
     Cast: Emile – Maurice Chevalier; Jacques – François Périer;
       Madeleine – Marcelle Derrien; Lucette – Dany Robin;
       Duperrier – Robert Pizani; Curly – Raymond Cordy;
       Cashier – Paul Olivier

1946   LE ROI (France). 100 minutes.
     Director: Marc-Gilbert Sauvajon
     Script: M-G Sauvajon, from the play *Le Roi* by Flers and
       Caillavet.
     Photography: Robert LeFebvre
     Music: Jean Marion
     Cast: The King – Maurice Chevalier; Thérèse Marnix – Annie
       Ducaux; Mme Beaudrier – Sophie Desmarets

1950   MA POMME (France). 90 minutes.
     Director: Marc-Gilbert Sauvajon
     Script: M-G Sauvajon
     Photography: Henri Alekan
     Cast: Ma Pomme – Maurice Chevalier; M. Peuchat – Jean Wall;
       Mme Peuchat – Sophie Desmarets

1950 PARIS 1900 (France). 76 minutes.
Director/Writer: Nicole Vedrès
Shows various leading personalities between 1900 and 1914, including Chevalier and Mistinguett.

1953 SCHLAGER–PARADE (Germany). 100 minutes.
Guest appearance.

1954 CENTO ANNI D'AMORE (Italy). 110 minutes.
Guest appearance in the last of six episodes portraying love from 1854 to 1954.

1954 J'AVAIS SEPT FILLES (France and Italy). 98 minutes.
Director: Jean Boyer
Script: Serge Veber, Jean Des Vallières, based on a story by Aldo de Benedetti.
Music: Fred Freed
Cast: Count André – Maurice Chevalier; Luisella – Delia Scala; Linda – Colette Ripert

1957 RENDEZVOUS WITH MAURICE CHEVALIER (France).
Director: Maurice Regamey
Six programmes of a series originally made for television and then shown in cinemas.

1957 THE HAPPY ROAD (USA). 100 minutes.
Film with Gene Kelly, Barbara Laage and Michael Redgrave, for which Chevalier sang the title song.

1957 LOVE IN THE AFTERNOON (USA). 125 minutes.
Producer/Director: Billy Wilder
Script: Billy Wilder, I.A.L. Diamond, based on the novel *Ariane* by Claude Anet.
Photography: William Mellor
Music: Franz Waxman and Marchetti
Art direction: Alexander Trauner
Cast: Frank Flannagan – Gary Cooper; Ariane Chavasse – Audrey Hepburn; Claude Chavasse – Maurice Chevalier

1958 GIGI (USA). 115 minutes.
Director: Vincente Minnelli
Script: Alan Jay Lerner, based on Anita Loos' dramatization of the Colette novel.
Photography: Joseph Ruttenberg
Music: Frederick Loewe
Art direction: William A. Horning and Preston Ames
Costumes and scenery: Cecil Beaton

Cast: Gigi – Leslie Caron; Honoré Lachaille – Maurice Chevalier; Gaston Lachaille – Louis Jourdan; Mme Alvarez – Hermione Gingold; Liane d'Exelmans – Eva Gabor; Sandomir – Jacques Bergerac; Aunt Alicia – Isabel Jeans

1959   COUNT YOUR BLESSINGS (USA). 102 minutes.
Director: Jean Negulesco
Script: Karl Tunberg, based on the Nancy Mitford novel *The Blessing*.
Photography: Milton Krasner, George J. Fölsey
Music: Franz Waxman
Art Direction: William A. Horning
Cast: Grace Allingham – Deborah Kerr; Charles-Edouard de Valhubert – Rossano Brazzi; Duc de St-Cloud – Maurice Chevalier; Sir Conrad Allingham – Ronald Squire.

1960   CAN–CAN (USA). 134 minutes.
Director: Walter Lang
Script: Dorothy Kingsley, Charles Lederer, based on the Cole Porter musical.
Photography: William H. Daniels
Music: Cole Porter
Art direction: Lyle Wheeler, Jack Martin Smith
Cast: François Durnais – Frank Sinatra; Simone Pistache – Shirley MacLaine; Paul Barrière – Maurice Chevalier; Philippe Forestier – Louis Jourdan; Claudine – Juliet Prowse

1960   UN, DEUX, TROIS, QUATRE! (France). 140 minutes.
Four ballets featuring Zizi Jeanmaire, Roland Petit, Moira Shearer and Cyd Charisse, introduced by Maurice Chevalier.

1960   A BREATH OF SCANDAL (Italy). 98 minutes.
Director: Michael Curtiz
Script: Walter Bernstein, based on Molnar play *Olympia*.
Photography: Mario Montuori
Music: B. Cicognini, Robert Stolz, Al Stillman
Art Direction: Hal Pereira, Eugene Allan
Cast: Olympia – Sophia Loren; Charlie – John Gavin; Philip – Maurice Chevalier; Eugénie – Isabel Jeans; Lina – Angela Lansbury

1960   PEPE (USA).
Guest appearance.

1961 FANNY (USA). 133 minutes.
   Producer/Director: Joshua Logan
   Script: Julius J. Epstein, based on the play by S.N. Behrmann and
       Joshua Logan, inspired by Marcel Pagnol play and film.
   Photography: Jack Cardiff
   Music: Harold Rome
   Art direction: Rino Mondellini
   Cast: Fanny – Leslie Caron; Panisse – Maurice Chevalier; César
       – Charles Boyer; Marius – Horst Buchholtz

1962 JESSICA (USA). 105 minutes.
   Producer/Director: Jean Negulesco
   Script: Edith Sommers from the novel *The Midwife of Pont Cléry*
       by Flora Sandstrom.
   Photography: Piero Portalupi
   Music: Mario Nascimbeni, Marguerite Monnot, Dusty
       Negulesco
   Art direction: Giulio Bongini
   Cast: Jessica – Angie Dickinson; Father Antonio – Maurice
       Chevalier; Old Crupi – Noel-Noel; Edmondo Raumo –
       Gabriele Ferzetti; Nunzia Tuffi – Sylvia Koscina; Maria
       Lombardo – Agnes Moorehead

1962 IN SEARCH OF THE CASTAWAYS (USA). 100 minutes.
   Director: Robert Stevenson
   Script: Lowell S. Hawley, based on Jules Verne's novel *The*
       Children of Captain Grant.
   Photography: Paul Beeson
   Music: William Alwyn
   Art direction: Michael Stringer
   Cast: Professor Jacques Paganel – Maurice Chevalier; Mary
       Grant – Hayley Mills; Thomas Ayerton – George Sanders;
       Lord Glenarvon – Wilfred Hyde-White; John Glenarvon –
       Michael Anderson Jnr; Bill Gaye – Wilfrid Brambell

1963 A NEW KIND OF LOVE
   Guest appearance singing "Louise" and "Mimi" during the credit titles of this film staring Paul Newman and Joanne Wood-
   ward.

1964 PANIC BUTTON (Italy). 90 minutes.
   Director: George Sherman
   Script: Hal Biller, based on a story by Ron Gorton.
   Photography: Enzo Sarafin
   Music: Georges Gavarantz
   Cast: Phillipe Fontaine – Maurice Chevalier; Louise Harris –
       Eleanor Parker; Angela – Jayne Mansfield

1964   I'D RATHER BE RICH (USA). 96 minutes.
   Director: Jack Smight
   Script: Oscar Brodney, Norman Krasna, Leo Townsend
   Photography: Russell Metty
   Music: Percy Faith
   Art direction: Alexander Golitzen, George Webb
   Cast: Cynthia – Sandra Dee; Philip Dulaine – Maurice
         Chevalier; Paul – Robert Goulet; Warren – Andy Wil-
         liams; Dr Crandall – Charles Ruggles; Martin Wood –
         Gene Raymond; Miss Grimshaw – Hermione Gingold

1967   MONKEYS GO HOME! (USA). 101 minutes.
   Director: Andrew V. McLagen
   Script: Maurice Tombragel, based on the novel *The Monkeys* by
         G.K. Wilkinson.
   Photography: William Snyder
   Music: Robert F. Brunner, Robert B. and Richard M. Sherman
   Art direction: Carroll Clark, John B. Mansbridge
   Cast: Father Sylvain – Maurice Chevalier; Hank Dussard – Dean
         Jones; Maria Riserau – Yvette Mimieux.

1970   THE ARISTOCATS (USA). 78½ minutes.
   Title song sung by Maurice Chevalier.

Newsreel Footage

Various shots from newsreel and documentary films have also been used
in *La Bataille de France* (1964), *La Naissance* (1970), and *Le Chagrin et la Pitié*
(1972).

Bibliography

Manuscript sources

Nineteen signed autograph letters and envelopes, two signed letters, 1932–1956, and nine telegrams from Chevalier to Mistinguett; three signed autograph letters from Chevalier to Mistinguett's family. Twelve drafts of replies from Mistinguett. (*Collection André Bernard.*)

Printed sources

Bodin, Thierry, Autograph Catalogues.

Boyer, William, *The Romantic Life of Maurice Chevalier*, Hutchinson, 1937.

Brambell, Wilfrid, *All Above Board*, W.H. Allen, 1976.

Bridge, Joe, *Nos Vedettes*, Editions Joe Bridge, n.d.

Brunschwig, Chantal, Calvet, Louis Jean and Klein, Jean-Claude, *Cent Ans de Chanson Française*, Editions du Seuil, 1972.

Bruyas, Florian, *Histoire de l'Opérette en France, 1855-1965*, Emmanuel Vitte, Lyon, 1974.

Castans, Raymond, *Fernandel m'a raconté*, Editions de Provence/Editions de la Table Ronde, 1976.

Charavay, Jacques, Etienne and Noël, Autograph Catalogues.

Charles, Jacques, *Le Caf' Conc'*, Flammarion, 1966.

Charles, Jacques, *Cent ans de music-hall*, Ichéber, 1956.

Charles, Jacques, *De Dranem à Maurice Chevalier. Souvenirs*, Oeuvres Libres, 1951.

Charles, Jacques, *De Gaby Deslys à Mistinguett*, NRF, 1933.

Charles, Jacques, *Le Music-hall en France*, Oeuvres Libres, 1953.

Charles, Jacques, *La Naissance du Music-hall*, Fayard, 1952.

Charles, Jacques, *La Revue de ma vie*, Fayard, 1958.

Chevalier, Maurice, *La Louque*, Julliard, 1946.

Chevalier, Maurice, *Londres-Hollywood-Paris*, Julliard, 1947.

Chevalier, Maurice, *Tempes grises*, Julliard, 1948.

Chevalier, Maurice, *Par çi, par là*, Julliard, 1950.

Chevalier, Maurice, *Y a Tant d'amour*, Julliard, 1952.

Chevalier, Maurice, *Noces d'or*, Julliard, 1954.

Chevalier, Maurice, *Artisan de France*, Julliard, 1957.

Chevalier, Maurice, *C'est l'amour*, Julliard, 1960.

Chevalier, Maurice, *Soixante-quinze Berges*, Julliard, 1963.

Chevalier, Maurice, *Quatre-vingts Berges*, Julliard, 1967.

Chevalier, Maurice, *Môme à cheveux blancs*, Presses de la Cité, 1969.

Chevalier, Maurice, *Les Pensées de Momo*, Presses de la Cité, 1970.

Clair, René, *Cinéma d'hier, cinéma d'aujourd'hui*, Gallimard, 1970.

Cocteau, Jean, *Foyer des artistes*, Plon, 1947.

Colette, *La Vagabonde*, Albin Michel, 1911.

Colette, *L'Envers du music-hall*, Flammarion, 1913.

Cudlipp, Percy, *Maurice Chevalier's Own Story*, Odhams, 1930.

Feschotte, Jacques, *Histoire du music-hall*, Presses Universitaires de France, 1965.

Greene, Graham, *The Pleasure-Dome*, Secker & Warburg, 1972.

Guitry, Sacha, "Discours de Réception", Gala programme, Théâtre des Variétés, 1950.

Halimi, André, *Chantons sous l'Occupation*, Olivier Orban, 1976.

Harding, James, *Sacha Guitry, The Last Boulevardier*, Methuen, 1968.

Harding, James, *Folies de Paris*, Chappell/Elm Tree Books, 1979.

Jando, Dominique, *Histoire mondiale du music-hall*, Delarge, n.d.

Le Boterf, Hervé, *La vie parisienne pendant l'Occupation*, 2 vols, Editions France Empire, 1974, 1975.

Lerner, Alan Jay, *The Street Where I live*, Hodder & Stoughton, 1978.

Leslie, Peter, *A Hard Act To Follow*, Paddington Press, 1978.

Librairie de l'Abbaye, Autograph Catalogues.

Lorcey, Jacques, *Marcel Achard,* Editions France Empire, 1977.

Marshall, Michael, *Top Hat and Tails: The Story of Jack Buchanan*, Elm Tree Books, 1978.

Mistinguett, *Toute ma vie*, Julliard, 1954.

Morssen, Pierre, *Autograph Catalogues*.

Prasteau, Jean, *La merveilleuse aventure du Casino de Paris*, Denöel, 1975.

Ringgold, Gene, and Bodeen, de Witt, *The Films and Career of Maurice Chevalier*, The Citadel Press, 1973.

Rivollet, André, *Maurice Chevalier. De Ménilmontant au Casino de Paris*, Grasset, 1927.

Rodgers, Richard, *Love Me Tonight*, W.H. Allen, 1976.

Sablon, Jean, *De France ou bien d'ailleurs*, Robert Laffont, 1979.

Saka, P., *La Chanson Française des origines à nos jours*, Fernand Nathan, 1980.

Willemetz, Albert, *Maurice Chevalier*, Editions René Kistler, 1954.

Willemetz, Albert, *Dans mon rétroviseur*, La Table Ronde, 1967.

Tabet, Georges, *Vivre deux fois*, Robert Laffont, n.d.

Van Parys, Georges, *Les Jours comme ils viennent*, Plon, 1969.

Sound archive

Chancel, Jacques, "Radioscopie avec Maurice Chevalier", 3.12.69, Cassette 231 P253 19, Archives de l'INA.
Lama, Serge (presenter), "Maurice de Paris", five-part radio series, France-Inter, December 1981.

Index

Alfonso XIII, King of Spain
(1886–1941), 22–23, 167

Antoine (Antoine Muracciolli), singer
(b. 1944), 175

Arletty (Léonie Bathiat), actress (b
1898), 148–149

Arnaud, Yvonne, actress (1892–1958),
158

Aznavour, Charles (Aznavourian),
singer (b. 1924), 133, 154, 163–165,
167, 196

Badet, Régina, dancer and singer (c.
1880–?), 45, 46

Baker, Joséphine, singer (1906–1974),
58, 72, 142.

Bard, Wilkie, comedian and singer
(1870–1944), 50

Barrymore, John, actor (1882–1942), 94

Beaton, Sir Cecil, designer and
photographer (1904–1980), 183–184,
185

Beery, Wallace, film actor (1886–1949),
111

Berlin, Iriving, composer (1888–1964),
26

Blore, Eric, film actor (1887–1959), 126
and n.

Boucot, Louis-Jacques, composer and
singer (1884–1949), 12–13

Boulanger, Georges, General
(1837–1891), 1, 3

Bow, Clara, film actress (1905–1965),
94–95, 103

Boyer, Charles, actor (1899–1980),
113–114, 125, 128, 154, 159, 175, 188,
198.

Brambell, Wilfrid, actor (b. 1912), xi,
190

Brassens, Georges, composer and
singer (1921–1981), 163, 175

Brook, Clive (Clifford), actor
(1891–1974), 103–104

Buchanan, Jack, actor and impresario
(1891–1957), 138–139

Buchholz, Horst, film actor (b. 1932),
188

Butt, Sir Alfred, impresario, 56

Carnot, Sadi, politician (1837–1894),
1–2, 3

Caron, Leslie, film actress (b. 1931),
184, 185, 188

Carton, Pauline (Biarez), actress
(1884–1974), 91

Chaplin, Sir Charles, film actor and
producer (1889–1977), 35, 91, 93, 95,
180

Charles, Jacques, impresario and
producer, 60–61, 62, 63, 102

Chase, Charley, film actor (1893–1940),
91

Chevalier, Charles, brother of Maurice,
3, 5

Chevalier, Joséphine, mother (d. 1931),
"La Louque", 3, 4, 5, 6, 7, 8, 9, 10, 11,
12, 13, 14, 17, 18, 19, 28, 37, 44–45,
48–49, 52, 54, 55, 73, 76, 77, 78, 79,
85, 88, 102, 110, 114, 134–135, 161,
173, 174–175, 200, 201

Chevalier, Maurice (1888–1972): FILMS:
Aristocats, The, 199–200; *Avec le
sourire*, 135; *Bedtime Story*, 120–122;
Beloved Vagabond, The, 135, 136; *Big
Pond, The*, 104; *Bonjour, New York!*,
94; *Break The News*, 138–139; *Breath
of Scandal, A*, 187; *Can-Can*, 186;
Count Your Blessings, 186–187; *El*

Cliente Seductor, 104–105; *Fanny*, 188–189; *Folies-Bergère*, 125–126; *Gigi*, 181–186; *L'Homme du jour*, 135; *I'd Rather be Rich*, 189; *In Search of The Castaways*, 189, 190; *Innocents of Paris*, 96–98, 101; *J'avais sept filles*, 179; *Jessica*, 189; *Love in The Afternoon*, 181–182, 186; *Love Me Tonight*, 114–117, 124; *Love Parade, The* 99–101, 103, 104, 123, 140, 152, 195; *Ma Pomme*, 169; *Make Me a Star*, 117; *Merry Widow, The*, 123–124; *One Hour With You*, 109; *Panic Button*, 189; *Paramount On Parade*, 103–104; *Playboy of Paris*, 106, 109; *Roi, Le*, 168–169; *Silence est d'or, Le*, 150–152, 153, 184, 199; *Smiling Lieutenant, The*, 104; *Stolen Jools, The*, 110; *Toboggan*, 117; *Valse Renversante, La*, 91; *Way To Love, The*, 122
SONGS: "Ali Ben Baba", 147; "Ananas, Les", 96; "Ça sent si bon, la France", 145; "Dans le vie faut pas s'en faire", 70, 199; "Donnez-moi la main, mam'zelle", 130, 164; "I'm Glad I'm Not Young Any More", 184; "Le premier, le seul, le vrai Paradis c'est Paris", 77–78; "Louise", 96–97, 98, 106, 114, 175, 177; "Ma Pomme", 135, 145, 169, 197; "Marche de Ménilmontant, La", 145; "Mimi", 115, 116; "Paris sera toujours Paris", 101, 142; "Paris je t'aime", 197; "Prosper", 129, 144–145, 197; "Quand on est deux", 82; "Quand un vicomte", 126; "Symphonie des semelles de bois", 145; "Thank Heaven For Little Girls", xiv, 184, 186; "Valentine", xiv, 83–84, 85, 96, 97, 114, 126, 167, 175, 197
Chevalier, Paul, brother, 3, 5, 9, 10, 14, 18, 19, 161, 174, 176
Chevalier, Victor Charles, father, 3–4, 5, 48–49, 76
Christiné, Henri (Henri Marius), composer (1867–1941): 68–69, 83; *Dédé*, 69–70, 71, 72, 73, 76, 136; *Phi-Phi*, 68, 69, 78; "Viens Poupoule", 25, 68

Clair, René (Chomette), film director (1898–1981): xi, 91, 116, 138–139, 199, 150–152; *A Nous la liberté*, 139–151; *Break The News*, 138–139; *Deux Timides, Les*, 151; *Paris qui dort*, 91; *Quatorze juillet*, 151; *Silence est d'or, Le*, 150–151, 152, 199; *Sous les toits de Paris*, 91, 139
Cocteau, Jean Maurice, poet (1889–1963), xvii, 145, 165 and n., 166, 175, 192
Colbert, Claudette (Lily Chauchoin), film actress (*b*. 1905), 104, 196
Colette, Sidonie Gabrielle, novelist (1873–1954): 39–40, 41, 156–157, 182; *Claudine à Paris*, 39; *Gigi*, 157, 182; *Vagabonde, La*, 40
Cooper, Gary (Frank J.), film actor (1901–1961), 93, 104, 107, 111, 117, 181
Cordy, Raymond (Cordiaux), film actor (1898–1956), 151
Coward, Sir Noël Peirce, playwright, composer, actor (1899–1973), 150 and n., 196, 200
Crawford, Joan (Lucille Le Sueur), film actress (1906–1977), 111
Criqui, Eugène, boxer (*b*. 1893), 134
Cukor, George, film director (*b*. 1899), 109

Darty, Paulette, singer (*d*. 1940), 11–12
Dearly, Max, actor (1874–1942), xiii, 47–48, 50, 74
Delysia, Alice (Lapize), singer (1889–?), 27
Diamant-Berger, Henri, film producer (*b*. 1895), 91
Dietrich, Marlene (Maria Magdalena Dietrich von Losch), film actress (*b*. 1901), 94, 107–108, 109, 113, 140, 149–50 and n., 177, 180
Dillingham, Charles Bancroft, impresario (1868–1934), 71–72, 73, 98, 127
Dranem (Armand Ménard), comedian (1869–1935), 33, 40, 77, 130, 133
Dufrenne, Oscar, impresario, 130
Dumas *fils*, Alexandre, writer (1824–1895), 1

Duvivier, Julien, film director (1896–1976), 135

Eiffel, Gustave, engineer (1832–1923), 1, 2
Ellington, Duke, bandleader (1899–1974), 99
Erté (Romain de Tirtoff), designer (*b.* 1892), 58, 59, 193

Fairbanks, Douglas Senior, film actor (1883–1939), 71, 72, 93, 111–112, 127, 190
Fairbanks, Douglas Junior, film actor (*b.* 1909), 111, 177
Fernandel (Contandin), comedian (1903–1971), 133
Field, Sid, comedian (1904–1950), 157–158
Fields, W.C. (William Claude Dukinfield), comedian (1879–1946), 45, 121
Fitzgerald, F. Scott, novelist (1896–1940): 89; *The Last Tycoon*, 89
Flers, P.L., producer and impresario, 34, 36–37, 38
Fragson, Harry (Victor Léon Philippe Pot), singer (1869–1913), xiii, 26–27, 28, 29, 47, 68–69, 84, 131
Franc-Nohain (Maurice Legrand), writer (1873–1934), 129
Francis, Kay (Katherine Gibbs), film actress (1906–1968), 109–110, 126
Franck, François Esposito, impresario, 29, 30, 31
Freed, Fred, accompanist to M.C., 171, 177, 192, 194
Fréhel (Marguerite Boulc'h), singer (1891–1951), 196
Fresnay, Pierre (Laudenbach), actor (1897–1975), 188

Gabin, Jean (Alexandre Moncorgé), film actor (1904–1980), 158
Garbo, Greta (Gustafsson), film actress (*b.* 1905), 112–113
Gaulle, Charles de, Brigadier-General (1890–1970), 143
Gingold, Hermione, actress (*b.* 1897), 184, 185

Goldwyn, Sam (Goldfish), film producer (1884–1974), 90, 93
Gounod, Charles-François, composer (1818–1893), 1
Grant, Cary (Archibald Leach), film actor (*b.* 1904), 109
Greene, Henry Graham, novelist (*b.* 1904), 135, 140
Grévy, Jules, politician (1807–1891), 1
Grey, "Monsewer" Eddie, comedian, 168
Grossmith, George, actor and singer (1847–1912), xiii, 50, 189
Guitry, Sacha (Alexandre Georges), playwright and actor (1885–1957), 1, 100, 123, 144, n., 148, 152, 167

Hamel, "le Père", café proprietor, 18
Hardy, Oliver Nowell, film actor (1892–1957), 91
Harlow, Jean (Harlean Carpenter), film actress (1911–1937), 101, 113
Hart, Lorenz, lyricist (1895–1943), 114, 115, 123–124, 164, 182
Hearst, William Randolph, newspaper-owner (1863–1951), 93
Henson, Leslie, comedian (1891–1957), 84, 158, 189
Hepburn, Audrey (Edda Hepburn von Heemstra), film actress (*b.* 1929), 181, 196
Herbert, Victor, composer (1859–1924), 99
Horton, Edward Everett, film actor (1886–1970), 110, 121 and no., 122
Hylton, Jack, bandleader and impresario, 83, 156

Janis, Elsie, actress (1889–1956), 55, 56, 62, 84, 187–188
Jannings, Emil (Theodor Friedrich Emil Janenz), actor (1884–1950), 95
Jeans, Isabel, actress (*b.* 1891), 184
Jouhandeau, Elise, dancer and writer (1891–1971), 192
Jouhandeau, Marcel writer (1888–1980): 192–193; *Réflexions sur la vie et le bonheur*, 192
Jourdan, Louis (Gendre), film actor (*b.* 1919), 184, 185, 187

Karno, Fred (Wescott), impresario (1866–1941), 35

Keaton, Buster (Joseph Francis), film actor (1895–1966), 111

Kennedy, Ronald, English friend of M.C., 53, 56, 168

Kerr, Deborah (Kerr-Trimmer), film actress (b. 1921), xi, 186

Korda, Sir Alexander, film producer (1893–1956), 126

Lafont, Henri, collaborator, 147

Lamarr, Hedy (Hedwig Kiesler), film actress (b. 1914), 113

Lane, Lupino (Henry George Lupino), actor (1892–1959), 101

Lasky, Jesse L., film producer (1880–1958), 90, 91, 94, 98, 106

Laurel, Stan (Arthur Stanley Jefferson), film actor (1890–1965), 91, 111

Laval, Pierre, politician (1883–1945), 143

Léautaud, Paul, writer (1872–1956), 152

Lehár, Franz, composer (1870–1940): 99; *The Merry Widow*, 122, 123, 124

Lerner, Alan Jay, lyricist (b. 1918), 182, 183, 184 and n.

Leroy, "Baby" (Le Roy Winnebrenner), film actor (b. 1932), 120–121, 185

Leslie, Earl, dancer, 65, 72, 73, 127

Leslie, Lew, impresario, 84, 85

Levey, Ethel, actress, 50

Linder, Max (Gabriel Leuvielle), film actor (1883–1925), 91, 106

Little Tich (Harry Relph), actor (1868–1928), xi, xiii, 24, 83, 132

Locke, W.J., novelist (1863–1930), 135

Lockwood, Margaret, film actress (b. 1916), 135

Loewe, Frederick, composer (b. 1901), 182, 183, 184 and no., 185

Loren, Sophia (Sofia Scicolone), film actress (b. 1934), 186, 187

Louis XVI, king (1754–1793), 2

Lubitsch, Ernst, film director (1892–1947), 94, 99, 101–101, 103, 104, 109, 115, 123, 124, 125, 181, 195, 199

Lumière, Auguste, film pioneer (1862–1954), 150

Lumière, Louis, film pioneer (1864–1948), 150

MacDonald, Jeanette, film actress (1903–1965), 100, 101, 109, 114, 116, 123, 185

Mamoulian, Rouben, film director (b. 1898), 114, 115, 117

Mathieu, Mireille, singer (b. 1947), 174, 194

Matisse, Henri, artist (1869–1954), 156

Maugham, William Somerset, novelist (1874–1965), 126 no.; *The Moon and Sixpence*, 126 n.

Maupassant, Guy de, writer (1850–1892), 1

Mayer, Louis B., film producer (1885–1957), 89, 92, 144

Mayol, Félix, singer (1872–1941), xiii, 25–26, 31–32, 46, 68, 84, 131, 174, 194

Méliès, Georges, film pioneer (1861–1938), 150

Mendès, Catulle Abraham, writer (1841–1909), 22

Menjou, Adolphe, film actor (1890–1963), 95, 97, 98, 100

Mille, Cecil Blount de, film director (1881–1959), 94

Mireille (Mireille Hartuch), composer and singer (b. 1906), 129

Mistinguett (Jeanne Bourgeois), singer (1873–1956), xi, xiii–xiv, 20–23, 38–39, 40, 41, 42–45, 47, 49–50, 51, 52, 53–54, 55, 57, 58–59, 61–66, 67, 71, 72, 73, 82, 86, 91, 117–120, 121, 122, 125, 127, 132, 138, 140, 144, 145, 149, 157, 162, 171, 174, 179, 180–181, 187, 194, 200

Modot, Gaston, actor (1887–1970), 151

Molière, Jean Baptiste-Poquelin, dramatist (1622–1673): 151, 152; *L'Ecole des femmes*, 151

Montaigne, Michel Eyquem de, writer (1533–1592), 114, 173, 198, 199

Montel, comedian, 33–34

Moore, Grace, singer (1901–1947), 122, 124, 140

Moreno, Marguerite (Monceau), actress (1871–1948), 91

Morgan, Michèle (Simone Roussel), actress (b. 1920), 175

Napoleon I, tyrant (1769–1821), 11, 43, 57, 62

Nohain, Jean (Jaboune Legrand), writer (b. 1900), 129–130

Oberon, Merle (Estelle Merle O'Brien Thompson), film actress (1911–1979), 125

Offenbach, Jacques (Jakob), composer (1819–1880): 42, 47, 69, 77, 187; *La Vie parisienne*, 77

Olivier, Paul, actor, 151

Ophüls, Max (Oppenheimer), film director (1902–1957), 113

Pagnol, Marcel, writer, playwright and film director (1895–1974), 188

Pallette, Eugène, film actor (1889–1954), 101, 106

Paquet, Félix, actor, 142, 176, 200

Paquet, Maryse, 176

Parsons, Louella, writer and critic (b. 1890), 121

Patachou (Henriette Ragon), singer (b. 1918), 162–163, 164, 170, 171

Patterson, Pat (Madame Charles Boyer), 113, 125, 128

Périer, François (Pillu), actor (b. 1919), 151

Pétain, Philippe, Maréchal de France (1856–1951), 143

Peyrefitte, Roger, novelist (b. 1907), 26 n.

Piaf, Edith (Giovanna Gassion), singer (1915–1963), 148, 162, 165–166, 167

Pickford, Mary (Gladys Marie Smith), film actress (1893–1979), 71, 112

Poiret, Paul, dressmaker, (1879–1949), 69, 86

Popesco, Elvire, actress (b. 1896), 135

Porter, Cole, composer (1893–1964), 56, 129, 187

Powell, William, film actor (b. 1892), 104

Préjean, Albert, film actor (b. 1898), 91

Printemps, Yvonne (Wigniolle), actress (1894–1976), 42, 148

Raimu (Jean Auguste César Muraire), actor (1883–1946), 46–47, 74, 168, 188

Raya, Nita, singer, 138, 139, 140, 141–142, 143, 147, 149, 153, 154

Reinhardt, Max, theatre producer (1873–1943), 99

Renoir, Jean, film director (1894–1980): 151–152; *La Grande illusion*, 151–152

Roach, Hal, film director (b. 1892), 91

Robey, Sir George, comedian (1869–1954), xiii, 50, 84, 158, 188

Robinson, Edward G. (Emmanuel Goldenberg), film actor (b. 1893), 111

Rodgers, Richard, composer (b. 1902), 114, 115, 117, 124, 164, 182

Rossi, Tino (Constantin), singer (b. 1907), 148

Roth, Lillian, actress (b. 1911), 101

Rousseau, Jean-Jacques, writer (1712–1778), 114

Sablon, Jean, singer (b. 1906), 118, 162

Saint-Marcel, writer, 21–22

Sanders, George, actor (1906–1978), 121 n.

Schertzinger, Victor, film director and composer (1880–1941), 99–100

Scotto, Vincent, composer (1876–1952), 129

Shaw, George Bernard, dramatist and Irishman (1856–1950), 71, 105, 182

Shearer, Norma, actress (b. 1900), 89–90, 110, 184

"Simone", mistress of M.C., 65, 73, 75, 82

Sinatra, Frank, singer (b. 1915), 187

Smith, Sir C. Aubrey, actor (1863–1948), 116

Sorel, Cécile (Seurre), actress (1873–1966), 113

Sothern, Ann, actress (b. 1909), 125–126

Stanwyck, Barbara, film actress (b. 1907), 110

Sternberg, Josef von, film director

(1894–1969), 94, 107, 108

Straus, Oscar, composer (1869–1954), 104, 109

Stroheim, Erich von, actor and film director (1885–1957), 89, 123, 140–141

Swaffer, Hannen, journalist, 157 and n.

Swanson, Gloria, film actress (*b*. 1918), 94

Thalberg, Irving, film producer (1899–1936), 89–90, 122, 124–125, 126, 158

Tucker, Sophie, singer (1888–1966), 83, 180, 181

Turpin, Ben, film actor (1874–1940), 101, 117

Utrillo, Maurice, artist (1883–1955), 156, 174, 192

Vallée, Yvonne (Madame Maurice Chevalier), 78, 79, 80, 81, 82, 84, 85, 86, 87–89, 90, 93, 94, 95, 101, 106–107, 108

Vals, François, secretary to M.C., xi, 161–162, 176, 188, 194, 201

Vals, Madame Madeleine, xi, 161–162, 176, 188, 194

Van Parys, Georges, composer (1902–1971), xi, 150

Varna, Henri, impresario, 130, 139, 145

Verneuil, Louis, dramatist (1893–1952), 135

Vilmorin, Louise de, writer (1902–1978), 175

Voltaire (François Marie Arouet), writer (1694–1774), 114

Volterra, Léon, impresario and race-horse owner, 59–60, 61, 64, 67, 68, 82, 98, 130

Volterra, Madame Suzy, 67, 189, 198

Waugh, Evelyn (Arthur St John), writer (1903–1966): 166; *The Loved One*, 116

West, Mae, film actress (1892–1980), 122

Whiteman, Paul, bandleader (1891–1967), 102

Whiting, Richard A., composer, 97, 106

Wilder, Billy, film director (*b*. 1906), 169–170, 171, 180, 182

Willemetz, Albert, writer, dramatist, impresario (1887–1964), 62, 63, 68, 69, 83

Willy (Henri Gauthier-Villars), critic (1859–1931), 39

Wray, Fay, film actress (*b*. 1907), 104

Young, Loretta, film actress (*b*. 1913), 111

Yvain, Maurice, composer (1891–1965): 51, 62, 63, 76, 77; *Là-Haut*, 76, 77, 78; *Ta bouche*, 76

Zanuck, Darryl F., film procedure (*b*. 1902), 125

Ziegfeld, Florenz, impresario (1869–1932), 98–99

Zukor, Adolphe, film producer (1873–1976), 92, 94, 98, 114